MEXICAN STANDOFF

OSCAR KING

NINE
ELMS

Mexican Standoff

First published in 2017 by
Nine Elms Books Ltd
6B Clapham North Arts Centre
26-32 Voltaire Road
London
SW4 6DH

Email: inquiries@bene-factum.co.uk
www.bene-factum.co.uk

ISBN: 978-1-910533-32-1

Cover design by Tony Hannaford
Book design by Dominic Horsfall

Set in Borgia Pro
Printed and bound in the UK

After a successful and varied career in the British Special Forces and service with the American military and government, Oscar King now works in the security and risk resolution sector in London, the Middle and the Far East. When not working or adventuring, King writes. Having previously written military non-fiction for Bene Factum, he has now successfully turned his hand to fiction.

Mexican Standoff is the third and final chapter of the Harry Linley series, following *Persian Roulette* and *Moscow Payback*.

For the very lovely Miss Mina Lisa Vito

And in memory of my friend
Dr. Robert F. Perry MD (Doctor Bob)

"When a wise man dies a library is burned."

MEXICAN STANDOFF

"A confrontation between two or more parties in which no participant can proceed or retreat without being exposed to danger."
Wikipedia

"He who advances without seeking fame,
Who retreats without escaping blame,
He whose one aim is to protect his people and serve his lord,
The man is a jewel of the Realm"
Sun Tzu, The Art of War

"Nobody ever did,
or ever will,
escape the consequences of his choices."
Alfred A. Montapart

Contents

Characters

Bunny – a Persian cat

Soraya – Bunny's Kitten

Alexei Delimkov – imprisoned Godfather of Delimkov cartel

Ivanna Delimkova – wife of Alexei and interim leader of the cartel

Harry Linley – security professional, former SAS officer

Nazrin* Sultanova – Harry's wife

Shaheen Soroush – Iranian expatriate, TV channel owner

Lee Lai Xian – Shaheen's girlfriend

Oleana Katayeva – Delimkov cartel fixer

Isaak Rabinovich – Delimkov cartel accountant

Maria Sedova – Delimkov cartel assassin

Willie Swanson – Delimkov cartel's London fixer

Mikhail – Godfather, Solntsevskaya Bratva cartel

Warrant Officer Omar Shamoon – CID, Dubai Police

Detective Sergeant Maryam Seyadin – CID, Dubai Police

Archivaldo – leader of Mexican Sinaloa cartel

Jorge González – Sinaloa cartel lawyer

Sheetal Khan – Indian IT professional

Graham Tree – security company director, former SRR soldier

Sid Easton – Harry's security company business partner

Mac Harris – electronic bank funds extractor, former MI5 technician

Beki Harris – Mac's wife

Toby Sotheby – MI6, Regional Head, Middle East

Mr G – Italian mob boss in London

Nicco '*il Toro*' – Mr G's thug

Panos – Mr G's IT guy

Alejandra – Sinaloa cartel's sleeper agent in London

Giovanni – waiter

Tarisai – MI6, executive assistant to Sotheby

The Cellist – godfather to the President of Russia's daughter

Artur Kiselev – fellow former prison inmate to Alexei

Alfredo Peniche – Mexican bank manager

Tarana – friend of Nazrin

★ *Note to readers of the first edition of Persian Roulette: Out of courtesy, the first name of this character has been voluntarily changed. The Author regrets any confusion caused by this amendment.*

Abbreviations

BARF – Bank Access Retrieval of Funds

CID – Criminal Investigations Division

CTSFO – Counter Terrorist Specialist Firearms Officers

DEA – Drug Enforcement Agency

FATCA – Foreign Account Tax Compliance Act

GCHQ – General Communications Headquarters

GRU Spetsnaz – Main Intelligence Directorate Special Forces (Russian)

MI5 – Military Intelligence, Section 5

MI6 – Military Intelligence, Section 6

MOE – Methods of Entry

NSA – National Security Agency (USA)

RFID – Radio Frequency Identification

SAS – Special Air Service

SF – Special Forces

SRR – Special Reconnaissance Regiment

STA – Special Treatments Area

SVR – Foreign Intelligence Service (Russia)

VSI – Very Seriously Injured

PROLOGUE
A Marriage Too Soon,
A Mistress Too Far?

H arry Linley had an all too familiar problem – a suspicious wife and a jealous lover.

Since their chance meeting in Belgravia's Antelope pub, both Harry and Ivanna Delimkova had known that their affair was a high-stakes game. What he didn't know, however, was that she had a Russian husband in a Russian prison and his cartel to run. And when Harry's wife Nazrin returned from Dubai to live in London, the affair reached new levels of complication.

From Ivanna's side, operations were going from strength to strength under her command. Her accountant maintained efficiency and cover, her assassins were effective, and her access to the highly illegal but extremely effective Bank Account Retrieval of Funds scheme (or 'BARF') had made her hundreds of millions of dollars from its victims – all lesser criminals who couldn't afford to report such thefts for fear of attracting the wrath of the anti-money-launderers.

Ivanna enjoyed her power and her lover, so was in no rush to expedite her husband's inevitable release from the gulag – at least not while Harry, as her new and exciting point of infatuation, filled her bed, her body and her heart once a week.

For his part, Harry was confused by the equal depth of his attraction to this voluptuous Russian millionairess, and couldn't help but wonder if he had, once again, wandered too soon into a marriage too far. Another divorce would mean yet another split of his assets, which were as substantial as they had ever been in his life, and – more importantly – if things were to go pear-shaped, who would get custody of his son Charlie…not to mention Bunny the cat?

The only thing certain about Harry's situation was that nothing was certain; and it was only about to get a whole lot worse.

CHAPTER ONE
Gallardo Splash

From the moment Alfredo Peniche set eyes on the bright yellow Lamborghini Gallardo, he knew he should absolutely not buy it. In fact, every nerve ending and every piece of banking logic and survival instinct in his Mexican DNA told him to walk away and be content with his dark blue BMW M5. Sadly for Alfredo, and in common with so many human beings faced with similar temptations, he swiftly managed to overcome any modicum of common sense he'd ever accumulated.

Even as he handed over the banker's cheque for 3,800,000 Mexican pesos, he felt like he was jumping off a cliff; but he did it anyway.

In the ensuing months, however, all the doubts and reservations Alfredo had ever had about the transaction were gone. The car had changed his life, and he cursed his previous hesitations about displaying his newfound wealth. The Gallardo transformed him from a dull, married, grey-suited bank manager to a designer-suited 'silver fox' playing the field behind his wife's uncaring back.

In short, the car was a Mexico City babe-magnet of the highest order, and it didn't matter to Alfredo that the women being so magnetised were also pay-and-play. He had a bright yellow V10, a steady supply of blue tablets, and a wife who'd learned not to ask questions the answers to which she might not like.

Alfredo became a discreet 'overnight regular' at the Gran Hotel Ciudad de Mexico, which was to be one of several strikes against him. So it was perhaps ironic that none of his immoral indiscretions would be the cause of his demise. In fact, at the very moment Alfredo Peniche's dominoes were starting to tumble, and just as he was paying off an immaculate-looking tag team of hookers in his hotel room overlooking the Zócalo, the man's nemesis was out walking his springer spaniel on a dew-sodden recreation ground in the village of Liss in England, completely unaware that Alfredo Peniche, in his human form, even existed.

Two weeks after walking the dog on that particular morning, Mac Harris was sitting in his basement enjoying a lunchtime bacon sandwich. He peered across at his two supercomputers, fully conscious of the fact that, in all likelihood, they had just six months' more life expectancy identifying criminal bank account activity and syphoning the illicit funds via dispersed bank transfers to the Delimkov cartel, for whom he worked. What Mac didn't realise was that his computers' technical 'sell by date' happened to be five months and twenty-nine days longer than that of one señor Alfredo Peniche.

It was a Tuesday morning and Alfredo was concerned about some very recent events at the branch of Banco Inbursa he had, to date, managed impeccably. The modest branch on Fray Servando Teresa de Mier had shown significant profit over the past three years and Alfredo was the golden boy among all branch managers. He had in the past eighteen months turned down two promotions from head office, not because he didn't want them, but rather because he couldn't actually take them.

Alfredo managed a number of choice accounts out of his branch, the application processes for which rather surpassed the stringent 'know your client' compliance processes of the applicant by head office; and these accounts had since flourished.

Sadly, the same couldn't be said for the individuals who'd opened these accounts at Alfredo's branch in the first place, because the home address tied to any sole trader clean account Alfredo deemed suitable for takeover was transmitted to his 'handler', and within weeks the account's owner would simply disappear or die of 'natural causes'. These deaths went unreported to the bank's head office, and the accounts became Alfredo's sole responsibility, over which either he or whomever his handler designated assumed de facto power of attorney.

These accounts then thrived from cash deposits at a lucrative though believable rate, and retained their holdings in Mexican pesos, avoiding any transaction involving US currency, citizens or residents. In this way, they remained out of reach of the Foreign Account Tax Compliance Act (or 'FATCA'), the US Government's international financial 'big brother' law to monitor all such accounts and dealings.

As soon as any of the dead men's accounts reached a pre-determined size, the account holder would invest in 'real-estate' outside Mexico in order to launder the money, which, in reality, was sourced from the country's largest and most powerful drug cartel – Sinaloa.

Alfredo's immediate concern on that particular Tuesday morning was that, two weeks previously, multiple mysterious but significant transfers had been made out of four of the accounts over which he held signatory authority to accounts in Panama, Brazil and Peru. The transactions were immediately flagged to his computer, and he simply assumed the cartel's accounts handler had been the one to make them. So when he called his handler to confirm that sums representing tens of millions of dollars had left the accounts, he was understandably shocked at the response.

Up to that moment, his handler had been very respectful, even friendly to Alfredo; but now he saw a different side to this individual. The response stated unequivocally that he had just seven days to retrieve the amounts or the handler would be forced to inform his boss that this was no banking glitch. This warning had come ten days ago now, and Alfredo should have sensed a further indication of his own horoscope when the handler had turned up unexpectedly at the bank the previous Friday and taken full control of the main accounts.

Following such an encounter, a less naive man would have simply driven his Gallardo the short distance to the international airport and got on a plane to wherever his Mexican passport would allow him to travel. However, Alfredo was a banker not a gangster, and he had no inkling of the unforgiving events that had occurred while he had been trying to figure out what the hell had happened to the money.

Alfredo could not have known that assassinations seldom happened on a Monday, because any run-of-the-mill target, and bank workers in particular, tended to start and finish each working week in one way only – pure, undiluted routine.

So at 8.15 am on Monday he failed to notice the 'dicker' loitering at the end of his street, who in contrast clocked him as he emerged out of his villa onto Calle 1862, avoiding the one-way flow on Lorenzo Boturini, and taking Nivel instead along to Lázaro Pavia, where he could exercise the pipes on the Gallardo for about forty-five seconds before pulling into his assigned parking space at the bank.

So, the following day, on Tuesday, having unwittingly confirmed his week's route to his murderers, Alfredo kissed his wife goodbye for the very last time. Had he known this, he would have regretted that his last words to her were a lie, having told her he would be home late because of a business dinner later that evening. Unbeknown to him, the events pending would result in his regular, spectacular hooker knocking on his hotel room door to no avail.

This time, as Alfredo pulled the Gallardo onto Nivel, there was no dicker; there didn't need to be. The motorcycle rider and his pillion passenger had done what they were about to do at least a score of times before. When it came to hitting their prey and effecting their escape, they were second to none.

The powerful and responsive KTM 1190 had been completely stripped down, lowered, and all accoutrements removed, with the frame and bike simply sprayed matt black with no markings. On this particular morning, the tank had a red plastic cover, which matched the rider's helmet cover. The rear number plate was a 'ringer' from a legally owned dispatch rider's bike, which had been velcroed over the legitimate plate.

The rider sat relaxed astride the bike on the side road skirting the local playground and park, opposite the road from which the Gallardo would in all likelihood emerge. Both he and his pillion knew that, if the target didn't show himself that day, they'd come back the next; the conclusion either way was inevitable. The KTM's immaculately serviced engine was ticking over; the pillion passenger stood, as if chatting to the rider, electronic cigarette in his left hand, taking no chance of leaving DNA behind on a discarded cigarette butt. His right hand, complete with black golf glove, was tucked into his jacket pocket holding the most powerful production revolver money could buy.

The Smith & Wesson Model 500 only held five .500 S&W cartridges, which, based on the pillion's track record, was four more rounds than he would need to earn his pay-out that day. The four-inch barrel variant of the revolver made the weapon additionally suited for the concealment needs of its owner, and the lack of an ejected cartridge case would leave one less link in the forensic trail.

The two men had only been in position for twelve minutes when they heard the sound of Alfredo's car.

"*Aquí, vamos*," the pillion said calmly as he replaced the e-cigarette in the left pocket of his leather jacket and simultaneously felt the thumb of his right hand pull back the trigger of the revolver. He flicked down his helmet visor and was on the pillion seat of the KTM in a single movement. He had total confidence in his rider; the two operated as one on the bike.

They saw the yellow Gallardo appear at the end of the street where it spent its dormant nights, and watched fixated as Alfredo gunned the accelerator, letting the V-10 engine respond in noise and movement in equal measure. The rider flicked the KTM into first gear and rode gently up to the junction onto Nivel, along which their mark was now accelerating.

Alfredo failed to register the motorbike approaching the junction, only spotting it as he was slowing to a stop to turn left onto the main street leading straight to his bank. As the ABS braking system brought him to a smooth and efficient halt, he saw the bike indicating left and assumed it would draw up alongside him. He hadn't seen the pillion passenger pull the Smith & Wesson revolver from his pocket, nor would he ever be aware that, with the hammer retracted, the gun was effectively hair-trigger, with less than three pounds of pull to release it onto the waiting chamber.

It was all too easy; as the bike slowed alongside the Gallardo, the rider ensured his pillion was in the perfect position. The end of the pistol was no more than half a metre from the target's head when it discharged its devastating round.

The driver's window of the Gallardo was instantly shattered and it did not alter the trajectory of the bullet in any significant manner that would help Alfredo. The .500 round, which was designed to fall a brown bear as a hunter's weapon of last resort, simply tore Alfredo's skull apart leaving only his jaw where nature had put it in relation to his body. The far side of his skull and the brains and sinew within, were scattered like contemporary art over the black leather interior and headliner of the Lamborghini, leaving only the car's glass to show discernible but very ample blood splash.

With one shot and job done, the KTM did not turn left as indicated. It simply pulled around the front of the Gallardo and headed south at a conservative speed that would not attract undue attention. The rider took the first available left and right turns that were not impeded by traffic, and as he did so the pillion removed the rider's red helmet cover, revealing a grey helmet beneath. And just before they pulled onto the main street that would bring them to Mixiuhca subway station, the rider pulled off the KTM's red tank cover and handed it back to the pillion rider.

The rider pulled up just thirty metres past the Mixiuhca entrance and the pillion got off. In a single motion he pulled off the ringer plate to reveal another. He then walked over to a waiting taxi, which was driven by a man he recognised from similar previous events. He removed his jacket and helmet and placed them in the taxi through the open passenger window. He noticed the KTM had already disappeared towards the safety of the main highway and its throngs of traffic that was Río de la Piedad. The taxi pulled away to return the pistol to one of the cartel's quartermasters and the pillion casually crossed the road to enter the subway station. He would head to where there was safety in numbers, to the crowds of Centro Médico, the hub of Mexico City.

Job done.

CHAPTER TWO
Tunnel Rat

The drug lord of Sinaloa was many things, but not stupid. His ruthless path to becoming head of Mexico's most feared cartel had been made by a combination of three factors; strategic brilliance, pathological savagery, and above all else, his unwavering ability to deliver whatever action – or threat – he promised.

Whether death or drugs, if the man simply known as 'Archivaldo' said it was coming your way, that was exactly what would happen. As a result, even standing as he did at barely 165 centimetres in his socks, Archivaldo was not only the most wanted and feared criminal in Mexico, but had also made his way onto Forbes' World's Most Powerful People rankings several years in a row, until finally the DEA forced his exclusion. And all this just eight years after his first escape from a Mexican maximum security prison in a laundry van.

From that moment, Archivaldo was smart enough to know that he would, one day, be caught again. So together with his lawyer, who through everything had remained his most faithful right-hand man, they had studied which prisons were most likely to be his future holding pen. There was only one: the Altiplano supermax, considered Mexico's most inescapable bastion, and so the planning started right away.

They quickly ascertained that, if he were re-imprisoned in Altiplano, he would be resident in the highest security 'Special

Treatments Area', and subject to 24-hour surveillance and daily cell and body searches. The STA was the most impregnable area of this most impregnable prison, save for just one or two vulnerabilities. It had just twenty cells, and was therefore compact and concentrated in structure – and it was at ground level.

Archivaldo's team quickly recognised the weakness, and with over $3 billion a year in drug revenues at their disposal, it wasn't long before the very best mining and tunnel engineers money could buy had been assembled to work together with the full-time cartel miners who built and controlled over 127 border-busting tunnels from Tijuana to San Diego Boulevard, and for three hundred miles east. It was not difficult to redirect sufficient resources.

The '*túnel de reserva*', as it became known, was envisioned long before Archivaldo would ever grace the cells of Altiplano. Having taken control of the Almoloya de Juárez farmland sandwiched between the prison and an army base, the cartel developed the simple cover of a farm equipment repair workshop before construction began. The tunnel ran some six metres underground and over two kilometres in length to the perimeter of the prison, its engineers working undetected as they shifted over 3,250 tonnes of earth. They even ensured to build the tunnel 1.7 metres tall, which represented the five centimetres of headroom necessary to permit their vertically challenged boss to walk upright to freedom.

Work on the *túnel de reserva* to nowhere ceased just twenty-five metres short of the Special Treatments Area. The tunnel entrance in the pseudo workshop was then covered, cemented over and mothballed, while the workshop itself continued 'business as usual'.

Archivaldo hoped beyond all hope that the tunnel would never have to be used but was reassured by its presence and the fact that there was no more than a few metres of digging required to bring it under any one of twenty showers, each of which stood en suite to a cell in the STA.

In February of 2014 Archivaldo's luck ran out, when he was betrayed by a man who was subsequently skinned alive and decapitated. Neither the judiciary nor the media could understand Archivaldo's calm demeanour when, under propaganda fanfare, he was consigned to an inescapable life sentence in Altiplano's STA.

Within three months of Archivaldo being placed in Cell 20 the *túnel de reserva* had been completed, and a significant amount of Sinaloa cartel business and communication was conducted by way of a live (spoken) or dead (written) letterbox arrangement underneath the cell's shower's drain tray. Meanwhile, arrangements were made in Costa Rica and Liberia for the covert relocation of the cartel's entire operational command team.

Additionally, the fact that Archivaldo knew he could walk out of the prison on just about any night he chose kept him amused, allowing him to perpetrate hideous crimes against his enemies for which he could never be held accountable. He had the perfect alibi – he was serving life in the supermax!

That, however, all came to an end one July evening, when the voice under the floor of the shower reported that tens of millions of dollars had gone missing from their multiple laundering accounts in Banco Inbursa. At first this was blamed on the Lamborghini-driving, whoremongering bank manager, whom Archivaldo pronounced a dead man walking with a simple "*Mátalo*".

However, even after the successful hit on Alfredo Peniche, the outflow of similar accounts continued, and now from multiple bank branches. Someone or something was bleeding the cartel of their hard-earned drug money, and no one could figure out who or how. Archivaldo ordered all but a few of the main accounts to be depleted or closed, but given that all the named account holders were actually dead, the latter was by no means going to be a quick or easy process.

So by 8.45 pm a few July evenings later, Archivaldo had made up his mind to take things into his own hands and personally supervise operations.

That night, the prison guards, who normally worked in shifts, inexplicably decided to go to the canteen together for dinner. Archivaldo sat on his cell bed, removed his prison slippers and put on a pair of shoes, before finally removing his electronic ankle bracelet. At 8.51 pm he rose from the bed and walked to the shower, where a one-metre high splash-wall concealed the shower tray from the cell's dedicated surveillance camera. He had practised this routine scores of times before, and the entire façade ensured nothing would appear unusual to the observant monitor, who would, from previous scrutiny, assume it was simply Archivaldo's evening masturbation ritual. However, this time the prisoner would not re-emerge within a few minutes adjusting his trousers.

This time, he simply crouched, lifted the floor, and descended through the half-metre square hole onto the nine-metre ladder that led down to the *túnel de reserva*. Greeted by his cousin, he then scurried for seventeen breath-cramping minutes along the underground tunnel and up to the surface again to two awaiting vehicles, one of which was a decoy. He climbed into one, which bore him the 90-minute drive to a makeshift airfield just outside San Juan del Río, where two identically liveried Cessna Caravans were expecting him. One aircraft departed, again as a decoy, towards Los Mochis; the other flew Archivaldo to the freedom of his new operational hideout on the outskirts of Limón, Costa Rica. He was already in the air enjoying a cold beer by the time the alarm had been raised in Altiplano.

That night, his only focus was to have sex with the two awaiting magnificent Costa Rican beauties so ably arranged by his loyal and brilliant lawyer, Jorge González, who had executed the entire operation.

Thereafter, however, Archivaldo's sole intent was to seek out whichever people or organisation had stolen his money, and make them pay through abject pain and an abhorrent death, the likes of which only the Sinaloa cartel could promise and most assuredly deliver.

CHAPTER THREE
Nice Is Nice

As an accountant, Isaak Rabinovich was happy, and as an accountant who cared more about the bottom line than anything else, he was ecstatic. Previously he'd thought Alexei Delimkov was the most brilliant of all godfathers, and by the time he'd become the Delimkov cartel's chief bean-counter, he never thought that anything could have convinced him otherwise. All that had changed, however, since Alexei had entered the gulag with a ten-year sentence, compliments of the President of Russian Federation.

Alexei's downfall and his wife's subsequent ascendancy had brought new energy to the cartel. He wasn't certain whether it was female intuition, luck, coincidence or guile, but the whole character of the cartel had changed. Ivanna had brokered peace between rival Russian mafia groups. She was even on speaking terms with the Solntsevskaya Bratva cartel, something her husband could never have achieved.

Ivanna's feminine logic had told her to never fight a man at anything in which he could beat you. Far better to let him do what he liked and was good at, and to let him feel unchallenged, than to lose ground trying to better him at his own game.

Isaak was not surprised, therefore, when Ivanna had asked him to accompany her to Monte Carlo, where they'd been taken by a Viking 55 Cruiser, the most seaworthy of vessels in its size, to a rendezvous in international waters with a German flagged super-yacht to meet with its principal passenger, the infamous *Bratva* boss, Mikhail.

During the 30-minute transit to the meeting, Isaak's inclination to be seasick was surpassed by the underlying thought that he, Ivanna and her *byki* bodyguards were all going to end up at the bottom of the Mediterranean. He just hoped to God that when the end came, it would be quick, and not by drowning. Perhaps they would shoot him before weighting him down and throwing him overboard.

However, nothing could have been further from his fears. Ivanna's party were welcomed on board, and while the *byki* and Isaak were frisked for weapons before being seated out of hearing range, Ivanna proceeded to pour on her charm while Mikhail poured the Beluga vodka.

The meeting lasted a little over an hour, and Isaak watched Ivanna politely hug and kiss Mikhail on each cheek as they said their goodbyes. As the Viking yacht slipped its tether to the super-yacht to make course at speed back to Monte Carlo and the luxury of the Hotel Metropole, Ivanna smiled at Isaak and simply said, "It's done." She paused, expecting him to ask the obvious, but he didn't, so she continued. "We have a cartel truce. I've promised to stay out of the refugee and human trafficking into Europe, and away from narcotics for one year; he's agreed to stay out of alcohol and cigarette counterfeiting."

Isaak gave her a puzzled look. "But we weren't in human trafficking, and we've never been a factor in narcotics."

"Oh Isaak, I know that, but it gets better," she said with a knowing smile. "I told him our cyber-unit will go all-out for the next six months, then we'll go silent while we restructure. He agreed to curtail all his cyber fraud activity for six months, on the assurance that we then go nowhere near any of his accounts." She handed Isaak a piece of paper. "Here are the branches to avoid. We'll reconvene after six months. It's perfect, don't you see?"

"I do," nodded Isaak. "We'll have to shut Mac down in six months anyway, so you've given him nothing beyond what we would have already had to do."

"I gave him nothing and everything, Isaak, and because I'm a woman, I don't think he really cared. He's making a fortune running the migrants into Europe; he even admitted to me that many of them are mules for narcotics and munitions into Greece, and his boys take over the goods from there. Even though the authorities can close the borders to non-paying migrants, there are no such restrictions for the cartel-sponsored variants!" She grinned. "Thankfully the officials in the Balkans have never changed; they can still be bought. And he's cleaning up as a result."

Ivanna looked beyond the bow of the boat towards the harbour and the backdrop that was Monte Carlo.

"Harry was right about this boat," she said. "It just cuts through the waves."

"Harry who?" asked Isaak.

Ivanna could have kicked herself. "Oh no one really," she blurted. "Just some boat expert Willie introduced me to in London." She hoped Isaak believed her.

He didn't, because Isaak knew that Willie the 'fixer' in London would only ever retrieve the information from such an individual, and certainly not introduce him to the boss. But he simply nodded and tucked the now common albeit still princely British name into the back of his mind, just in case it ever came up again.

The reality for Ivanna was that, despite the significance of the meeting, she was genuinely distracted by the thought of getting back to her mews house in London's Belgravia for a discreet rendezvous with Harry Linley. Ivanna was a woman in secret love, and as with all women that hid their love, every now and then it would inadvertently sneak to the surface.

It was about a week later when Isaak strolled through the white contemporary façade of the Boscolo Exedra Hotel in Nice into the cool summer evening air.

He had left his mobile in the hotel and knew that the man he was meeting would have done the same. The rendezvous was at 8.20 pm – no meeting of this kind was ever arranged around a cardinal point of the clock. He meandered through the busy little streets of Nice until he found himself on Rue Massena, where he turned right and approached the restaurant, noting that the al fresco seats were all taken. He couldn't care less.

A waiter looked up at him expectantly as he walked through the dining families outside into the restaurant. "I'm meeting a friend upstairs," he said dismissively. The waiter ushered him to a small lift that took him to the first floor. As he exited the lift, another waiter greeted him. "I'm meeting a friend," Isaak repeated, trying not to seem pissed off. He scanned the tables by the windows and then thought better, so looked around the lift shaft towards the back of the restaurant. Mac Harris was already seated drinking a beer and pulling apart some French bread.

Mac smiled as Isaak approached and rose slightly out of his chair to shake his hand. "Nice is nice, isn't it," he said with an appreciative grin.

"You've been here before?" asked Isaak.

"I'm a geek not an international playboy like yourself, Isaak!" Mac chortled. "This place is a bit lively for me."

"Well, it was handy for me, Mac," Isaak said, ignoring the fact that the man was taking the piss out of him; he knew Mac had no inkling of the wild sex life he had arranged for himself. "I had a meeting here a few days ago and I figured if there were any watchers, they'd have either got fed up or compromised themselves by now."

"Are we phone-free?" Mac asked.

"Completely," Isaak replied. "It's back at the hotel, SIM card removed."

"Good." Mac smiled. "I removed mine in Paris and took the train down here. It's a nice trip."

The waiter arrived. They each ordered a pizza and beer, and then Isaak got down to business.

"Ramp up BARF, Mac," he said plainly, "but be ready to shut it down overnight if needs be."

"Any reason?" asked Mac.

"Yes. You told Ivanna we needed to shut it down before it was compromised, which would be around the two-year point." He took a swig of his beer. "We're over a year in and it's been a spectacular run. You've earned every penny we've paid you. But it's been so good that she doesn't want to overcook it, so she's said do everything you can for six months, then shut it down."

He paused for effect and slid a piece of paper across the table towards Mac. "One more thing." He watched Mac's eyes leave the piece of paper and come back to him. "These bank branches in Cyprus – don't go anywhere near any account in them. No exceptions."

Mac took the piece of paper and slid it into his back pocket; he'd read it later out of sight of the restaurant's security cameras.

Isaak picked up his beer again. "So we're in the final lap and then it's game over for BARF, Mac. How do you say? Cancel the milk and put the cat out?" He smiled at his own weak sense of humour. "I think you've earned the premium on your retirement."

Mac cracked a courtesy grin. "It's been fun," he said. "I'll be sad to shut it down. But all good things…" He trailed off and took a sip of his beer.

Isaak stared at him blankly. "All good things what?"

"…must come to an end, Isaak!" Mac summed up with amusement. "We knew this would have to happen." He reflected for a moment as if debating whether to speak his mind, and then said, "But hey, I've come across some really lucrative stuff in Central America lately."

"Like what?" Isaak had to ask.

"Well, after our success in Costa Rica and Bermuda when you first hired me, I decided to scan out some lesser known banks in Panama and Mexico."

At that moment, the waiter delivered two massive pizzas to their table, and both men promptly nodded in unison when the waiter asked if they wanted another beer.

Mac made sure he was out of earshot before continuing. "Small business accounts that pool tens of millions in pesos, then make significant transfers to other Central American or Middle Eastern banks, and the funds used to buy property at the other end. Once they're in the Middle East bank accounts, the pesos are converted to a local currency that's pegged to the US Dollar, so that these 'shadow dollar' transactions avoid US jurisdiction and the Feds' scrutiny."

"And?" interjected Isaak as he bit into his first slice of pizza.

"And these business accounts appear to have common electronic signatures for each bank branch." Mac took a bite of his own pizza and spoke on through his mouthful excitedly. "And none of these accounts have normal business transaction flow. All the funds come inbound by cash, and there are no normal business expenses; so my guess is it's a network of tax evaders or money launderers."

The waiter brought their refills, and Mac used the forced interruption to wolf down more pizza. "I extracted some small amounts, there was no response, so I've started to clean out similar accounts because, clearly, whoever controls them can't afford to report the loss to the authorities."

"How much are we talking about?" asked Isaak.

"No less than $25 million from each branch, even when the accounts aren't fully loaded with higher amounts; I've found up to fifty accounts in each branch over three branches in Mexico City alone. Panama has similar or even greater numbers because they're not signed up to FATCA."

Isaak stopped eating; he knew that Panama was one of the few countries that hadn't signed up to America's intrusive FATCA tax enforcement programme on US citizens holding foreign accounts. "That's significant. It has to be drug money. Can you pull it out without them being able to track it? You'll need to be careful – those Mexican bastards are crazy."

Mac sipped his beer. "No worries, I can cover our tracks; and in any case, the Mexicans might be all powerful in Mexico – but not in the UK or Russia. They only have reach on the American continent, and on top of that, they don't appear to be too tech-savvy."

"Let's do it," Isaak instructed. "And when you've got whatever you can, we must shut it down. Agreed?" He needed Mac to confirm the instruction.

"No problem, I'll be careful, but these guys have no way of finding us. Especially if we shut it down soon." Mac was clearly confident.

Isaak had decided the pizza was too big for him, so he resorted to gulping down his beer. "You're going to be a very rich man, Mac. Sounds like the perfect crime."

He drained his bottle and stood up abruptly, throwing a 100-euro note onto the table. "Let's meet when it's over." He reached over and shook Mac's hand before walking out into the Nice evening with his thoughts turned to his concubine in Moscow.

Mac would finish his beer and pizza, and return to Paris the following day. Both men felt the thrilling anticipation of almost certain success. Neither could have imagined that a 27-year-old IT geek from India was about to make their lives a lot less certain.

CHAPTER FOUR
Double Lives

Since his early days serving in the Special Air Service Regiment, Harry Linley had got so used to leading a double life that, whenever it reverted to plain vanilla, he genuinely missed it. Fortunately, this was not very often.

In the SAS, such an undercover existence had been a legitimate part of his job; never admitting in public what he really did for a living; saying he was going to one place while actually going to another; total denial of involvement in operations exposed by the media, and so on. In common with so many of his colleagues in the Special Forces, his professional double life quickly came to mirror itself in his personal one, becoming especially compatible with his addiction for loving women. His resistance to their advances was equivalent to the breaking strain of a warm Kit Kat, a foible that had made Harry's somewhat complicated life what it now was.

Harry was ensconced in a second marriage with the beautiful and worthy Nazrin, with whom he should have been content. Her Azerbaijani genes ensured a beauty and elegance that had the potential to be ageless. She had a Western woman's style, but a Middle-Eastern woman's values. She didn't walk into a room, she glided into it. This would inevitably turn any head fuelled by testosterone, which might otherwise have been a problem for Harry were it not for her culture. She was fiercely loyal to her husband, having previously even thrown her former friend (and Harry's mistress) under the metaphorical bus to save him from the Dubai Police and the complicated predicament with the Iranians and now infamous Shaheen Soroush they had pinned on him. Harry should have been both grateful to and satisfied with Nazrin; but sadly that just wasn't Harry.

Even Harry himself had tried to analyse why he now found himself in a passionate affair with a wealthy, married Russian woman. He reasoned that she was beautiful and, though not as young as his wife, she just oozed sex. When he was with her, everything led to the bedroom – or whatever piece of furniture or wall they could use. From the moment they had met, on any given afternoon or evening, anything they did was simply foreplay to an inevitable sexual conclusion. It didn't matter whether it was a glass of wine in the Antelope pub where they had met, a light lunch in a Sloane Square restaurant, or even just sharing a taxi; Harry knew, as soon as he and Ivanna rendezvoused, the finale was inevitable. They would walk to her home in Eaton Mews, where they would have wild sex until Ivanna was satisfied or Harry was spent, or, more often than not, both.

On most occasions after spending time with Ivanna, Harry would walk the short distance to Sloane Square underground station and catch the tube to Richmond. It was then just a brisk walk halfway up Richmond Hill to the charming apartment that was now the Linley family home.

On entering, Harry would never have to feign exhaustion, just the reason for it. Nazrin would always have food ready for him, no matter what time of day or night he arrived home, and their son Charlie, now two years old, was as peaceful when he was sleeping as he was a human hand grenade with the pin out when he was awake – an apple that hadn't fallen far from the Harry tree.

Bunny, their stunning white Persian cat, was as comfortable in Richmond as she'd ever been in Dubai. She had always preferred to be an inside cat in any case. When she wasn't avoiding Charlie's clumsy and often painful attempts at affection during the day, she would be tucked up with Harry on the sofa or in-between his legs in bed.

The domestic picture had all the elements of perfection, and if the husband had been anyone else except Harry it probably could have been so. His new work as a partner in a well-funded, high-end security solutions company gave him the perfect alibi for absences of hours or days, and the confidentiality he owed to the company's clients had been adequately explained to Nazrin by Harry's partner Sid Easton.

For her part, Nazrin had felt privileged when the former naval commander and SRR officer had taken her for a five-star 'fusion' curry at the Gymkhana restaurant in London's Albemarle Street. Here he spent the afternoon with her to explain the role of the company solving complex security scenarios for high net-worth clients and corporations. After Sid had bid her goodbye, she had sat on the tube feeling justifiably proud that Harry had transitioned from the dreariness of the financial industry in Dubai to the excitement of international problem-solving. It also didn't hurt that Harry had exited making a small but notable fortune in Dubai thanks to his business with Shaheen Soroush, the Iranian pornography tycoon, and that this current job was very well paid too.

She would have been less proud had she known that, while Sid was wining and dining her, Harry was exploring every inch of Ivanna's body a little over a mile and a half across town. Nor would she have been impressed to learn that the previous week Harry had taken Sid's wife to lunch in St James's. Both men had realised that their wives were inclined to be less suspicious of anything they were told in terms of excuses if these didn't come directly from their husbands. It was a calculated plan concocted to buy them a professional alibi each, and it didn't bother Sid too much if Harry also used it for the purposes of extracurricular carnal exploration.

What Sid didn't know was the extent of Harry's relationship with Ivanna. Sid had been with them in the Antelope when the two had met, and he was pleased when Ivanna had contacted him to open a client consultancy contract with their company, which included a very healthy retainer. Sid was no fool, so he knew that if past performance was indicative of future results, he could safely suspect that Harry had scored a one-off as a result of the pub meeting, and that it was this that had probably caused her to buy into the company; but that was as far as his assumption went.

Harry had instinctively taken the decision not to tell Sid about the extent of the relationship for two reasons: the first was that Harry considered Sid to be happily married and a bit on the sensible side when it came to domestic affairs, so he might not approve of Harry's romps with a married woman. Harry would have been doubly right if either one of them had known that she ran one of Russia's most powerful mafias. In any case, he'd wrongly assumed that, what Sid didn't know about, he couldn't be drawn into.

In reality, even if Harry had come clean with Sid, it would have been of little consequence, because Harry would only be able to provide his own inept interpretation of the depth of the relationship. To him it was a 'fun affair' involving two consenting adults after lust, and to Harry's mind, that was it.

This, of course, was anything but Ivanna's interpretation.

Ivanna was in love, and not just a little. She wasn't sure whether it had happened because she was lonely and needed an intimate confidante; whether it was because Harry was different to any Russian man she had ever met; or whether it was just the danger of the affair. In any case, the reason was fast becoming irrelevant. She thought of Harry nearly every moment of every day, longed for his next text or call, and planned each detail of their rendezvous as the meticulous seductress she'd become.

She hadn't felt so alive for as long as she could remember, but she was also acutely aware of how very dead she'd be if her imprisoned husband ever discovered the affair. To that end, she too kept the relationship a total secret from everyone around her. All Willie Swanson, her London fixer, even knew was that Ivanna had taken the precaution of retaining Harry's company for security consultancy, from which Harry had manoeuvred himself into the position of her personal 'account executive' – a perfect cover to see each other for 'business'.

Even so, Harry's number on her phone was labelled '*Fitness trainer*', just in case Willie or Isaak were in line of sight when it went off. Messages such as '*Fitness, 2 pm Wed gym*' meant that Harry would meet her at her house. '*Park jog*' was their code for meeting elsewhere, which would be followed up with a call from the receiver to propose the venue of their next meeting.

Ivanna was confident that Alexei would never find out about her dalliance, and the fact that he still had over half of his ten-year sentence to serve in a Russian jail gave her the comfort she needed that she could keep this most precious secret secret.

The only flaw in Ivanna's entire plan was that she had lost control of her feelings. She wanted more than just a few hours a week with Harry. She also felt insanely jealous whenever he left her to go home to that Azerbaijani bitch she had never met. She was fast embodying jealousy through simultaneous love and hate. It was a dangerous condition that was making her blind to all she didn't want to see, and all while running a greedy, vicious, complex cartel.

CHAPTER FIVE
Team Revenge

Oleana Katayeva, the now dormant Dubai fixer of the Delimkov cartel, sat in the Dubai courts awaiting her turn in front of a bench comprised of one fat Egyptian and two thin Sudanese judges. The six months she had spent in Al Aweer central jail had just three positive aspects: she had learned a decent smattering of Arabic; she'd had time to figure out how to spend the roughly $3 million she'd stolen from Shaheen Soroush's apartment in Singapore; and she'd planned her revenge on those who'd caused her arrest and imprisonment in Dubai on suspicion of 'crimes contrary to the interests of the Emirate'.

Her time in jail had been a living hell because of what she assumed was police orders, and she was given no favours. Also, because she was Russian, the mostly obese female prison guards interpreted this as meaning 'prostitute', and so she was treated as such. She shared a 4 x 7-metre cell with five other women, of which, very fortunately, one happened to be a Russian – human-trafficked – prostitute, who'd been caught on the street without a visa.

Oleana had lost almost five kilos thanks to the gruel standard of food. The monotony of her incarceration was broken only by two monthly events: her visit to the courts, which would in a matter of seconds approve the extension of her detention for another month; and her periodic interviews conducted by the CID, led by Warrant Officer Omar Shamoon and Detective Sergeant Maryam Seyadin.

With time, both the detectives had seemed to become increasingly mellow towards her. Their initial aggressive line of questioning had revolved around the notion she was working for the Russian government in connection to a uranium enrichment deal with the Iranians. But her repeated denials, combined with the fact there had been no response whatsoever from the Russians in regard to her arrest, started to introduce doubt to that theory. Additionally, and purposely, Omar knew that a stint in Al Aweer would soften up almost anyone enough to talk their way to securing a release. She had laughed at them when they'd accused her of tracking the Iranian, Shaheen Soroush, out of and into Dubai; and they were gobsmacked when she admitted to having been Shaheen's ex-wife's lover before the latter and her daughter had been tragically killed in the Malaysian air crash in Ukraine.

During the weeks of questioning, Oleana described her friendship with Harry Linley as being just that, but with expired benefits. And both detectives gradually became convinced she was telling the truth when she claimed to be the unwitting victim of Harry's jealous wife who'd framed her in order to save her marriage and her useless husband. She was equally persuasive in her denial of all prior knowledge of the two Iranian men who'd attacked Shaheen Soroush in a Dubai car park (which was true), and her denial of being present at said event (which was untrue).

Following what transpired to be the last time Oleana was interviewed by the CID in the prison, as she was being taken back to her fully occupied cell, she would have been genuinely surprised to hear Shamoon telling his sergeant and partner, "I think we might have made a mistake. Either that or she's so well trained we'll never crack her. We have to release her and see who she contacts; that's the only way we're going to get to the bottom of whatever she and her partners in crime are up to."

The sergeant agreed. "She's lost a lot of weight. She was a beautiful woman, but not anymore. I think she has secrets but knows that, if she told them, a lot more harm would come to her from elsewhere than anything we can ever do to her. Let's face it, it would be no effort for the Russians to arrange for her to be killed while she's locked up in Al Aweer."

As the detectives got into their unmarked BMW 3 Series, Omar Shamoon sighed. "Let's go to the courts and see if we can find our counsel."

Two weeks later it was time for Oleana's scheduled continuance hearing, for which she was duly lined up and then seated in the courtroom flanked by eight other female prisoners dressed in their identical clean, pink, pyjama-style *salwar kameez* prison uniforms. Each end of the line-up was flanked by a large and angry-looking female prison guard.

As each prisoner was brought forward, the obese Egyptian judge, wearing his red, white and black sash and speaking in Arabic, asked the attending lawyers if they had anything to say. In at least half the cases the appearing prisoners seemed not even to have a defence lawyer, so despite the pleading of the prisoner for bail, each case was 'continued' in a matter of seconds, and each weeping woman in pyjamas would be returned to the pink, seated line. Oleana was resigned to the fact that her appearance would yield the same result as the previous five, but she was determined not to beg or cry.

Her case number was called along with her name and she stepped forward to be recognised by the judges as the accused. She looked at her defence lawyer, willing him to stand up and at least try for bail. Frustratingly, and by now predictably, he remained seated, staring at the written brief before him.

The fat judge again spoke in Arabic, and she could understand enough to know that he was asking for an update. She saw him look towards the back of the room where a distinguished-looking Emirati in a kandura spoke up and asked to approach the bench. Alongside him was another Arab; he looked familiar, but it took several seconds for her to realise it was Warrant Officer Omar Shamoon – she had never before seen him in Arab dress. Both men walked towards the judge, but Shamoon stopped at the front row; he was not a lawyer, so could go no further.

The other man went all the way to the bench and spoke in a subdued voice to the fat Egyptian judge. Oleana strained her ears and looked at the court interpreter for a clue, but he just shrugged his shoulders. She looked at Shamoon; he looked back and gave her what she thought was the vaguest of reassuring smiles. All of a sudden she was scared. What now? Oh God, what else?

She watched the judge pick up a thick file, presumably hers; he opened it as the Emirati continued to mutter to him in Arabic and pointed towards Shamoon. It was the first time since she'd been in the courts that she'd seen the judge look at any file. She turned back towards Shamoon again, but he was fixated on the bench.

The judge spoke authoritatively to Omar: "*Hatha Iqterahak?*"

Oleana looked at the translator, who mumbled back to her, "This is your recommendation?"

"*Naam, hu sayidi.*"

Oleana's Arabic was good enough to know Shamoon had just said "Yes, sir".

The judge looked at each of the Sudanese judges alongside him, who up to now had been looking both stoic and lethargic at the same time. One nodded in turn while the other merely shrugged his shoulders to whatever had just been asked of them. The judge then picked up his pen and scribbled something on the file.

He looked over at Oleana and declared, "*Ma alaik etihamat.*"

As he spoke, Oleana thought she understood, but his Egyptian pronunciation was confusing and she didn't dare to assume. But the interpreter smiled as he relayed back to her, "The charges are dropped, you are free to go."

Oleana had prepared herself not to cry when they sent her back to jail but this she hadn't expected. She felt tears of relief well up in her eyes and looked up at the judge. "*Shukran, sayidi, shukran.*" She was almost weeping.

The judge smiled slightly and nodded; the fat man wasn't used to releasing prisoners.

At this stage Oleana didn't know whether to return to her seat or not, but suddenly she noticed a slim woman in an abaya with an ID card attached on the front beckon over to her.

"Oleana" the woman said with a smile. "Come with me and we'll process you." It was Detective Sergeant Seyadin. Oleana had never seen her in Arabic attire or a headscarf before either; she too looked very different, though also far more elegant than in Western dress.

It seemed the CID had arranged for all Oleana's belongings to be brought to the court. She was permitted to change out of her prison clothing and into the jeans and T-shirt she'd been wearing the day of her arrest. It was only then that she realised how much weight she'd lost. She looked in the bathroom mirror – she was gaunt and looked awful, but she didn't give a shit. She was going to be free.

Once Oleana had changed, Sergeant Seyadin walked her to one of the offices along the busy corridors of the courts. There sat Omar Shamoon and the Emirati who had spoken to the judge on her behalf.

Shamoon offered her a cup of tea and a seat, both of which she gratefully accepted.

"Oleana." He had got used to calling her by her first name. "Please appreciate the fact that, if we believe there is some sort of action happening against our country, we must react. Our country is threatened from many directions and we can't take any chances on any count. It now seems that your presence and the events that transpired while you were in Dubai were a coincidence. For you that was very unfortunate, but you have to realise that we were simply responding to events *and* information received." He took a deep breath. "But with you it seemed we made a mistake, and I am personally very sorry for that." He picked up an envelope from the desk and handed it to her. "Here's enough money for you to get yourself back on your feet, and to get you home." He then picked up one red and one blue passport, both hers. "You entered Dubai on your Saint Kitts and Nevis passport, so we've renewed your tourist visa, and you have thirty days from yesterday to renew your visa again or to leave the country." Finally he pulled over a large padded envelope. "Here are your phones, purse, cards and belongings that you had on you when you were placed in custody; and here is your handbag." He glanced over at Sergeant Seyadin. "These are our business cards; if you have any problems from here on out, please call us and let us know. We'll do anything we can to help."

Oleana was still in shock, and there was a part of her that wanted to explode in rage, but the warrant officer was being so kind, and he had clearly taken efforts to arrange her freedom, so for now she decided to remain gracious. She looked up all three Arabs before her, making eye contact with each of them in turn, and simply said, "Thank you; thank you; thank you." She gave a tired sigh. "Can I go now?"

"Sergeant Seyadin will walk you to the entrance, this place can be a maze, and we don't want you wandering into the wrong area." Shamoon and the counsel both stood to shake her hand.

Oleana smiled weakly and left the room, searching for her sunglasses in the padded envelope, as she was escorted toward the bright sunlight of Dubai.

Back in the office, Omar looked at the lead counsel attached to the CID. "Prison couldn't crack her, but I'm damned sure her newfound freedom will give us we need to find out what she really is."

"She's had her silver bullet," the counsel replied. "I hope for her sake you don't have to lift her again."

Both men finished their tea and moved promptly onto that evening's Premier League match between Liverpool and Manchester City.

Outside the court, for the first time since she'd been in Dubai, Oleana found herself with no clue of where to go or what to do.

She'd told the taxi to take her towards Emirates Towers, but less than a mile into the journey she decided to head for Dubai Mall, where she could find a hairdresser, clothes and a manicure. She checked the envelope with the money; it had 30,000 dirhams in it. This equated to 5,000 for each month served. She figured it must be CID source money normally reserved for their touts.

She emerged from the mall at 6 pm with a clutch of shopping bags feeling a little more like the pre-prison Oleana. She was also delighted that she'd tried out her Emirates NBD ATM card in the mall and it had actually worked; to her relief, she'd managed to keep it active while she was in jail. She had ample funds in the account but was acutely aware that she also needed to retrieve the cash she'd previously hidden in the safe house.

However, that could wait until tomorrow. On this particular evening she simply walked the short distance to the Palace Hotel and booked herself a five-star room for three nights. Tomorrow she would take in the spa and then seek to enter the house to retrieve her cash. She smiled to think that it would be barely twenty-four hours of freedom before she might have to break another of Dubai's laws.

That night she dined in-room, but of all the luxury the hotel could offer, what she most enjoyed was undoubtedly the privacy of her en suite toilet, which was without stench or audience.

As she was about to fall asleep, she relished the thought that, for the first time in months, no one knew where she was. She then slept so deeply in the huge soft bed that her body and mind were refuelled, to such an extent that she awoke later feeling as if she'd come back from the dead, which wasn't far from the truth.

For the sake of her resurrection, it was just as well that Oleana didn't know about the GPS tracker beacon sewn into the lining of her handbag, nor about the two Dubai detectives who were smiling as they imagined her wallowing in the luxury of Downtown's Palace Hotel.

Shaheen Soroush's life had settled down since his return to Singapore from Dubai. His son Aryan was now studying happily at the prestigious but unfortunately named ISS International School; and in the meantime Shaheen had fallen in love with a local woman, Lee Lai Xian, whom Shaheen had met while she'd been working as a cosmetics sales assistant by day and a high-end escort by night. Shaheen had never bought cosmetics from her.

Lai Xian now lived in the Ascott Raffles Place residence with Shaheen, Aryan, and their pristine Persian cat Soraya (gifted to Shaheen by Harry in memory of his beloved and apparently murdered Bunny). This woman was by any measure the very best thing that could have ever happened to the widower and his bereaved son. She was kind, gentle, affectionate and caring, with a doll-like beauty almost unique to Singaporean women – the positive effect of the genetic crossroads the island city has come to represent.

Lai Xian had never really wanted to get into a relationship with one of her clients, but there was something so vulnerable about Shaheen that had brought out all her motherly instincts. So when she discovered he had lost both his wife and daughter in one of the notorious Malaysia Airlines plane crashes, and that he was ridiculously affluent, the combination had been enough to change her mind. It hadn't taken long for her to stay at the apartment for days on end fulfilling all of Shaheen's needs before she had become *the* item in Shaheen's life. When he'd asked her to give up the escort business and move in with him, it had been a no-brainer, and she concurrently quit her day job too.

From that moment on, she was able to concentrate on three things: looking after the two new men in her life; spending the healthy allowance Shaheen provided on the very best designer items; and spending two and a half hours, five days a week at the gym perfecting her skills in mixed martial arts. Lai Xian held a sixth degree black belt in MMA, and had just one more grade to 'Master' and winning the coveted red and black belt of her lethal art.

Standing only 1.6 metres tall and weighing just fifty-two kilos, Lai Xian did not exactly appear intimidating. But, if attacked, her power, technique and speed could dispatch a man over three times her weight in less than three seconds. The elegant oriental dragon and flower tattoo that covered her beautiful, slender back in its entirety might have been a telling clue as to her tolerance for pain, but Shaheen had no idea as to its significance or her activities in the gym; both imagined her regime involved little more than Pilates, a yoga mat and the odd pedicure.

Shaheen's business had gone from strength to strength since he had left Dubai; his adult internet and TV distribution business was making strong inroads in Indonesia, and the royalties were rolling in. He had an employee force of over three hundred individuals and offices based on four continents. He was still on the Iranian regime's wanted list for un-Islamic activities, so he had to be extremely careful about the airlines on which he flew. Any over which the Iranians might have influence were avoided; he couldn't chance any flight on which he might end up being forcibly diverted into Iran.

He had never really got to the bottom of why he was attacked in a car park during his last visit to Dubai, or why one of the men who'd attacked him had remained in a coma ever since. He recalled practically nothing of the attack, but simply knew that, by the time he'd returned from Dubai, over $30 million in gold, cash and diamonds had been stolen from the multiple safes he kept in his apartment. Shaheen had studied the copy of the Ascott's security videos from that period over a hundred times. There was no doubt that the two glamourous women entering the complex empty-handed and leaving with what appeared to be full handbags were his dead wife's former lover Oleana and her Russian friend Maria, both of whom had been with him in Dubai when he'd been attacked. His lone recovery had taken nearly a week while he awaited the return of his dead daughter's iPad from Oleana, which had been his sole reason for being in Dubai in the first place.

There was no doubt now that these women must have concocted the plan to have him attacked and drugged, but clearly neither they, nor even Shaheen himself, had realised that he could fight so instinctively and with such lethal effect as to permanently down his two attackers. It was a shame that he couldn't actually recall how he'd achieved it. All he did know was that Oleana must have found out about his safes through his dead wife and hatched her plan to rob him.

There was, however, one matter that eluded him and that he found himself questioning over and over again: how the fuck did they manage to shift the entire loot in just two handbags? It just didn't make any sense. He had wondered if they'd used the communal garbage chute, but there was no evidence of any unusual activity to reflect that. He'd speculated that they could have used additional bags and lowered them by rope from the sixth-floor balcony, but they'd entered and left his apartment complex in broad daylight, so such activity would have been readily noticed on the busy streets below. He just couldn't figure it out.

All he did know was that those Russian bitches had stolen his easily earned and tax-evaded millions, and therefore any revenge could not be meted out by law enforcement. He'd now figured out a way he could make them pay, but it was taking considerable patience for the necessary stars to align in order to put his plan into action. His first problem was that Oleana was banged up in Dubai's women's jail; his second that he didn't have a clue where Maria was. So he was elated when his phone rang one Wednesday afternoon from a Dubai number he recognised.

"Oleana's out," were the simple words uttered to him by Graham Tree, by now Shaheen's retained though unofficial private investigator in Dubai.

"No kidding! Do we know why?" Shaheen asked, conscious of the lack of initial greeting between the men.

"The charges have been dropped. Rumour has it they've even given back her passports. So she might not stay for long."

"Why dropped?"

Why do you give a shit, Graham Tree thought to himself at his end of the line, though he answered, "I'm not sure yet, but I'd guess she got tired of wallowing in jail and cut some sort of deal. She's a smart woman, you know that."

Shaheen wondered what such a deal could possibly consist of, instantly worrying that Oleana might have implicated him in something. "Okay Graham, see if you can find her and befriend her. I feel very sorry for what's happened to her," Shaheen lied. "Let's make sure she's okay…for old times' sake."

"Leave it with me, Shaheen. Just give me a few days, okay?" Graham needed to buy some time.

"That's fine, but keep me posted on any developments. And by the way," he added, trying to sound casual. "Did you ever hear anything about her dark-haired friend? I can't remember her name."

"Maria," Graham replied, visualising as he did so the very same woman riding his penis like there'd been no tomorrow. Christ, she'd been sexy. "Don't know where she went, Shaheen. Russia, I expect; I think she was from Moscow. When I talk to Oleana, I'll ask her."

"Just out of interest," Shaheen reinforced, trying to conceal his level of interest, little realising Graham would have asked anyway, just on the off-chance of gaining a repeat session of his previous encounter with her.

After he hung up, Shaheen smiled. He'd known this call would come one day, but even so, it had been a pleasant and unexpected surprise that had brightened his day considerably. He just hoped to hell Oleana hadn't stitched him up to that far too smart and tenacious Dubai detective.

Fifteen minutes later Shaheen called Lai Xian to tell her he'd booked his usual table for them at Gunther's; he would meet her there direct from work. She almost squealed with approval.

CHAPTER SIX
Safe House Rules

Archivaldo's transition into Costa Rica had been perfectly executed by his most faithful lieutenant, Jorge González, who also served as the cartel's lawyer.

It was often a source of much amusement across the cartel that the equivalent of their Chief Operating Officer was a lawyer who had graduated *magna cum laude* from Glendale University College of Law in California. It was somewhat ironic that Jorge had never been stripped of his honours or qualifications for the simple reason that he had never been convicted of any crime.

Jorge compared himself to the Wall Street bankers that had collectively brought down the world's economy in 2008. Not one of those executives had even been charged with a crime, and while the world's working masses suffered terribly as a direct result of their deeds, the men that had caused the problems simply got richer and invariably remained free. Jorge was that type of guy.

However, the biggest difference between Jorge and the bankers was twofold: he had broken far more laws than any of them would do in their entire lifetime; and unlike the soft-bellied, spineless bankers, he was willing to kill or maim anyone to preserve the integrity of the organisation he so ably protected and operated.

The large, four-bedroomed detached house in the high ground of Limón's Lomas de Recope had been carefully chosen. Its only shortfall was that it had a red roof, whereas all the surrounding houses had green or grey roofs. This distinguishing feature was, however, offset by the discreet guest house located behind it. This structure was out of view of the road that formed the cul-de-sac in front of the main house. The distance from the house to the guest house was only twenty-five metres, and the tunnel engineers had quickly succeeded in linking the two properties.

Additionally, and ever mindful that 'an escape route is everything', Jorge had purchased at premium price a less prestigious property with a small workshop at the rear of the hideout that was located in La Loma de Moín. This was situated just two hundred metres downhill and through a wooded area from Archivaldo's guest villa, and it proved no difficulty for the engineers to covertly construct a shallow 'rat-line' down through the woods to the workshop.

With that work complete, a stripped and sprayed KTM 1190 Adventure R motorbike and an Ultra 300LX Kawasaki jet ski were brought into the workshop under cover of darkness.

A respectable couple in their late thirties then moved into the house with their twin 19-year-old son and daughter. Of course, in reality, none of them was related; both men were tried and tested cross-country motorcycle riders and both women were light and expert on what was one of the fastest production jet skis in the world. All four had used their skills for the cartel in delivering death or drugs prior to their current assignment. Jorge had been exacting in his instructions, and they knew he was not in the least tolerant of fuck-ups.

He'd instructed that there must be one man and one woman in the house at all times, no exceptions. They had to keep up the façade of a normal family coming and going around that one restriction. The engineers had run a panic-button wire into the house and attached it to a smoke detector. If the smoke detector sounded, or they received a call or text that simply said '*caballo rápido*', then they were under orders to have the KTM engine running and ready to go in all respects. Their cargo would give them instruction en route. If they received the message '*delfín rápido*', then the immediate action was to tow the jet ski down to the breakwater end of Puerto Moín where there was a makeshift boat ramp. The KTM rider or a car would deliver the cargo to the jet ski, and that cargo would instruct a north, south or easterly course. It was imperative that they have the jet ski, the KTM and their pick-up truck fuelled and ready to go 24/7.

None of the occupants knew who their cargo might be, nor where he was coming from, nor did they know about the rat-line tunnel. All they knew was that they would follow their orders to the letter and get well paid for doing so. Failure or disobedience was not an option they could or would even consider, not least because they had seen the violent repercussions for incompetence or disobedience.

In the villa two hundred metres up the hill from the getaway team Archivaldo was just finishing his second breakfast of freedom when Jorge walked in and sat down at the kitchen bar opposite his boss.

"*¿Qué está pasando?*" Archivaldo spoke with his mouth still full of honey melon.

"We pulled the head of IT security at Banco Inbursa." Jorge smiled as a scantily clad Costa Rican beauty poured him a coffee. "At first he denied there was any fault with his system, so we made him examine it again from a computer we'd set up for him. He concentrated on the branch run by our 'Lamborghini manager'. It looks like that idiot and his handler fucked up."

"No kidding, genius." Archivaldo looked menacing. "That playboy fucker cost me millions."

"The accounts the funds went missing from all had something in common. They had the same initial online passwords and were all linked by the same encryption key. They also had multiple cash deposit inflows, but only debited to other Latin American countries or the Middle East in amounts that could be used to buy property."

"So who could see those characteristics?" Archivaldo took another sip of coffee.

"We don't know yet. If it's the DEA, we'll find out through the guys we have on the inside in Miami or San Diego. If we draw a blank there, then we have to assume it's not the Feds who've cracked the bank system."

"And then what?" Archivaldo needed to get to the bottom of the problem.

"The bank guy said there are a few experts in the world who might be able to hack and track, but we'll need to find the best, and he thinks we'll only find that kind of talent in the US, India or China."

"Go for India, nobody will suspect we're using anyone there." This was an assumption but Archivaldo was correct. He glanced out of the window towards the woods as he thought. "So find our Indian geek, then reduce the amounts in the accounts down to something negligible, except for one bank branch where we'll increase the balances. Have him monitor those accounts, and let's hope whoever the bastard is stealing my money tries it again. Then we track him down and kill him, and his employers if he has any."

Jorge nodded, already thinking about the cartel's access to India.

"One more thing," Archivaldo said, interrupting the lawyer's thoughts. "How much did the handler lose us?"

"North of forty million dollars." Jorge already knew the order that was about to be spoken.

"Take control of the accounts, then have his fingers and feet cut off." The drug lord paused without looking up from his plate of melon. "And then kill him."

Within forty-eight hours, the handler was just another unfortunate soul to die a miserable death in the sprawl of Mexico City.

Oleana had woken up to Dubai's bright sun piercing the discreet curtains of her five-star bedroom. She was trying to recall when she had last slept so well, only now realising just how precious the commodity of privacy had become to her. She grabbed the pen and pad from the side table and jotted down a number of 'to-dos' for the day. How the day panned out would decide whether or not she'd stay in the opulence of the Palace Hotel for more than just a few nights.

She stood in front of the mirror and wanted to cry, but she stopped herself. Her body was no longer toned and smooth, she had lost just about every inch of fat and her muscles were no longer strong. She knew she now had to eat well and start an exercise regime, as well as topping up on vitamins of which she was surely deficient.

She put on the new but inexpensive clothes she'd bought in the mall the previous day, well aware that they would probably no longer fit her skinny body within a month. Her make-up helped her win back some of her beauty, and the breakfast offered up by the hotel's Ewaan restaurant quickly filled her shrunken stomach.

She walked out of the hotel and hailed a taxi to the Mercato shopping centre. From here she walked the familiar route to the safe house, wondering whether it would be empty, or if the landlord had reclaimed it.

About fifty metres short of the property's gate, which took the form of a metal door, she retrieved the front door key from her purse. On reaching the property, she eased open the gate and peered inside. There were no signs of life; everything looked quite neglected. She left the gate open and walked the three metres to the front door and rang the doorbell. If anyone answered, she'd already rehearsed her 'right number – wrong street' routine. She waited about twenty seconds and rang the bell again. Still no signs of life. She leaned over and looked into the kitchen window; the house looked dormant. She rang the doorbell one more time.

Oleana then pushed the key into the lock hoping the locks hadn't been changed. Half-expecting the key not to turn, she was pleasantly surprised when she felt the mechanism give way and the door seal crack open. She pushed the door open and in her friendliest voice called out into the house, "Hello, is anyone home? It's the real-estate agent? Hello?" There was no response.

She left the front door open in case she needed to make a quick exit, walked to the bottom of the stairs and called out again. Still no answer. The place looked unused and was covered in dust. However, the air-conditioning was doing its job keeping circulation in the house, and Oleana thanked herself for having decided to pay the utilities by direct debit, which had also kept her Dubai account active.

Making her way upstairs, she immediately checked the wardrobes and quickly realised that all the high end handbags and two of the largest suitcases were gone. She assumed rightly that Maria, the woman who'd been sent to replace her as the Delimkov cartel's fixer in Dubai, had clearly fled town with everything she deemed valuable in the house. Oleana wasn't angry; she knew she'd have done the same and was just glad Maria had got out while she still could.

Oleana then went downstairs, now with bated breath. Had Maria discovered and taken the money she'd hidden in the house? She closed the front door and went to the freezer, removed the large frozen pizza box inside and tore it open. As she emptied the contents she felt tears of relief well up in her eyes. The eight wraps of $100-bills fell frozen onto the kitchen counter. She looked at each one in turn but made sure not to tamper with it. Each bundle would have to thaw before she could take the risk of separating the notes.

She then walked to the window at the back of the lounge and inspected the bottom corner of the curtains, feeling for the slit where she'd previously cut open the stitches of the hem – all three rolls of money she'd hidden were there. She eased each one out and replaced the curtain back into its original position, before placing the bundles next to the wraps in the kitchen.

Finally Oleana went back upstairs, packed up the clothes she'd left behind in two of the remaining Rimowa suitcases, and carried them one at a time down to the kitchen, where she inserted the money into the dividing sleeve of one of the cases.

She opened the front door, threw the empty pizza box into the outside bin and retrieved the cases, before trolleying her four-wheeled cases out to what she knew as 77B Street. Here she hailed a taxi that would return her to the Palace over a million dollars the richer.

Oleana would never return to the safe house; it had more than served its purpose. When she arrived at the hotel she informed the receptionist that she would like to extend her stay by a week, and then scheduled daily appointments at the hotel's spa.

As she lay in the tranquillity of the massage parlour, she reasoned that six months in jail for an unencumbered million-plus was not bad work – though she definitely didn't want to do it again.

Across town Omar Shamoon was looking at the GPS tracker. "If she goes back there to live in a few days, then that'll make sense. If not, she must have gone there to retrieve something." He paused and looked over at Sergeant Seyadin with a knowing smile. "Perhaps you should pay her a visit at her hotel and see what you can find out. After all, we know she responds well to women."

CHAPTER SEVEN
Size Is Everything

Isaak's return to Moscow from Nice had been uneventful. He now frequently reflected on how, since Ivanna had assumed control of the cartel, his life had become considerably less stressful. She was not the micro-manager and mob-boss her husband had been, nor did she tend to play the same mind games with those who caused her problems; she simply, quickly and quietly got rid of them. Since she wasn't bothered about ego or trademark, under her control the cartel's imposed deaths seldom looked like murder; they were either 'accident' or 'suicide', hence the repercussions were few. Additionally, in the past few months that Ivanna had been living in London, her entire persona had changed. She was no longer the serious, intense Ivanna of old. These days she seemed, and was, far more relaxed, and looked as good as she ever had. Ultimately, she was a far easier boss than Alexei, and Isaak half-dreaded the day when Alexei would be released from the gulag to bring stress back into his life.

The other factor having significant influence on Isaak's life was the inclusion in it of Maria, the cartel's most efficient female assassin, or 'torpedo' as she was known within the organisation. When Isaak had found out that Maria had stolen money meant for the cartel, they had struck a deal. His silence for her sex, and he frequently collected his payment in Moscow or wherever Maria happened to be.

Isaak had reached the stage where he foolishly believed his relationship with Maria to be genuine, so he frequently wined and dined her before accepting her 'favours'. For her part, she always looked immaculate, and didn't seem to mind the fact that, because she was so beautiful, he tended to orgasm early on in the proceedings.

He would have been utterly staggered to learn, however, that every time he penetrated her she considered it outright rape. Although the word 'no' was never said, this was sex under duress. And for his sake, of all the people to be fucking against their will, Maria should definitely have been the last. She had a plan, and when the timing was right she would, sure as hell, carry it out without mercy.

Although she was very much aware that the timing for Isaak's demise was being determined by external factors, as she showered down in Isaak's apartment ensuring every particle of smell and semen had been flushed from her body, she knew her patience was running out. She needed him out of her life and silenced for good.

She walked into the lounge in her tight jeans, heels and Zoe Karssen lip-print T-shirt to find him still in his bathrobe, presumably still naked underneath. With a concealed shudder, she picked up her Victoria Beckham bag. "Isaak, I have to dash. I have a shit-load of things to do before I head off to London in two days."

"You're going to London?" Isaak said with a note of surprise, setting his coffee down on the side table.

"Yes, Ivanna has called me over. I'm not sure why. She just asked me to come."

Isaak was mildly irritated. Why hadn't Ivanna told him about this? In days gone past, she would have always confided everything in him, but it seemed those days were over.

"How long will you be gone?"

"I'm not sure. If you find out, let me know!" She let out a slight laugh.

"Maybe I should come too..." Isaak half-asked, hoping to get some encouragement.

Jesus Christ! Maria cringed inwardly. "I don't think there's any need for that," she said in the nicest tone she could muster at this stage, trying to look as relaxed as possible. "It didn't sound like it was going to be a long trip, but I'll let you know as soon as I know.

Isaak got up and walked over to her, placing his hands around her thin, firm waist. "I just don't like us to be apart, Maria," he said, delusion across his face. "You know I've become very fond of you."

Maria wanted to punch the rapist bastard right there and then in the face, but she knew just one word from him about her theft and she would be lucky to escape with her life. She composed herself.

"I miss you when we're apart too. But I liked it when you used to send me those sexy texts and emails. *They* used to turn me on." The words made her wince inside.

Isaak grinned. "You like that?"

"Mmm-hmm."

"In that case, I aim to please." He leaned forward and kissed her on the lips.

She kissed him back dutifully and told him, "You take care while I'm away – and keep away from other women!"

"I'll do my best!" He laughed as she slipped from his grip, said goodbye and let herself out of the apartment.

He sat back down and resumed his coffee. "Who'd have thought it?" he said to himself. "A beauty like that falling for me." He opened up his robe and looked down. "I guess you must be bigger than she's had before."

As Maria walked into the underground car park towards her Porsche 911 4S she knew she could find solace in two things at least: she would make sure her situation was irreversibly finite – and at least the bastard had a small dick.

Jorge had really not wanted to go to India because he detested the diet and its bowel-churning consequences. However, such was his boss's level of irritation that to entrust this particular trip and its requirements to anyone else would have been a major career foul.

He decided to use his Dominican passport and the visa was expedited from India's consulate in Mexico City via the cartel's 'brown envelope' application process. Jorge then spent the next twenty-three hours on Air Canada and Lufthansa planes semi-circumnavigating the globe.

By the time he emerged from Mumbai Airport's new Terminal 2 building and caught a taxi to the Taj Lands End Hotel in Bandra, his body clock no longer knew whether to drink or sleep, so he did a bit of both.

The following day he sat in the spacious lobby feeling unusually relaxed. He knew the cartel had no business whatsoever in India since the opium trail from Afghanistan provided over eighty percent of drugs into the EU, and that supply was run by the Asians and the Russians; the Mexicans had little interest except via the African route, so he was definitely off his 'patch'.

At 11 am he saw one of the hotel lobby staff point two Indians dressed in business attire towards him. "Mr George?" one of them asked on approach.

"Close enough," Jorge replied, and the two men introduced themselves as the CEO and COO of Ascentity IT Solutions and Outsourcing. They explained that they were based in Thane about thirty kilometres to the north-east.

Both men ordered tea, and once everyone was settled and the small talk complete, the CEO asked, "Now, how can we help?"

Jorge explained that he was the lead counsel for a large corporate that had business interests in Mexico, and despite having what they thought had been the highest security protocols, someone or some entity had managed to hack into their systems and divert funds. "As a result," he continued, "I'm here looking for the very best counter-hacker money can buy and I've been told you have a former MIT graduate in quantum computing working for you."

"We do indeed. But why choose India, Mr George?" asked the COO. "Surely there are such people in the USA?"

"That may be so, señor," replied Jorge, "but as we all know, compliments of Mr Snowden, they also have the most intrusive of any governments when it comes to surveillance. So, although we've done nothing wrong of course, in Mexico we are very sensitive about the nosiness of Uncle Sam next door."

"How much went missing?" the CEO asked.

"About five million," Jorge lied. He knew he needed to make it an amount that was serious but not so high as to push their price up.

The two men spoke briefly in Hindi; Jorge heard one of them mutter what sounded like, "*Ham paanch pratishat le lenge!*" He guessed correctly that they'd just calculated their fee.

"I want to know, gentlemen," Jorge interrupted, "if you have such a person on your team, as your website advertises, that can look into and counter-hack the highest level of protocols in order to find out who stole our money?"

The CEO looked at him. "We have such a man. We think he's the best in India."

"Good," said Jorge. "Then why don't you bring him here this afternoon and we'll see what he can do. Please make sure he brings any equipment he might need to hack into an account."

Four hours later the two Indian executives knocked on the door of Jorge's hotel room, along with a gangly man in his mid to late twenties. The young Indian was introduced as Sheetal Khan. "This is the MIT man you asked about," the COO told Jorge.

Jorge had his own laptop set up on his desk. He did not even bother to greet Sheetal. "I have an account at this bank in Mexico in my name," he told him, showing the young man his passport, "so I'm not asking you to do anything illegal. The first thing I want you to do is get into my bank account."

"Am I allowed to ask you any other questions, sir?" Sheetal asked Jorge.

"Not for the moment, let's just see how you do. You can go into any part of the computer if it helps."

"But sir!" The Indian's head nodded side to side. "This equipment is very limited in its power to do what you ask."

"No problem," Jorge reassured him. "I just need to see if you can get anywhere close."

Almost instantly Sheetal brought up a screen and format on the computer that Jorge had never seen before. He then scrolled down through reams of code appearing to search for one particular element, before plugging a device into the USB port of the laptop, which brought up yet another display.

"I can do this a lot faster if I have multiple screens," Sheetal said without glancing away from the screen. "Also the computers I would recommend are so vastly better than this one that there really is no comparison." His fingers moved so fast across the keyboard they were almost a blur. He switched between displays several times until finally he said, "I'm through stage one."

Jorge checked the screen – the kid was right, he was in. "Okay, Sheetal, but can you get through the verification?"

Sheetal reached over for his smart phone and hit an app. "This is trickier," he said. "I only have three shots that the bank detects and then your account gets locked. Will I need to work out the encryption key codes on whatever you need me to do?"

"Probably not, but I'd like to see if you can do it." Jorge replied.

"I have done it before, sir, but if I have key code examples, it's much easier. So if the job is to break into an account, that's one thing, but if the job is to find out who's stealing from it, then that's another thing entirely." Sheetal looked away from the screen and at Jorge. "Which would you like me to do?"

"The latter." Jorge handed him the access key, somewhat disappointed that this 'genius' hadn't simply hacked in. At least the guy wasn't a bluffer, he reasoned to himself.

Once Sheetal had full sight of the account, Jorge pointed to a transaction. "Tell me everything you can about that one." It had been purposely set up to test the geek.

Within minutes Sheetal had established the details of the transaction, including the IP address from which the instructions had been issued that indicated Turkey.

"Do you think you can get to the next level?" asked Jorge.

"What do you mean?" Sheetal was confused.

"Can you track the money through accounts?" explained Jorge. "Whoever stole our money sure as hell isn't going to put it through their own VPN or account."

"I don't think I need to go that route with this computer." Sheetal was thinking laterally. "If I can identify the IP shield mechanisms the thief is using, and if I have enough computing power, then I can track him that way. If he's stolen from you more than once, there'll be a commonality, and the more often he does it the more chance he'll give me of identifying his protocols." Sheetal turned back to Jorge. "Is the thief still active?"

"We hope so," replied Jorge.

"How long do I have to find him?" the young Indian asked.

"I'd guess a couple of weeks."

"I know I can help you." Sheetal explained, "but a lot will depend on the complexity of the hack. In order to find the passcodes into the various accounts, the combinations are almost infinite; but with the right computer, I could have these in seconds. However…" He paused a moment. "Machines like that are known as quantum computers and they're very expensive – only you can judge the bang for your buck."

"How much for the best?" Jorge asked.

"Several hundred thousand for conventional computers, up to $15 million for the best quantum computer."

Jorge put out an expression of shock but his mind was racing. If the cartel could harness such computer power and expertise, the cybercrime potential could be inordinate; but he couldn't let on to the Indians in the room.

"We'll go lower-end," he lied, "and see what you can do."

The CEO intervened. "So shall we do a deal, Mr George?"

Jorge nodded. "Okay, what's the cost?"

The CEO looked at Sheetal and instructed him to wait outside. He waited until the door was closed behind his employee.

"You said you had lost $5 million? If we're able to recover it, then why don't we say you pay us five percent. However, our fixed fee is $250,000, non-refundable, to start the work." The CEO was convinced he was cutting a hard deal. Jorge quickly concluded that the Indian had never dealt with a Mexican, so he concealed his pleasure at the pricing.

"I don't care about recovering the money, I just want to find out who stole it." He had just thrown a stick in the Indians' spokes. "I'll pay you $100,000 upfront, but the geek comes to Mexico as soon as we can get him there. I need him in the same time zone. Also," he added, "if the kid does the job, we pay you guys a balance up to $200,000, then he gets a direct additional payment from us for $100,000. No side deals, and you have no claim on what we pay him provided we cover your fees. I need the kid incentivised to watch and work around the clock. If you don't agree, I'll have one of your competitors here tomorrow."

The CEO looked to the COO for reassurance; they hated the fact their employee would get paid so much, but there was a sideways nod between them for their take. "Okay, Mr George, but you pay all the costs for Sheetal's travel and all his hardware needs, which, as you know, are likely to be state of the art and not cheap, right?"

Jorge nodded. "*Sí.*"

"In that case I'll go downstairs and pen the deal, and get you the bank details for the first payment."

"Okay," said Jorge, "but no need for the bank transfer." He reached into his bag by the desk. "Here's the $100,000. I'll pay you when you bring the contract back. Now let's get the kid back in."

The CEO left the room and Jorge explained the deal to Sheetal; he wanted to make very sure the young man knew the Indian executives had no claim to his part of the incentive payment. He then asked Sheetal to write down his 'dream-sheet' of every piece of equipment he would need to do the job, and told him to be ready to take his passport to the Mexican Consulate the next day for his visa.

The CEO returned with the handwritten contract. Jorge made some requisite lawyer-like changes to it and they all signed. The Indians left and Jorge called in a favour for Sheetal's visa – it was a done deal. He then emailed one of the cartel's quartermasters in Mexico City with Sheetal's list. It would be ready to go.

Jorge amended his flight to leave the day after Sheetal would almost certainly have his visa issued, and booked him onto the same flights. He would instruct Sheetal not to associate with him on the flight or anywhere else until they got to Mexico City, where, unbeknown to this young Indian hacker, Jorge's organisation owned pretty much every official it needed.

Sheetal didn't know it yet, but he was destined for the town of Los Mochis in northern Sinaloa, where his activities would cause the downfall of his paymaster and the unexpected ascendancy of a new and, apparently, populist world order.

CHAPTER EIGHT
Dinner Stakes

Oleana was lounging by the pool of the Palace Hotel, enjoying the almost vertical upward view of the world's tallest tower. She was procrastinating making the phone call she knew she needed to make to Moscow. On the one hand, she was wallowing in the sojourn of not having to answer or explain her movements to anyone; on the other, she knew she needed to inform the cartel she was out of jail before they discovered it for themselves. She was also fully aware that she'd be called in for a debrief to explain what she'd been asked by the authorities while she was inside and whether it had any implications for the organisation.

The thought of being judged by her own kind was about as daunting as the process she'd been subjected to in the Arab courts. However, at least she knew these people, and there would be no kicking the can down the road with the Russians. They would quickly decide if she was still useful to them, and if not, at best she'd be expelled, and at worst…well, she just didn't want to think about that eventuality just yet.

She was just hoping to hell she'd get a chance to spend her newfound wealth and was thinking about where exactly when her thoughts were broken by her phone ringing; it was the first call she'd received since getting out. She looked down at the screen and was surprised to see the name '*Graham*'; she swiped green to pick up.

A pensive "Hello?" was all she said.

"Oleana, it's Graham Tree." He was not so presumptuous as to think she'd have saved his number, going so far as to qualify even further: "Harry Linley's friend."

"Hi Graham, how are you?" She wasn't sure why but found herself smiling.

"Never mind about me," Graham answered, "How are *you*? I hear they put you away, but now you're out."

"They dropped the case, Graham, but only after six fucking months." By now her face had fallen. "Harry's bitch of a wife set me up; we'd arranged to meet for coffee so I could see their baby boy. She never showed but the police sure did, and the next thing I knew I was being investigated for activities 'contrary to the interests of the state'."

Graham listened, but he really didn't want her in a bad mood; he needed to lighten the atmosphere and change the subject. "So where are you now?"

She told him and he tried to set a positive trend on the conversation. "Oh, that's a lovely place, have you tried the Argentinian restaurant?"

"Well, it's not much fun dining alone, so no I haven't." Her response had not meant to sound the way it came out – she knew straight away what would come next.

"Well I can help fix that. Why don't we catch up tonight over dinner? I've got loads to tell you." Graham didn't really have very much of anything at all to tell her, but knew that if he threw out some bait, she'd probably bite.

There was a pause. Oleana was thinking how she still looked awful and whether she even wanted Graham to see her so underweight and gaunt. However, within seconds she'd concluded perhaps a couple of hours with him would give her some information she didn't know, and she could certainly do with the nourishment of a good Argentinian steak. "Okay," she said, "would around eight work? I can't have a late night." In one fell swoop, she had just taken sex off the menu, and Graham knew it, but he wasn't bothered. Conquering Oleana after the likes of Harry Linley had already been there did not appeal to him.

"Sounds good. The restaurant's called *Asado*. I'll book a table for eight o'clock and meet you in the hotel lobby."

Oleana agreed, and as the call ended she checked the time – it was 3 pm. She would call her Russian employer tomorrow after she'd extracted some updates from Graham.

In his office, no sooner had he hung up on Oleana than Graham was making another call.

"Shaheen, it's Graham. I just spoke to her, she's staying in the Palace Hotel in Downtown Dubai. I'm having dinner with her tonight, so I'll be able to find out more."

"How long is she staying?" Shaheen asked.

"I didn't ask but I'll find out this evening. All she said was that the charges had been dropped and that she blamed Harry's wife for having got her banged up."

"In that case, I need to thank her." Shaheen was dead serious. "It's a shame they didn't throw the key away."

Graham assumed the bitterness Shaheen expressed was because perhaps the rumour Oleana had been his dead wife's lover was true; he had no idea that the man also blamed her for the theft of millions of dollars' worth of his tax-evading gains.

"None of us can turn back the clock, Shaheen, mate. I'm not an advocate of 'forgive' but I do think it helps to 'forget' past stuff there's no solution for."

"She took things from me, Graham. Deliberately and calculatedly." Shaheen was thinking of his money; Graham was thinking of his wife. "Do not have sympathy for this woman, she's wreaked havoc on my life since I met her, and the fact that I happen to be here in a good place with a new woman is in spite not because of her. If we can teach Oleana the meaning of the word 'consequences', I think we'll both be doing her a big favour in life, and *that* is why I've been paying you a retainer, Graham."

"Don't get me wrong, Shaheen, I'm your man and I'll get you the information you need. I'd only add what the old Chinese saying says about revenge – '*When a man goes and seeks revenge, he'd better dig two graves*'. I wouldn't want you to go after her and end up having her cause even more trouble for you, that's all."

"I appreciate your concern, Graham, but just find out everything you can tonight and then I can make a decision."

Graham hadn't heard Shaheen this irritated before, but he felt he'd been able to say his piece. Now, if anything went wrong with whatever Shaheen had in mind for Oleana, at least Graham could say, "I told you so." He thought about calling Harry, but decided it could wait until tomorrow when he knew more.

As Shaheen placed his phone down on the coffee table, Lai Xian peered over at him from across the kitchen counter. "Is everything okay, baby?" she asked.

"I don't know yet." Shaheen looked vulnerable. "There's a score to settle; I know how; I just don't know where or when."

Lai Xian walked into the lounge and sat on his knee. She leaned forward and kissed him. "Don't worry, my baby," she said soothingly. "Whenever and wherever, I'll be there with you. Maybe I can even help."

Shaheen felt her light but firm body on his knee and now in his hands; he knew that if the shit ever did go down, then she would be of little to no use to him, so he simply said, "That's good, sweetie, at least I'll have someone with me I can trust." He smiled into her eyes. "Now, let's have a quickie."

Lai Xian chuckled and looked at her watch. "It'll have to be. Aryan's back from soccer in half an hour." She sprang to her feet, lifted up her skirt and removed her panties, knelt down in front of Shaheen and began to undo his belt.

He was no longer thinking of Oleana.

Harry's was sitting in his new firm's Old Broad Street office when his phone rang.

"Graham, you big wanker! Where are you?"

"I'm in Dubai, mate, and guess who I'm taking to dinner tonight?"

"Go on," Harry urged.

"Only Oleana. She's out of jail, mate." Graham said 'mate' a lot.

Harry's mind raced. His instinct was to be happy for her, but he knew well enough it had been his wife who'd stitched Oleana up to the police, and now she might be out for revenge. "Well, give her my love when you see her. How long has she been out?" He was keen to know whether she'd have had any time to start on a revenge plan.

"I'm not sure, but not long." Graham paused. "Look mate – Shaheen Soroush still has a serious axe to grind with her; I don't know why but he seems to loathe her."

"See if you can find out her plans." Harry has asked the obvious. "And do tell her you've spoken to me and that I was asking after her to find out if she's okay." He hoped that might soften her up.

"I'll do that," Graham replied.

"And try not to shag her, you bastard!" Harry added with a laugh.

"Hey mate, you know me – I'd take a jagged hole in a rusty tin can if it had a female body attached to it. Anyway, perhaps she could do with a real man for a change, hey?"

"You know she's going to look at it and say, 'Oooh Graham, it's just like Harry's penis but smaller'." Harry put on his sultriest Russian accent.

"It's not the size that counts, mate, otherwise you'd still be a virgin," Graham countered.

"I've never heard a diamond dealer or a woman say that size doesn't matter – only guys with small dicks!" Harry was on a roll.

"Go fuck yourself, Harry, while you think of me plundering your well-trodden ground later."

"Alright bud," chuckled Harry, calling the proceedings to a good-natured end. "You have fun, but make sure to give me the full monty when you have it." He put down the phone and immediately received a WhatsApp – '*Keep fit, 4 pm*'. He smiled; Ivanna must have arrived back from Monaco.

He called Nazrin to say he was delayed at work.

CHAPTER NINE
Inmate's Out Mate

In Moscow's Voentorg Building, just five hundred metres from the Kremlin, Isaak sat in his third-floor accountancy firm's office. He listened intently and with concealed irritation to Ivanna, who was calling him from London.

She explained to Isaak that she'd asked Maria to come to London, but as she spoke she couldn't stop thinking of the 'keep fit' text she'd just sent Harry, thrilled at the prospect of the evening's activity. In a tone that didn't match her expression, she continued to explain to her accountant that she was promoting Maria within the cartel and that she'd decided she should become her attaché in London in order to act as an extra pair of eyes and ears over operations. Of course she couldn't mention her real reason was that she craved a female confidante and companion.

Isaak wanted to protest, more for reasons of satisfying his lust than anything professional, but he restrained himself. He really didn't want Maria away from Moscow, and he certainly didn't want her closer to Ivanna. However, it was quickly explained to him by the intuitive Godmother that she needed him able to concentrate one hundred percent on the accounts and 'cleaning', and that Maria assisting her in London would ease his load by alleviating the necessity for long calls such as this one.

As he heard the words, he couldn't help but think that with Maria in London, the only thing easing his load in the immediate future would be his own right hand.

Having been dismissed, Isaak slung his phone down onto the couch and exclaimed, "Fuck!" All thoughts of money and sex were suddenly driven from his mind by the attractive Regus receptionist knocking at his door and then awaiting his instruction to "*Vohdite!*"

As she half-opened the door he couldn't help but notice the tightness of her dress, the effect of which on men she knew full well. Her lips were devoid of lipstick but pouting nonetheless and still beautiful. "Mr Kiselev is here to see you," she said.

Isaak immediately linked the name to how much he'd like to kiss those lips, but instead smiled politely and said, "Oh yes, please send him in."

As Artur Kiselev entered the room he might well have sensed Isaak's fear and, justifiably so. Artur was clearly not a man to fuck with. He was just thirty-four years old and sported a nose that had never recovered from being severely broken several times. His hair was dark but no longer than three millimetres anywhere on his head, and he was quite unshaven. His shoulders were broad, his waist thin, and at a glance Isaak judged him to be about 185 centimetres tall. He was dressed in a black jacket, black shirt and black jeans.

As he held out his self-tattooed hand to shake Isaak's, the former convict simply said, "*Zdravstvuyte*, Mr Rabinovich, nice to finally meet you."

Isaak gestured for the man to sit down, unable to conceal his curiosity. "I'm sorry, Mr Kiselev, I was intrigued by the urgency of your call and your demand to meet me regarding 'company business'. But the fact is I've never heard of you, so I'm not sure why you would want to *finally* meet me. After all, I am just a humble accountant."

"First of all, Mr Rabinovich, you should call me Artur. I don't like being called by my last name. I hope it's also okay if I call you Isaak?"

"Please do," nodded Isaak politely.

"You see, Isaak, we share the same boss, so we are in fact colleagues."

Isaak became indignant. "Oh I don't think so, Artur; I only have one boss and I know all our employees, given the fact I happen to oversee all their salaries. So I don't see how we can be fellow employees."

Artur smiled to reveal his stained teeth which would have better suited a man twice his age. "But my boss – our boss – is Alexei Delimkov, and he has been for the last two years."

Isaak immediately cut in. "Well, I don't see how that can be – Mr Delimkov has been…"

"In Krasnoyarsk prison, with me," Artur interrupted. "Except I was in there for the last ten years." He now had Isaak's undivided attention. "When Alexei arrived at the jail, it was clear straight away he wasn't one of my kind; he's a very smart man, and now he runs our camp number. As it happens, he and I have become good friends. I have this letter from him." He reached across the desk, offering a cheap brown envelope to Isaak, who seized it and opened it.

My dear Isaak,

It has been a tough two-plus years and I know that, for the sake of company security, I was not to be contacted by any of you except Ivanna, who as my wife would raise no suspicion. However, her letters are now few and far between and I am concerned. Is she all right and does she still miss me? My lawyer says she does but also that she has moved to London. I assume this is because it is unsafe for her in Moscow.

Do not tell Ivanna, but I believe I have a very good chance of having my sentence reduced. It may cost me up to $20 million to certain parties. Therefore, please have this money ready and on hand whenever the instructions are given.

The man who has delivered this letter is Artur Kiselev, he has the word 'CEBEP' tattooed just above his right wrist. He has been a good and loyal protector to me in prison, please put him on the payroll and pay him 4 million roubles.

I will see you soon, my dear friend, to personally thank you for safeguarding my business. And please – I want to surprise Ivanna, so not a word to her about any chance of my possible release.

Alexei.

"Could you show me your right wrist please, Artur?" Isaak asked.

Artur pulled up his sleeve to reveal a heavily tattooed forearm, and the word '*CEBEP*' was clearly visible just above his right wrist.

Isaak pulled open his drawer and selected one of six cheque books. As he wrote, he said, "This cheque is for four million roubles, that's about $60,000, so it should last you well, Artur. I can't pay you any more without direct instruction from Alexei, which is unlikely to happen unless he gets out of prison, so please spend this wisely." He pushed the cheque across the table.

Artur read it and smiled. "It's good to be on the same team, Isaak." He folded the cheque and put it in his jacket pocket.

Isaak cringed as he heard the words, but concealed his distaste. He despised overt criminals, and this guy fell right into that category. The only comforting thought was that Mr Kiselev would in all likelihood fuck up again and wind up right back where he'd just come from. He reached over to shake the man's hand. "Welcome aboard, Artur! You have my number, but please only call me in an emergency – or if you have news of Alexei." He was relieved to see Artur almost skip out of his office with glee.

Isaak spun in his chair, somewhat shell-shocked by the encounter. Alexei out in three years instead of ten for a pay-off of $20 million! Should he tell Ivanna or follow instructions? He tried to assess which was the more hazardous choice. He'd have to side with Alexei, who after all was the long-term play. At the end of the day, no matter how good an interim boss Ivanna had made, he only had to survive with her until Alexei got out; for him this game was a lifelong insurance plan.

He called Maria to probe her some more about her role change and arranged a 'dinner date' that night so he could 'seduce' her just one more time before she left for London.

It was just gone 4 pm when Harry turned the corner into Eaton Terrace and smiled fondly at the sight of the Antelope, the venue of his first meeting with Ivanna.

As he crossed over the road towards the entrance of Eaton Terrace Mews, he used the opportunity to check his tail for anyone observing him. With nothing immediately registering as a problem, he strolled on up the mews and rang the doorbell of Number 9.

Ivanna opened the door looking and smelling stunning. She was wearing an Agent Provocateur Rosette Blue dress that left nothing to the imagination, under which he glimpsed matching bra and panties concealing only what was most important; and to complete the ensemble, a pair of black Christian Louboutin heels. Harry adored women who dressed for bed and the effect on him was almost instantaneous. The front door was no sooner shut than they were kissing; she could feel his excitement against her pelvis. She placed her hand against his fly, feeling the extent of his manhood.

"Let's get my little Harry upstairs," she whispered through her teeth in her most alluring Russian accent,

She went ahead of him, knowing he would be fixated on her legs and behind, showcased to perfection by her dress. As she led him into the bedroom, she simply asked, "Shoes on or off?"

Harry smiled and kissed her. "Yours on, mine off." He was already pulling his shirt off over his head, his Montblanc belt long undone.

Ivanna fell purposely down onto the bed and looked up at him. "Fuck me, Harry" were the last words she said before Harry eased up her dress, she raised her pelvis subtly towards him, and he entered her body. Ivanna couldn't remember when she'd last been so happy, or so much in love.

Harry couldn't remember when a woman had tried so hard to please him.

CHAPTER TEN
Casino Charity

With his drug lord apparently safely holed up in Costa Rica, Jorge González had decided to personally supervise Sheetal's installation in the remote wilds of the Golden Triangle on the border of Durango and Sinaloa states, an area where Archivaldo and his reach were revered and rightly feared.

The procurement of the D-Wave 2X quantum computer had taken a bit of doing. However, the supplier had been convinced that the buyer was a group of hedge fund entrepreneurs based in Chapel Hill, North Carolina. Supposedly they required the speed and lowest denominator characteristics of the computer to produce an artificial intelligence application to the stock market. In this way, and by paying off a bunch of intelligent – but utterly corrupt – idiots in Carolina to front the well-funded shell company, Jorge and the cartel had got it done.

The movement and installation of the hardware would have been problematic for just about any other organisation but the Sinaloa cartel. Because, after all, here was an outfit that could push $3 billion worth of hard drugs across the US border every year; getting something – even a quantum computer – across the border in the opposite direction was a veritable piece of cake.

The installation of the closed-cycle dilution refrigeration cooling equipment and the accompanying power source into the brand new complex opposite the International Paper plant in Los Mochis was perfect cover. All the D-Wave logos had been removed from the equipment, which had subsequently been repacked in refrigeration unit containers, so no onlooker or deliveryman would think for a moment that the town was acquiring the most powerful computer in Central and South America.

The culture shock for Sheetal between Mumbai and Los Mochis was palpable. One was huge, vibrant and relatively safe for an Indian – the other precisely the opposite. He had been put up in a safe house villa with a housemaid and cook to enjoy. He was driven to and from work by two armed and heavily tattooed men who spoke only broken English. Unbeknown to Sheetal, both men were under threat of death to keep anything from happening to him.

Sheetal was pleasantly surprised, just three days after he'd starting configuring the '2X', when one of his protectors walked in and handed him his mobile phone. "It's for you."

"How are you settling in, Sheetal?" Jorge asked after they had exchange greetings.

"I must admit I'm a little bit homesick, Mr Jorge; this place is very different from my world." As Sheetal spoke, the protector couldn't help but notice the Indian's head doing an almost permanent sideways nod.

"You'll get used to it, my friend," said Jorge. "Just think about how you're going to spend all that money when you get home." His tone changed as he moved onto business. "Where are we at accessing and tracking the account movement?"

"I've just started in earnest, but we still need to try something just to test the tracking system. I also need to see if I can achieve our work unnoticed once the monies leave your accounts. I'll need to show you whenever you come here."

He sat down before the multiple screens containing vast amounts of information he knew went far beyond even Jorge's intelligent mind. He plugged his ear-piece into the phone.

"I've started to scan some accounts, Mr Jorge, in order to test my system, but none of these accounts have anything to do with ours. There's one for instance. It's in New York, it has $954 million in it, and it belongs to the Bangladesh Central Bank."

He highlighted a box on his screen containing data text and the dollar amount. "I've had the computer crosscheck potential passwords at random, and here's the password. The computer found it in less than two minutes so I've managed to breach their server and their codes."

Jorge wasn't sure he'd understood what was going on, but the Indian geek now had his full attention.

"If you'd like me to, I can push in a SWIFT from Bangladesh FX reserves for, let's say, $100 million. New York's Federal Reserve won't be able to gauge that the instruction isn't genuine, so we'll soon see if any alarm bells go off. They shouldn't, but if they do, then at least we'll test the visibility of the firewall protections I've built – these should ensure nobody can know that *we*, and not the Bangladeshis, have directed the transfer."

"Okay, so if you can do the transfer, where will you send it?" asked Jorge.

"Well, Mr Jorge, at the moment we don't want anyone to look at our accounts, so why don't we do a couple of things." He wished Jorge could see his impish smile. "I can send it somewhere innocuous but probably criminal, so let's say a casino or two in the Philippines? If they realise they've been given the money in error, they'll have it laundered within a day. So this will allow us to see whether our directions work, and if they don't, at least no one will know it's us directing the transfer. If all goes as planned, from there we can confidently turn our attention to your own accounts and the people who've been stealing from them. Once we're confident they can't detect us. What do you think?"

"Let's give it a go," Jorge said enthusiastically.

"Consider it done." Sheetal's fingers flashed over the keyboard. The call ended. He had just become a criminal.

The transfer went into motion, and three casinos in the Philippines were about to have a good day. It would only be some weeks later before someone in the Bangladesh Central Bank realised they were short $100 million and the alarm would be raised – by which time the money would be long gone.

Three days later, with no repercussions within the system, Jorge cleared Sheetal to go after the bastards who had stolen the

Sinaloa cartel's money, and he would arrange for deposits into a sole trader's account at Banco Inbursa's modest branch on Fray Servando Teresa de Mier.

The tethered goat was about to be in play.

At 8 pm Oleana was waiting nervously in the lobby of the Palace Hotel. She wasn't too sure why she was so agitated. It could be that she hadn't been out on what might be considered a dinner date since before her incarceration, or the fact that she hadn't had sex in all that time either. But she concluded it was more likely because, for what was probably one of the first times in her adult life, she didn't feel confident in her looks and appearance. She had made a real effort with her hair and make-up, and found a reasonably priced fluid silk knee-length Cedar dress from Reiss that went some way to concealing her weight loss.

But she needn't have worried. When Graham arrived, although he could see her face was considerably thinner than it had been the last time they'd met, he thought her more modelesque than skinny. They greeted each other and made their way along the stone-lined passage to the warm atmospherics and gentle musical entertainment of the Asado restaurant. It was the perfect ambiance to calm Oleana, and the quality of the food was exactly what her body craved.

As Graham ordered a bottle of 2013 Alamos Malbec, Oleana's mind flashed back to her night of wine and sex with Harry Linley in London, when he too had greeted her with a bottle of Malbec. She wondered if Graham was attempting to mimic Harry's class, but perhaps it was just coincidence. In any case, after the first glass, which went straight to her head, she didn't care.

Graham asked how she'd coped in prison.

"I'm Russian, Graham, so I'm a survivalist, but it was fucking awful. They had nothing on me though, so all I had to do was keep my mouth shut and play the long game."

"So what now?" he asked.

"Get the fuck out of here while I still have my passports. This whole experience has taught me one very important thing."

"And that is?"

"Never worry about how you're going to get into a foreign

country, only about how to get out of it. I should have seen this shit coming."

Graham could sense a hardness in her that he hadn't seen before, but he had her on a roll. "And where to from here?"

"I'm not sure," she lied. "I don't have much money." Another lie. "I'm thinking Saint Petersburg to live with my sister." She didn't have one. "Or maybe Moscow to see Maria." She knew Graham had slept with Maria so his response was wholly predictable.

"How is she?" he asked, trying to be innocuous but the perk in his tone quite obvious.

"How the fuck should I know, Graham, I've been in prison and she's in Moscow." There was a nervous pause, so she picked up her glass and smiled at him to dispel any awkwardness. "Have you heard from Harry?"

"I spoke to him today, he sends his love and wishes you well. He said he hopes to see you." Graham watch her smile fade.

"I'm fond of Harry, but I was meant to be meeting his bitch wife for coffee when I was arrested; so it had to be her who set me up."

"I don't know anything about that," Graham said, remaining truthful, "but if that's the case, then you can be sure she had no choice. The police here don't mess around when they decide to swoop."

"Well, I'd like to know for sure. This has completely fucked up my life." The waitress appeared and Oleana's mouth watered as she eyed the perfectly prepared fillet steak on her plate. "Please tell Harry I think he owes me big."

Graham said he would, before quickly changing the subject to his plans for a holiday that year. She soon brought him back to reality, however. "What about Shaheen? Do you hear from him?"

"Not often." It was now Graham's turn to lie. "But I hear he's still in Singapore. I get the impression he's rebuilding his life since his wife and daughter were killed. I suppose he doesn't really have much choice. What a waste."

"It really was," Oleana reflected. "His wife was very dear to me." She assumed Graham had no idea they had been lovers. "I think Shaheen somehow blames me for things I had nothing to do with, or at least had no control over, and I have no idea why." Once again she was planting the seeds to sway his outlook and loyalty if ever it came to that. Then she threw in the bluffing ace. "Look, if I go back to Moscow to stay with Maria, would you come visit?"

Bingo, thought Graham. "I'd love to."

They finished the meal and, as ever, Oleana being a woman had one clear advantage over any man on any date – she already knew how the evening was going to end.

There'd been a couple of moments when she'd seriously thought about inviting Graham up to her room for a nightcap, but the real fly in the ointment was that he'd grown a beard since their last encounter. Throughout the entire evening she'd tried to figure out what Graham saw when he looked in the mirror. She came to the conclusion that whatever he imagined was not what the rest of the world saw, at least not with that facial scruff. She'd have liked to tell him to shave it off, but thought what the hell. After all, the chance for a night in the lovely – and beardless – hotel bed by herself seemed much more alluring.

So by 10.45 pm she had pecked Graham goodnight in the lobby and gone up to her room, only to find a message from Sergeant Seyadin asking for a social meeting. Oleana knew she would have no choice but to meet with her, but also knew she had to get the hell out of this country. To that end she resolved to deposit as much money into her local bank account, in amounts that would not draw attention, just as quickly as the system would allow, then head to wherever Maria was hanging out; she would call her in the morning.

CHAPTER ELEVEN
Shampoo And Set

It was nearly 8.30 pm when Harry wandered downstairs and pulled himself a beer from Ivanna's fridge. After they had both climaxed, he'd dozed off while she'd lain with her head on his shoulder listening to his steady breathing.

Ivanna was now in the kitchen. Harry had showered while she changed out of her 'fuck-me' dress and into a silk robe. As he entered the kitchen she sauntered up to him, kissed him and took a sip from his beer. Harry smiled. "You know men have died for less?" he joked.

"As a matter of fact, I do, Harry." She kissed him again, knowing he had no clue that in her world she held power over life and death.

"Can we talk?" she asked.

"Sure. What's up?" Harry looked into her green eyes; she was so beautiful.

"Where are we going, Harry?" She'd been dying to ask him this while he slept.

"What do you mean?" He was thinking about the next time they would see each other.

"You and me, Harry? I know we love each other, so what's our plan?" Immediately she could see she'd taken Harry by complete surprise as the mood in the room suddenly shifted.

"Well, we are both married, babe, so don't you think it makes long-term planning a little bit awkward?" He was stating the obvious.

"But I could leave my husband; he's in jail for the next seven years so we have plenty of time to work things out; and you could move in here?" There was an element of pleading in her completely and utterly flawed proposal.

"Whoa, whoa!" Harry felt blindsided, "I can't get a divorce, babe, my wife would take me to the cleaners and I wouldn't be there to bring up my son." He thought better than to also mention Bunny, his beloved cat. Changing to a gentler tone, he then reiterated her point. "We have a great thing going on here, why mess it up?"

"Mess it up?" Her voice was raised. "Mess what up!? The fact we have to sneak sex and not tell anyone about our relationship? I want more!" She had just committed a mistress's cardinal sin – overreach.

"Well, I'm sorry, Ivanna, but for now this has to be it. I'm very fond of you but we can't go nuclear with this just yet." His misguided attempt to calm her had the opposite effect. She went ballistic.

"Fond? Fond! What the fuck does that mean? I'm fond of furniture and red wine and *you're* only fucking '*fond*' of me?" Now she was shouting.

"I didn't mean it that way, we Brits just have an aversion to the 'L' word, that's all. You know how much you mean to me!" Now Harry was trapped.

"Oh I do, Harry, four hours of fucking a week, that's all I mean to you." She paused, looking away defiantly. "You should leave now."

"Oh come on, don't be like that." He really didn't want to argue with her.

"Harry." She returned eye contact and took the beer bottle from his hand. "Go pick up your shit and leave."

"But, Ivanna…" He tried to reason.

"Now!" she yelled at the top of her voice.

Harry said nothing; he walked calmly up the stairs, put on his socks and shoes, and grabbed his jacket. Back downstairs, he stood at the kitchen door, looked at Ivanna, and spoke gently so as to throw out an olive branch. He would, however, regret his choice of words almost as soon as they left his lips.

"Keep fit tomorrow?" He was trying to throw some levity onto the situation.

The very next moment he ducked as what had been his beer bottle was hurled towards his head. He swerved and the bottle hit the wall, but somehow didn't break, and fell to the floor with a hollow clank.

He looked at Ivanna as he bent down to pick it up, before leaning forward to place it on the kitchen table, never taking his eyes off hers in case she launched again. "Are we done?" he asked, knowing the question could be applicable to either the fight or the affair.

Ivanna looked defiant. "The next object won't miss, Harry."

The situation was clear; Harry turned and walked out the front door without another word.

He walked up the mews, genuinely wondering what the fuck had just happened. How could a woman transition from the sexiest goddess on earth to a fucking lunatic in just the time he'd taken to have a nap and a shower? He walked to Sloane Square and caught the tube to Richmond. He hoped his little Charlie would still be awake by the time he reached home.

Ivanna sat in her kitchen and wept. She'd lost control of herself and already wanted him to come back; she'd been driven by her decision that she no longer wanted to be a prison-widow, but what could she do? She made two calls – one to Maria to tell her to expedite her transfer to London the very next day and to expect to stay close-by in the short term; the other to Willie, the London fixer, instructing him to book a table at the Bluebird for 10 pm, and for him to meet her there. Under the pretext of briefing him on Maria's arrival, she knew she could safely rely on him for an evening's much needed distraction.

When Maria received Ivanna's call, she too had just had sex and was also weeping, but her tears were out of anger. Every time she had to 'liaise' with Isaak the payback seemed worse and worse. If initially he'd made her skin crawl, now his lightest touch made it feel alive with parasites. She hated him more than he could ever imagine; there was no shower that could cleanse her, no vaginal douche that could rid her enough of his weak seed, so far as she could see, no end in sight save for one solution. She had to get this pervert off her back – literally. To cap it all, his demands in the bedroom had gone far beyond missionary sex and now all bets were off; this man was blinded by a love spelt 'l-u-s-t' and pronounced 'fuck', and he wasn't even good at it.

Maria recalled how her mother had once told her, "You should never hate anyone, because to do so is to wish them dead." She knew she hated Isaak.

So the call from Ivanna offered her three immediate lifelines: time, space and a way to lure this bastard away from his home turf to somewhere they hadn't been witnessed as a couple.

Once in London, Maria would get inside Ivanna's decision cycle, bide her time, and only then figure out how best to kill Isaak.

It was all under control, or so she thought.

It was 7 pm the following evening when Sergeant Maryam Seyadin glided into the Palace Hotel. Her figure-hugging abaya was open at the front revealing her skin-tight pleather trousers, and she was sporting a pair of red Gina platform stilettos that precisely matched the trim on her abaya, the red Prada bag she was carrying and the colour of her nail polish and lipstick.

She smiled broadly as she saw Oleana, who was visibly shocked that this woman who had always looked so plain at work could suddenly look so stunning when dressed to impress.

After the two women had 'air kissed' each other on both cheeks, they sat down, and Oleana opened the conversation. "I'm sorry, I started drinking my vodka while I was waiting, I hope you don't mind. Would you like one?"

Maryam could tell that lack of pause between sentences implied nervousness, so she tried to put Oleana at ease. "No problem, I figure you deserve a vodka or two."

"Can I order one for you?" Oleana asked again.

"Actually you can't, not while I'm dressed like this; but you can order me a water with lime and ice, and another double vodka and tonic for yourself." She leaned forward conspiratorially to whisper playfully. "And maybe while you're drinking yours, some of it can get muddled up with my water. That way you remain the decadent unbeliever, and I remain a model of Middle Eastern moral womanhood."

"Consider it done!" Oleana waved at the Indian waitress and ordered the drinks. Within five minutes, the policewoman was already feeling the 'Absolut' glow.

"I feel very sorry for you, Oleana." Maryam wanted to get Oleana talking about herself. "I don't think you got what you deserved." It was a deliberately open-ended statement.

"I learned long ago, Maryam," Oleana replied, "that you don't get what you deserve in life, you get what you negotiate. And I guess in this case I didn't negotiate too well." She conveniently neglected to mention the hundreds of thousands of dollars her time in prison had protected. If there were going to be any back-lash from the cartel, she'd have surely heard something by now.

"True." Maryam leaned forward and reached out for her hand. "But I'm guessing there's a lot more to you than meets the eye."

Oleana's – misguided – interpretation of what was happening hit her like a train – was Seyadin trying to play her for information because she knew about her previous lesbian relationship, or was this for real? Either way, Oleana instinctively hoped she could cap-italise on it, so she simply created a hand sandwich by placing her other hand on top of the detective's.

"Well, you're right about that, Maryam." Oleana's crystal-blue eyes were locked onto Maryam's two black pools, where pupil and iris were indistinguishable. "But you won't see any of that down here." She glanced around the bar lobby. "For that I think we should take the vodkas upstairs."

"Perfect." Maryam was certain that, if she could get Oleana into the privacy of her room, and with enough vodka, she'd forget she was talking to a policewoman. Oleana on the other hand could almost instantly feel the anticipation and excitement manifesting itself as a moistness between her legs.

Oleana stood up and picked up her vodka to down it in one. "Let's go!"

Maryam remained seated but did the same to her drink. The two women then walked towards the lifts that would take them the three floors to Oleana's room. Two glasses of water remained untouched on the table they'd just occupied. Hotel security noted that Oleana had a local female guest in her room. They were unlikely to interpret anything untoward.

★   ★   ★

Harry walked into the hallway of his house to find his young son Charlie holding himself up unsteadily on the door-guard that kept him imprisoned in their 'Charlie-proof' living room, duly sanitised by Nazrin to ensure no movables were in reach of their now energetically crawling son.

"Hello mate." Harry reached over the guard to pick his son up. "Where's your mum?"

"In the kitchen fixing your dinner," came the reply from behind the kitchen door, which was also barriered to keep Charlie confined to the lounge.

Harry hurdled into the lounge. "So what are we having?" he asked, as he climbed astride the second barrier, his content son still in his arms.

"It's lamb, baby. Your favourite." She turned to face him and smiled as only a wife and mother could towards the two most precious men in her life. As he came close to kiss her, she asked him how his day had been.

"It was good," he lied, trying to banish his row with Ivanna from his mind and life. He put his arm around Nazrin and suddenly felt a pang of guilt. She was such a good woman; he truly had no idea why he needed to stray, and especially not with a married woman.

Nazrin, for her part, felt a wave of contentment and kissed Harry on his neck and nuzzled his ear. But then she paused for just one moment; she almost said something, but caught herself, lingering just a little longer. There was no mistake – Harry's hair and ear smelt of fresh shampoo!

She calmed her thoughts and nuzzled again before saying, "Sit down, baby. Would you like a beer or a cup of tea?"

"Take a wild-arse guess!" Harry laughed as she was already on her way to the fridge, where she pulled out a bottle of Old Speckled Hen and used the opener that was magnetised to the fridge door.

"Bottle or glass?"

"Bottle's fine." Harry's attention was now with Charlie, who was sitting on his lap trying to reach out to every item on the kitchen table.

Nazrin handed Harry the beer, then kissed Charlie strategically on his little head. His hair smelt clean, but of hair. She kissed Harry on his head. The smell of fresh shampoo was unmistakeable, and it wasn't the Molton Brown *Ylang-Ylang* scented shower gel Harry favoured, which was a familiar smell in their bathroom every morning.

"Did you get to work out today?" She needed to ask.

"I wish!" Harry replied, unaware of the reason for the question. "I've been jammed all day business planning with Sid."

Nazrin remained composed, but not for the first time, every warning light in her 'man protection' instincts was flashing. Harry had showered either for no reason or for bad reason – either way she needed to find out why.

When they went to bed Harry was not in the mood for sex; he couldn't know then just how much he should have been.

CHAPTER TWELVE
Cellist Strings

J orge González had left his boss in Costa Rica, confident that the authorities had no clue he was there. He had left strict instructions with the security team that the boss was not to communicate with the outside world by any means that didn't have a protected VPN, and that he should also not use any computer he had ever used before. His SIM cards for his mobile would be changed every single day since anyone who knew him would know he seldom called on recognisable numbers anyway.

The flights to Sinaloa had gone without incident and Jorge had breezed through the airports at both ends. Once in Sinaloa, in any case, he owned the police (or at least all those that mattered). So he felt relaxed as he exited the Toyota RAV4 that had dropped him at the small warehouses opposite the International Paper plant. As he walked to the building he noticed the additional generators installed along its length and rightly assumed this served to enhance and back up the equipment inside that relied on a continuous supply of electrical power.

One of the cartel's security detail unlocked the two layers of doors that formed the entrance to the building and Jorge's senses were struck by two things. The first was the almost fridge-like temperature of the place; the second was the noise being emitted from whatever was in the room next door; something akin to a muted jet engine.

In front of him sat Sheetal Khan facing sixteen screens full of columns of numbers and code script. Such was the young Indian's focus that he hadn't heard Jorge come up behind him. He was startled when he felt a hand on his shoulder, and his boss asked, "So how's it going?"

"Mr Jorge, sir!" Sheetal leapt up to shake his hand. "I didn't know you were coming here."

Jorge smiled. "Well, I'm not in the habit of announcing my travel plans, Sheetal, especially not to an undisclosed location." He then pointed towards the open door that led to the adjacent room. "So is that my $15 million computer?"

"That it is, sir." Sheetal eagerly replied. "And I think she's worth every cent. I've never used this model before but I'm blown away by what it can do. Let me show it to you." Both men walked into the room and Jorge stood in awe before the black cube the size of a small room with what appeared to be server racks attached. The technical information binders alongside the computer's plain side simply read 'D-Wave' and nothing more.

"Is it as impressive as it looks?" Jorge asked. "Will it do the job?"

Sheetal led him back into the other room and closed the door to quell the noise. "It will work, sir, we just need whoever is stealing the money to take the bait and I think I'm ready."

"So explain to me – how?" Jorge knew instinctively he would likely understand very little of what Sheetal was about to explain to him.

"The financial world uses what is called the RSA encryption method." Sheetal was clearly excited just to explain. "And RSA includes a very difficult math problem related to factorisation. There's a 'private key' that contains the solution to that math problem. Theoretically, you could guess the answer by brute force decryption, where you simply keep guessing possible answers until you get the right one, but in practice this is impossible. To demonstrate, the average RSA key has 10^{302} possible answers. Not bad when you consider there are 10^{80} atoms in the observable universe. So if all the atoms in the universe were combined to create the world's most powerful CPU, it would still take 10^{211} years to achieve our aim by brute force. Mr Jorge, do you realise the universe is not even 10^{11} years old?"

"No, I didn't," replied Jorge, "but I do know we don't have that much time."

"Well, that's where you're in luck, Mr Jorge, because the way to solve the problem is by using something called Shor's algorithm."

"And the D5 can do that?" Jorge wanted to hurry him along to a conclusion.

"Well not quite Mr Jorge and that is why you need me because the D:Wave machine doesn't currently have the ability to decrypt RSA because it doesn't solve Shor's algorithm. It's currently used for deep learning slash neural network computing, which uses a different type of simpler math – principally linear regression. However, while I was at MIT I helped create quantum computers on a small scale that can solve Shor's algorithm for simple problems and nothing close to RSA's complexity, so I've programmed and altered the D-Wave machine to solve Shor's algorithm, combining the necessary computing power from D-Wave with the necessary programming to decrypt 99.99 percent of the world's encryption instantaneously. And that, Mr Jorge is how we are going to catch the entity stealing from you!"

Sheetal looked quite spent from his explanation; he was clearly proud and rightly so.

Jorge nodded. "Bien hecho, Sheetal. So is it ready?"

"I think it is," the Indian replied, beaming. "Now we just need the wolf to notice the tethered goat and to act.

Jorge nodded. "No problema, we're loading up this target account with $20 million in $5 million increments; we'll see whether our coyote turns up." He handed Sheetal a slip of paper with the Banco Inbursa account details. "If our thief takes the bait, I need you to track those funds wherever they end up, and I need you to crack the thief's IP or location. Can you do that?"

"I think I can." Sheetal nodded from side to side.

"Good. Because my boss is not a patient man." He handed Sheetal a cheap mobile phone. "There's just one number saved in this phone. When you have any results, call me on that number, but don't use my name on the line. You're to let me know when you have had a 'coyote in the garden', if he's taken anything, and if he left tracks. Do you understand?"

"I do, sir." Sheetal was already concentrating on not using Jorge's name.

"Good, we'll start loading the account tomorrow after midday, so make sure you're ready."

Sheetal nodded. "I'll be ready, sir."

Jorge smiled and glanced at the screens. "I have a feeling you will be." He headed for the exit, calling as he walked away from Sheetal, "Now catch me that coyote!"

Before leaving for Costa Rica, Jorge stopped over in Mexico City and met with the new bank manager of the Fray Servando Teresa de Mier branch of Banco Inbursa – the bait was laid.

In Moscow, the Delimkov cartel lawyer walked into the opulence of the Hotel National and smiled at the top-hatted and bow-tied doorman. This hotel would not have been his first choice, but he understood the reasons he'd been instructed to go to the venue. The Moskovsky restaurant was renowned in dubious but power-ful circles as the Cellist's favourite lunch spot when visiting from Saint Petersburg, and both the restaurant and hotel were only too pleased to accommodate his tastes and the block booking of a four-place table overlooking the Kremlin.

The sixties-style haircut and the mole above the left eye were identifiers enough for the lawyer to recognise the individual he'd never met before and hoped he would never meet again.

He introduced himself and shook his hand. The Cellist did not stand, but simply sipped a glass of 2008 Didier Dagueneau Silex, his favourite white wine, and gestured to the lawyer to sit down.

The waiter moved to place the napkin on the lawyer's lap but the Cellist intervened. "He's not eating, just pour him some wine, that's it." He'd drawn the lines of convention and the lawyer was under no illusions as to who was in control.

"Enjoy the wine." The Cellist was expressionless. "It's as good as you'll find anywhere."

"Thank you for seeing me, sir." The lawyer knew he was deal-ing with one of the most powerfully connected men in all of Rus-sia. He was acutely aware he couldn't afford to fuck this up from any angle. At best such event would cost him his job, at worst his liberty – or life.

The Cellist cut to the chase. "Your client pissed off my best friend. He had good favour, power and privilege, and he fucked it up by getting himself mixed up with an Iranian enrichment deal? Are you surprised he's in fucking jail?"

The lawyer knew he was on the back foot already. "I would say this, wouldn't I, but my client never had any dealings with the Iranians beyond property and iron ore, all of which was transparent to your boss, all of which has come to an end thanks to the US caving on the nuclear negotiations with Iran. My client had nothing to do with anything nuclear, and there's no evidence other than hearsay; it's an assumption to indicate anything to the contrary."

"Who gives a shit about evidence?" the Cellist replied in a low, menacing voice. "He fucked up and embarrassed the boss, he was lucky to only get ten years."

"I believe there is reasonable doubt, sir, and I also believe I wouldn't be sitting here if your…best friend and you didn't believe that too." The lawyer knew he'd just made a make-or-break statement.

"You might be right," the Cellist grunted, and sipped his wine. "But I suppose it's the level of reasonable doubt we're now discussing. How much do you think there is?"

"My client believes there's €10 million worth of such doubt, sir. Do you not think that reasonable?" The lawyer was starting to gain a bit of confidence.

"I do." The Cellist looked up from his wine. "But that would be €10 million for me and the same again for my best friend."

"But, sir, he's already spent nearly three years in Krasnoyarsk prison – surely that punishment is worth something?"

The Cellist knew he had all the power he needed. "Look, you little fucker," he said calmly. "Neither I nor my best friend give a shit if he spends another seven years there. I've given you the price for his freedom and a pardon – take it or leave it. Now finish your wine and let me enjoy my lunch and the view…alone."

The lawyer swigged his wine and placed the glass on the table as he stood up. "Very well, sir, we have an agreement. €20 million in total, but immediate release and pardon as soon as the money is in the accounts of your choosing. Do we have a deal?"

The Cellist looked up at the lawyer. "We do." He pulled an envelope from his jacket pocket and handed it to the lawyer. "These are the accounts where you should send the money. When it lands, your client will be released within a week."

The lawyer nodded and headed for the door. The Cellist watched him disappear from sight before reaching for his phone. It rang four times and a familiar voice greeted him. "Vlad, it's me. Spring Alexei Delimkov, we have ten big ones each."

The voice on the other end simply said, "Gotovo." It was done.

CHAPTER THIRTEEN
Long On London

Shaheen was relieved when Graham's call came. The fact (or so he thought) that Oleana and her accomplice had stolen so much from him had been consuming him, and not a day passed without him thinking of how to exact his retribution against her. If only he could figure out how he would do it.

To his credit though, Shaheen was far from a violent man, and he didn't relish the notion of any kind of physical revenge unless he was well removed from it. He would much rather damage her in terms of reputation or manipulate a permanent downfall. He was short on ideas but long on intent, so he listened carefully as Graham briefed him.

"Prison has clearly knocked the stuffing out of her, mate," explained Graham. "She looked thin and gaunt, even though she'd clearly made an effort to look nice for our dinner. She blames her being sent down on Harry's wife. She was apparently meant to meet her for coffee, but instead the police were there and she was immediately banged up."

"Is she right about that?" Shaheen was thinking that, not for the first time, he owed Harry Linley a big favour.

"I believe she is, and I say that because Harry had to leave the UAE the same day she was arrested, so that means one of three things..."

"Which are?"

"It means either it was a coincidence; or he was running away from the law; or the law told him to leave. And I don't happen to believe in the first option. So it has to be one of the latter two. And if I'm right? Then either Harry or his wife were in a pickle with the authorities, and one way or another Oleana became the sacrificial lamb."

"Do you think she's a criminal or a spy?" Shaheen asked. "Do we know what she was charged with?"

"She was charged with 'activities contrary to the interests of the state', whatever that means. I suppose it could be governmental but I'm guessing she's some sort of commercial spy. Anyway, they've dropped all charges, so it looks like she's innocent." He paused, "For now."

"You're wrong, Graham, she's a thief, and under the law no one is innocent, just guilty or not guilty." He was evidently irritated, but he hesitated for effect. "I don't want to tell you what she stole from me, but I have the evidence, and I strongly suspect she got caught doing something similar in Dubai and that's why she was arrested. Did she say how long she was going to stay?"

"Not explicitly," answered Graham, still wondering what the hell she could have stolen from Shaheen to get him so ruffled. "But I think she's going to head to Saint Petersburg, it's where she's from."

Shit, thought Shaheen. How the fuck was he going to get at her there? "Find out when and where she's going, Graham. I want her tracked and I'll pay you well for it."

"I'm on it, mate, give me a few days."

Shaheen put down the phone and gazed out the window of his Ascott Towers apartment overlooking Singapore's financial district. A soft voice broke his thoughts.

"Is everything okay, my baby?" Lai Xian had heard the call end and the irritation in Shaheen's voice.

"Everything's fine, Lai Xian," Shaheen replied in a calm tone. He turned and smiled at his Singaporean beauty. "Have you ever been to Russia?"

It was 2 am by the time Maryam Seyadin exited the lifts, although no one would know it was her. She had adjusted the thinly woven silk scarf of her hijab to form a full niqab across her face, so that not even her eyes were visible to an onlooker, but she could see well enough through the veil to exit the hotel and enter a taxi. From here she planned to go home and enjoy some sleep. She would brief Omar on her meeting with Oleana the following day but conveniently omit the fact she had been so tempted to let Oleana kiss her, simply to explore the experience. Ultimately, however, the combined forces of her upbringing and culture had led her to resist temptation, and she'd avoided an embroilment by evading the subject of sex every time Oleana had raised it – frequently.

For her part, Oleana was still reeling from the events of the evening. They'd retired to her room and ordered room service and wine, then attacked the minibar. Somehow along the proceedings both women had ended up drinking on the sofa, where she'd dropped every hint and made every move possible to see if she could win some physical contact with this most elegant of policewomen. At first she hadn't been sure whether Maryam's presence was a genuine act of friendship or sympathy, or just another tactic to gain information from her, but by the time the women had parted, all concerns regarding anything other than to perhaps orchestrate a future opportunity to have sex with her had become secondary.

Throughout their night talking and laughing together Oleana found herself reminded of Farah, Shaheen's dead wife, who'd been such a good lover and partner to her. And yet Maryam's features were Arabic, not Persian, which made her very different, but somehow equally attractive to Oleana. She reasoned that, if a Persian lover was considered off limits, then this Arabic woman represented forbidden fruits in the extreme. This made her want Maryam all the more, a feeling that was heightened when the policewoman had unexpectedly and spontaneously announced her departure in the early hours.

As the morning light had broken through the curtains, Oleana realised she was in bed alone but couldn't help but think of a pair of soft hands massaging her back. She purred mildly and moved her legs very slightly apart, substituting Maryam's imagined hand between them with her own.

Unbeknown to Oleana, she had at least succeeded in stirring total sexual intrigue and temptation in Maryam, along with an insatiable desire to see the Russian again, now helped by her certainty that Oleana must be an innocent party. Nothing in their drunken and intimate talk had revealed new information; Oleana had even told her she intended to stay in Dubai, find a job and apply for a residence visa.

But Oleana knew full well she needed to get the hell out of this country. She'd resisted, evaded or lied to just about every question asked of her during the evening. And added to that, if this policewoman now got some sort of jilted best friend syndrome, things could go pear-shaped very quickly for her, and she would doubtless be thrown back in jail in a heartbeat. She decided to call Maria to find out where she was and the latest score with the cartel.

Maria had just disembarked from her delayed 7.35 am Aeroflot flight from Moscow to Heathrow, so at just past 11 am London time she was sitting on the tube admiring its overground route into central London as it lumbered towards Boston Manor. She was mildly surprised when her phone rang and even more so to see Oleana's old number flashing up. She answered in a hushed tone so her voice wouldn't carry through the train carriage. "Oleana, how are you? *Where* are you?"

"I'm in Dubai and I'm okay, but I just got out of prison. Where are you?"

Maria explained she had literally just arrived in London and was about to become Ivanna Delimkova's right-hand woman. "What are your plans?"

"I need to get out of here," Oleana replied, "and I'm thinking Saint Petersburg, but I wanted to find out what was going on before I go anywhere."

"Thank God you called." Maria had by now placed her spare hand over her mouth so the conversation truly couldn't be overheard. "Isaak knows we got the money but he doesn't know how or where. He's been blackmailing me, demanding sex for his silence. It's not good, Oleana, not good at all. If Ivanna finds out, there'll be hell to pay, so this guy owns me right now, and once he knows you're out he'll want to own you too. He's a fucking pervert!"

"How the hell did he find out?" asked Oleana. "What do you want to do?"

"I'm not sure how he found out, but he clearly has information on our bank accounts in Russia. We need him gone and my new position with Ivanna might help that happen, but what I want to do and what we can do are two different things, girl; my best advice right now is don't, under any circumstances, go to Russia – come here to London. I won't tell anyone just yet, that way Isaak won't know you're out of jail. Then we can make a plan to clean up this mess." Maria knew she was getting close to a tunnel coming up ahead. "Look, I'm going to lose signal soon because I'm on a train and I think it's about to go underground. Call me when you get here."

"I'll do it," came Oleana's reply just before the line was cut off.

Oleana threw her phone on the bed. "Fuck!" she said out loud, reflecting how just when things were starting to look up, something always had to go wrong. She looked in the mirror and spoke to her skinny self. "If it wasn't for bad luck, you wouldn't have any luck at all!" She'd momentarily forgotten the fact that she was wealthy and would be beautiful again soon with the addition of a few kilos.

She caught a taxi to the Dnata Travel Centre on Sheikh Zayed Road and booked herself an economy ticket with the help of the polite Emirates Airlines staff on the first floor. She then went to Emirates NBD bank and deposited $80,000 dollars into her account, along with a forged receipt showing the private sale of a car. Finally she returned to the Palace Hotel and informed the reception she would be checking out the next day.

Within twenty-four hours she had exited the UAE and entered the UK on her Saint Kitts and Nevis passport. She had taken a chance carrying excess cash throughout her luggage; using a trolley, she followed very closely behind an immaculately dressed first-class female passenger as she walked through the 'nothing to declare' scanners. The clearly wealthy passenger was quickly pulled over by a customs officer who asked if she had any cash on her, and Oleana walked straight on undisturbed.

After checking into a single room in the My Hotel nestled between Chelsea and Knightsbridge, she sent a Maria a text informing her she was now '*in town*'.

★　★　★

By the time Warrant Officer Omar Shamoon had placed his coffee on his desk and logged into his computer, Oleana was at 36,000 feet above France, and he smiled when he saw the alert indicating she had passed through immigration some eight hours prior.

"Our bird has flown," he said out loud.

"Which bird?" asked Sergeant Seyadin.

"Oleana Katayeva, she's gone to the UK. She's about an hour and half out of London as we speak."

"You're not serious? The bitch!" Seyadin blurted with clear emotion in her tone.

Omar spun his chair around to face her. "You're angry she's gone?"

Maryam caught herself and calmed down. "Well, a bit," she explained. "She didn't give me any useful information when we met but she did say she planned to stay in Dubai. I really thought we would meet again."

"Well, I don't blame her for leaving," Omar replied. "She can't hold any affection for us now." He didn't realise he'd hit a sore nail on the head here with his colleague. "But why London and not Russia? Surely anyone who's been banged up and released would want to go home rather than visit a foreign city – and an expensive one at that! Let's just check to see what class she flew and if there's been any other internet or phone activity of interest."

"I'm on it," the sergeant replied as she returned to her desk. "My gut tells me it's not over for this lady yet." She sat down at her computer and saw that Omar had turned his attention back to his own screen. She tried to supress her disappointment; how could Oleana just jump on a plane like this? Was it because Maryam had evaded her advances? Was she running away from her in embarrassment or just from the country? Had she said something to spook her? Their whole intimate conversation had been a pleasant experience – how could this Russian just cast her offer of friendship aside? She desperately wanted to reach out to Oleana and ask why? In fact, she now realised how much she wanted to see her again. As she started entering the investigation data into her computer, she decided she would have to catch up with Oleana one way or the other; she needed a conclusion for herself as much as for the justice system.

She just hoped the bitch had taken her Chanel bag with her.

It was a little past midday when Graham Tree decided to call Oleana to ascertain when she'd be making her move to Russia. As his phone tried to connect to her UAE number, he waited for the familiar ring tone. It took longer than normal to connect, and when it did, it was not what he'd expected – a British ringtone. He immediately hung up, made an interim call, and then dialled another UK number to double-check. The other end picked up.

"Harry, it's Graham, how are you doing, mate?" he asked.

"Doing okay, mostly," Harry replied. "Work's good, a bit of woman trouble, so ops–normal, I suppose!"

"Wife playing up again?" Graham laughed slightly as he spoke.

"No, she's fine, mate. It's the away team that's playing up now! Women; you can't live with them and you can't live *with* them."

"So married life's going well in the UK then?" Graham persisted.

"It is. Nazrin's enjoying Richmond, Charlie's keeping her exhausted, and it seems like we've only been married for twenty minutes…underwater!" He laughed.

"Well, mate, if you think you've got women problems now, I think you might have a few more coming your way." Graham had Harry's full attention.

"Why's that?"

"Oleana's out of jail. I had that dinner with her the other evening," Graham explained. "She looks like shit and she's livid with Nazrin because she thinks it's all her fault she got thrown in jail. I told her it's bullshit but she wasn't having any of it. You need to watch your back, Harry. Hell hath no fury and all that crap."

"There's always at least one woman out to get me, one way or the other, mate, I don't think Oleana will be too much of a problem." Harry was reassuring himself more than anything.

"You don't understand, mate, I think she's in the UK. I tried her number this morning and it was a UK ringtone. Then I checked with her hotel in Dubai and she's checked out. She might be coming for revenge, mate!" Graham sounded genuinely concerned. "You know she has no boundaries – I don't have to tell you that of all people."

"Okay," said Harry. "I wouldn't mind betting she'll stay in the same hotel she stayed in last time she was in London."

"Which one's that?"

"The My Hotel in Chelsea. Although it's not really in Chelsea, more like South Ken, but that's the address. I dropped her off there last time we saw each other in London."

Graham had just got the information he required without paying for it or it being attributable to any source. He reiterated to Harry that he needed to watch his back, telling him he would let him know if he heard anything else. The friends said goodbye and promised to get together for a beer next time they found themselves in the same time zone.

Graham hung up and googled the My Hotel, called the number and asked for Miss Katayeva. The polite receptionist asked him to hold and redirected the call. The phone in Oleana's room rang just once and Graham hung up. He then dialled a Singapore number.

"Shaheen, it's Graham," he said, proving he was older than a millennial by the very fact he still instinctively introduce himself on the phone. "She's in London, staying at the My Hotel in Chelsea."

"How the fuck did you find that out?" asked Shaheen. "Does she know you know?"

"Not a Scooby," Graham answered, forgetting Shaheen would not understand London's rhyming slang.

"Not a what?"

"Oh sorry, not a Scooby Doo – clue," explained Graham. Silence on the other end. "She doesn't have a clue."

Shaheen had no idea what Graham was talking about, but jumped on his last sentence. "Perfect. Any idea how long she's staying?"

Graham was tempted to use the Scooby slang again, but thought better of it. "No clue on that one either, mate."

"Okay, good work, Graham, send me your bill. I'll call you if I need more info, but you please call me if you get anything else."

"I will," said Graham and hung up.

Shaheen shouted through to the bedroom. "Lai Xian?"

"Yes?" came the reply.

"Pack your stuff, we're going to London."

Lai Xian put her head around the door. "London? I thought you said Russia?"

"Change of plans, baby, and we're leaving tomorrow. We'll go via Dubai for a night, I want to see a guy there. Make sure to pack for a London summer – bring an umbrella."

CHAPTER FOURTEEN
Flash Flush

Mac Harris sipped tea from his mug as he scanned the columns of numbers on the six computer screens in front of him. He'd had a spectacular year with his BARF software and made the cartel hundreds of millions in diverted funds. His glow of satisfaction was made all the greater by the knowledge he could instinctively identify criminal accounts by their characteristics, and, so far as he knew, from his scanning financial alerts and even Bloomberg, none of the funds he'd siphoned had been reported.

Meanwhile, Isaak had been busy acquiring small banks in tier two countries whose currencies were pegged to the dollar, euro or pound. These destination accounts would be the backstop for the funds once they'd momentarily flowed through 'clean' accounts before reaching the cartel's coffers. Anything euro-denominated would eventually end up being transferred to a Djiboutian or Romanian bank. Anything that needed to be dollar-denominated would end up in Jordan or Bahrain; anything pegged to the pound would be destined for Gibraltar. All the banks were shadow-owned by the cartel, so no legal ownership documents gave any clue as to the banks' actual controllers, just an arrangement that would be signed off in blood if ever questioned by the documented and apparently clean owners.

Mac's BARF model monitored target bank accounts in a similar way to how Bloomberg's software monitored stocks. Mac would feed in the identifiers of any bank accounts he had identified as potentially vulnerable, and his model would then monitor two elements: account activity and their password-protected transactions. He had additionally created software capable of detecting any sort of reverse monitoring.

As the balances of the accounts rose, they would also rise in ascendancy on his screen columns; this way he could easily select which accounts warranted the majority of his attention. If the balance of the account was trending up, the balance was shown in green. If it was trending down, it would display in red, and no activity for a period of more than two weeks would result in a white font.

There had only been four occasions on which Mac had seen flashing red digits on display, and all had received his immediate attention because this was the alarm signal that someone was trying to penetrate his model. His immediate actions were to sever his servers from the web, go offline, delete the account from the model and reconnect to the internet via his secure server under a secure assumed VPN he had effectively developed by designing a complex version of Hotspot Shield's remote VPN model.

In all cases Mac knew it was safe to assume the attempted penetrations were standard bank cyber-scanning procedures seeking to identify any undue infiltration of their own systems. He knew from a wealth of experience that, if his access into their system were recognised for what it was, then their entire network would be immediately taken down 'for essential maintenance'. For this reason, he would survey the bank's responses and cyberactivity for any clues that might indicate they were onto him and his BARF, of which he was so proud.

With now just barely three months of further activity remaining to him, Mac was relieved this phase of his life was coming to an end. He justified his robbery by reassuring himself that, for the most part, he was stealing from the bad and giving it to the less bad. His personal income was now in the millions, so he was content he would retire after this last foray and breed working springer spaniels.

As he was reflecting on a passive and pleasurable future, one of the accounts changed its status, entering the top twenty on the watch list and displaying green. The De Domínguez Painting & Decorating Company had just received two deposits of 190 million pesos – about $10 million US – into its corporate account located in the Banco Inbursa's Fray Servando Teresa de Mier branch.

This was one of the accounts in the bank that had attracted Mac's attention. It was a sole ownership with single signatory authority, and it's activity was cash in and wire transfer out. There were never any withdrawals that would represent an actual painting and decorating company's costs, just sporadic large amounts in and out with the latter always resulting in a foreign transaction via Central America or the Middle East. This account smacked of money-laundering, avoided US dollar denomination, and would have been red-flagged by any bank that was not in on the deal.

Mac enacted the process of the splintering programme, which would siphon out multiple small amounts from the balance to innocent transit accounts before re-converging the fund to one of the cartel's selected banks. He decided he would use the euro as the target denomination, so he selected accounts in Mexico and Guatemala that held both euro and pesos accounts. This way he could effect an inter-account transfer before sending the funds Djibouti-bound.

Isaak was visibly shocked when Alexei's lawyer walked unannounced into his office, and even more surprised when the lawyer handed him the coordinates of two Cyprus bank accounts.

"I have an instruction from Alexei. You are to wire €10 million to these two accounts without delay. The reason for the transfer should simply state 'For attention of COO reference Loan 81024'. You should arrange for this transfer today. If there is any delay, I need to know. When the transfer is complete, I need to know. Is that clear?"

Isaak looked up from the paper on his desk. "How do I know this instruction is genuinely from Alexei?"

"Well, because I am his fucking lawyer, Isaak, that should be reason enough. However, he did say that, if you had any doubts, I should tell you 'Coco 1212' and you would know it came from him."

Isaak instantly knew the authentication was genuine. The term 'Coco' had long become a joke between him and Alexei because, before all the shit went down and the boss was thrown in jail, his favourite escort was a tall, elegant Russian with Far-Eastern features. Her name was Coco and she was in frequent receipt of Alexei's financial generosity, which was naturally transacted through Isaak. He paused momentarily as he pondered what had become of the oriental beauty. He wondered if she would ever turn up on the scene again, or whether her fondness for Alexei was inversely proportional to his woes.

His thoughts were broken by the lawyer. "Is there anything else you need?"

"I don't think so," Isaak answered, mildly irritated to have been distracted from his memories of Coco's figure. "I can instruct the bank today." He looked at his watch. "But at best it won't get transacted until tomorrow."

"Okay, but don't fuck it up or it'll be on you." The lawyer stood up as he spoke and picked up the folder he had brought in with him. "You have a good day." He didn't bother shaking hands; he didn't feel as if he had to. He despised Isaak because he could read men, and here, without any doubt, was a mean-minded miser with serious issues.

Isaak let a few seconds pass after the lawyer had left, before saying out loud, "Arsehole!" He reflected that the only thing he hated more than a lawyer was a lawyer with a superiority complex. He looked at the instructions on the paper and called his friendly bank manager who happened to be on the payroll. Both men double-checked the bank coordinates to make sure all the digits matched up. The manager agreed that the transfer would happen tomorrow and that no US dollar accounts would be used. Both men were all too aware of the fact that the use of dollars gave the Feds jurisdiction, and that was something to be avoided at all costs.

Isaak put down the phone and pondered what the payoff would be used for. He knew it was either a brave or powerful man that would put such amounts into a Cyprus account. The country was broke and even taxed savings, for Christ's sake! Something didn't add up. He picked up his mobile and dialled a UK number.

"Hullo," came the dull reply.

"Mac, Isaak, how's it going?" asked the accountant.

"Actually, funny you should ask that," Mac replied. "There's some movement on Op Fajita." This was his nickname for the Mexican accounts.

"How much?" asked Isaak.

"There's room for about ten orders and they'll suit a European palate."

Isaak understood exactly what Mac was telling him. "That's perfect timing; I've just had some unexpected costs at this end so please push ahead with that. And I need you to look at a couple of client ledgers in Cyprus as well. I'll WhatsApp you the coordinates. Please see if there's anything they can do for us."

It was Mac's turn now to understand the nuance. "No problem, I'll check it out. You can count on the Fajita delivery in the next couple of days."

"Good man." Isaak was happy he'd cut his losses from the outlay the lawyer had just ordered for Alexei's freedom, hoping he might have the chance to get some or more of this money from these other accounts.

At his end, Mac tapped into the Banco Inbursa account. He watched as the account started to reduce at a rate of slightly under $10,000 a cycle. He smiled as he watched the intermediary flow-through accounts start to build up similar amounts, before he activated the transaction software that would effect transfer out of those accounts to an innocuous Djibouti bank. He tapped in a halt on the transactions for when the source account hit $140,000. Knowing this would take a few minutes, he took the opportunity to go for a piss and make some tea.

He had barely been out of the room for thirty seconds when the Banco Inbursa account read-out started to flash red.

Upstairs Mac decided to let the dog out into the garden and he wandered out, mug of tea in hand, feeling thoroughly content with what his life had become and what it was about to be. He sat on his garden bench and revelled in the spaniel's sheer enthusiasm for just about anything he could smell. What must it be to be so easily pleased? He reflected that, because dogs had no expectations whatsoever, this was probably the key to their contentment. He clicked his fingers and the dog ran over to him obediently to be stroked. "Come on, boy, let's go back inside."

The dog followed him indoors and went straight to slurp water from his bowl. Mac placed his mug in the sink and figured he would take a look at these new accounts just as soon as Isaak had sent the coordinates, and then call it a day.

He made his way down into the cellar and sat down in front of his screens, putting on his glasses to see if the Banco Inbursa account had completed his drawdown.

"Jesus Christ!" he exclaimed in disbelief at the red flashing text showing just 2.9 million pesos in the account. "Jesus Christ!" he repeated. His hands were shaking as he directed his mouse towards the internet connection. "Oh shit! Come on!" The menu dropped down and he immediately disconnected. He then commenced shutdown of the entire computer. Only when this was complete did he lean back in his chair. How long had the attack been on his system? If it had just been seconds, he'd be safe, or if it had simply been the bank doing its normal cybersecurity checks, then the chances were that his various firewalls would make him untraceable. However, if this thing had gone on for minutes, then there could be a problem. He corrected himself – a gargantuan problem.

How could he have been so fucking stupid? It was what they called in the trade a 'Johnny English moment'. All spies and operators had one if they stayed in the business long enough; everyone made a stupid fuck-up sooner or later, no matter how well-trained.

For the most part he knew he'd have to be unlucky to get caught, but he couldn't ignore it. He reconfigured his online identity, then doubled up with a remote VPN and watched to see if the bank had closed down its system, which they would inevitably have done had they compromised him or suspected he was attacking them.

Within half an hour he was back in business and relieved to see the Banco Inbursa accounts showing normal activity, and that the flashing lights were back to steady. He reassured himself that he'd got away with it, and that another lesson had been learned even in this late stage of his career. "Thank fuck for that," he muttered to himself as he entered the Cyprus bank's coordinates into BARF. When the balances eventually displayed, he had to both check his system and ensure that the currency was indeed euro – there was over €600 million in each of the accounts. His mind had now moved on from the flashing red; these two accounts, if they had the right activity profile, could represent his swansong. He could surely suck some funds out, which would barely be noticed.

If Ivanna had looked at her phone once that morning, she'd looked at it a hundred times. Surely Harry would eventually call or text; surely he knew the words 'I'm sorry' weren't in the Russian vernacular. She was trying to focus on briefing Maria on her new duties, but it was as clear to her as to her now assistant that she was distracted.

"I'm having a tough time," she admitted to Maria.

"You must be missing your man," Maria replied, thinking of Alexei rotting in a Russian jail.

"I really am." Ivanna was not thinking of Alexei in the least. "I hope he comes back soon." She gazed out the window onto the mews. "What about you? Do you have a man in your life?"

"I do," confessed Maria, "but not one I really want to keep."

Ivanna dropped the subject and moved on to describing her daily routine and her expectations of Maria, which included managing her schedule, coordinating with Willie the fixer, and keeping an eye on her general security. As she watched Maria take notes, she couldn't help but notice how attractive to men she could be; she resolved there and then that Harry should not get to know this woman. Little did she know that he already did.

Harry walked into his Old Broad Street office, which his security company shared with a law firm. Sid was already sitting at his desk. "Anything new?"

"Yes, mate," Sid replied. "We've got a potential kidnap and ransom case in Lagos, a corporate escort job coming up in Iran, an asset-recovery tasking out of Scotland, and a hotel security review in town." He looked up. "Which one do you fancy?"

"I'll cover the London job," said Harry. "I need to keep the wife happy." While this was true, he was really thinking about a reunion with Ivanna.

"Great," Sid replied. "It's Brown's Hotel in Albemarle, the file from last year's review is on the Office 365 drive. You'll need to check in and conduct a covert review. The staff won't know until you arrive. The owners want the full gambit of checks."

"No problem, mate. Bread and butter." Harry was already wondering if he could somehow take Ivanna there. He double-checked his WhatsApp and texts – nothing from her. For the life of him, he could not understand women. Here was one that had thrown him out of her house because she'd wanted more to their relationship, and now she was giving him the silent treatment. He called to mind what he thought was an old Mae West saying: "If a woman thought the way to a man's heart was through his stomach, she was aiming a little high." Ivanna's aim had been just perfect until she'd raised it to his heart – and head.

Maria had been checked into the Sloane Square Hotel, which was very much the most convenient to Ivanna's house in Eaton Terrace Mews. The Club Room was perfect for her; it boasted a king-size bed and a small lounge in which she could set up her laptop.

As she sat and admired the surrounding architecture, she couldn't help but be pleased to be away from Isaak's clutches. The very thought of him on top of and inside her made her want to gag.

CHAPTER FIFTEEN
Coyote Hunt

J orge was having problems in the villa in Limón. His boss was bored, despite the flow of slender Costa Rican ladies who were paid to service him every day. Since escaping from prison, Archivaldo's appetite for women had been insatiable, and although he had his favourites, variety was proving to be the spice of life. However, the fact was that the splendid villa had become just another prison to him.

Jorge had broken up the routine a few times by driving his boss into Limón, and the change of hair colour and lack of moustache, combined with a baseball cap and glasses, was enough to reassure him no one had realised Mexico's most wanted was amongst them.

"I want to go back home," Archivaldo complained. "I want my Mexican mistress and the smell of Sinaloa, I want to drink with my lieutenants."

"You can't," Jorge advised. "It's just too fucking risky."

"You're kidding," his boss argued. "It's the last place anyone would look."

"I'm not worried about them looking, I'm worried about some bastard squealing," the lawyer countered. "The Feds are offering $5 million, the Mexicans $3.8 million. That kind of money can go a long way in Sinaloa."

"Not if your dead, it won't, and you know if anyone squeals, we'll find out who it is and chop their feet off just for starters."

Their conversation was broken by Jorge's phone ringing. He looked at the caller ID; it was Sheetal. "Stand by," he said, looking at Archivaldo. "It's our computer guy. Sheetal?" he said as he accepted the call.

"Is it okay to speak?" Sheetal asked.

"Go ahead."

Sheetal went straight to the point. "The coyote is in the garden."

"Did you locate him?" Jorge asked.

"I did, but I'm very suspicious," Sheetal replied. "The protective layering was about as good as I've ever seen. So good in fact, I can't believe whoever developed it hadn't set warning alarms so they can shut down their system in case someone like me tries to trace their IP and location."

"So what are you saying?" Jorge said with a slight tone of impatience.

"I'm saying our equipment did its job spectacularly and quickly, but even so it took me several minutes to penetrate his firewalls and shields. They left their system on despite my attack; in fact, I had nearly ten minutes to retrieve their data, backtrack the VPN to its source, and get a location. I just don't understand why they didn't see they were compromised and shut down their system before I had time to get what I needed and more. It could be a trap, sir." He deliberately avoided using Jorge's name. "That's all I can think."

"So where is it?" asked Jorge.

"Coyote is now in England, in a town called Liss. It's about eighty kilometres south-west of London. I have the street and I can probably narrow it down to about four houses because they back onto a field according to Google Maps."

"Okay, good work, Sheetal." Jorge's impatient tone had gone. "WhatsApp me the name of the street and town, as well as a band of house numbers where this computer could be."

"I will, but there is more thing, sir."

"Like what?"

"Well, when I was attacking their system, they'd penetrated two other bank accounts in Cyprus with very large balances, like €600 million each."

"Can we get any of it?" Jorge's first instinct was to steal.

"I'm not sure yet, but I think so," replied Sheetal. "If I can, I want to make it look like they did it. I need to analyse the codes they've written."

"Good man, Sheetal. Go back to work. I'll come and see you in a few days, but call me if you have anything else."

Jorge hung up and repeated the information Sheetal had given him to his boss. After about a minute, his WhatsApp pinged. He looked at his phone and read aloud. "Saint Mary's Road, Liss, Hampshire. Numbers, 1, 3, 5 or 7, they're on the left from the only entrance to the street."

Archivaldo walked over to the fridge, pulled out two Segua Red beers and popped the tops off with the opener hanging on a string next to the fridge door. He handed one to his lawyer. "I'm coming to Sinaloa with you, just for a few days. I want to see this computer that cost me $15 million and meet the guy who operates it. I also want to watch him monitor the accounts." He swigged his beer. "Get onto our brothers in London; we're going to have to pay for the hit. If we can narrow it down to two houses then we hit them both, but I want the bastard who thinks he can steal money from us to die a miserable death – and I want his bosses as well." Another swig. "You might also want to think about popping the Indian when we're done with him."

Jorge knew better than to argue with his boss, so he just pursed his lips and nodded slightly. "I suppose it's a case of how useful he becomes." He tried to soften the death sentence.

"Okay, let's wait and see," Archivaldo acquiesced. "If the geek knew he was operating that computer for his very life, would it help?"

It was just two days after Oleana had left Dubai that Omar's computer indicated that Shaheen Soroush had re-entered the country; this could be no coincidence. Soroush had told the immigration officer in Dubai airport he was staying for a couple of nights at the Taj Hotel, and Omar quickly checked the information to confirm both. Soroush had checked into the hotel taking a double room for just two nights, and he had a business class reservation on Emirates to London in just thirty-six hours.

"What the fuck are you up to?" Omar muttered to himself.

He looked around at Sergeant Seyadin. "Fancy some lunch at the Taj?"

"Well, it beats the canteen here," she answered.

"Good. Go put on your abaya, and I'll change into a kandura; we need to look like the locals we are today."

About an hour later they entered the lobby of the Taj Hotel. Sergeant Seyadin sat down in the lobby. Omar walked to the reception desk. "Is the duty manager here?" he asked, and the efficient receptionist immediately picked up her phone to call the same.

"Who shall I say is calling?"

"Warrant Officer Shamoon, Dubai Police," he answered, flashing his warrant card. "I'll be sitting over there." He pointed towards where Seyadin was seated.

It was just three minutes later when the polite duty manager approached the two detectives and asked how he could help.

"This is no big thing," Omar explained, but you have a short term VIP guest staying here and we'd like to ensure all the security cameras in your hotel are working. The guest himself won't indicate to you that he's anyone, but it's important to us that he's safe and secure while in the UAE."

"May I ask which guest?" asked the manager.

"A Mr Soroush from Singapore. He's a very wealthy man and an important business partner for Dubai. Sadly for us, he's also very modest." It was a natural talent for Omar to give the manager a false reason for his interest.

The manager excused himself, went over to the receptionist and then returned. "Indeed, sir, Mr Soroush checked in early this morning, accompanied by a Singapore national, a Ms Lee Lai Xian?" He handed a copy of Lai Xian's passport to Omar.

Pretty, Omar thought. What was it about these oriental women that was so alluring? He handed the paper to his sergeant.

She looked at the paper and nodded. "Can we keep this?"

The manager told her she could and asked if there was anything special they needed.

"No," said Omar. "We want him to be relaxed, so no fuss and not a word about us making sure he's okay. We'll just need all the camera coverage until he leaves, and we might choose to remain in the hotel for a few hours. Perhaps you could let us sit in your security monitoring room?"

"Of course, sir, let me show you the way and I'll arrange some coffee for you." The manager led the detectives to a discreet security room containing banks of monitors.

The detectives had only been in the room for about thirty minutes when a familiar figure entered the elevator on the nineteenth floor and exited on the third floor to go into the Tesaro Restaurant. He was alone.

Omar looked at Seyadin. "Fancy some lunch?".

Within minutes the two detectives were sat four tables way from Soroush, who was sitting alone, seemingly taking no interest in this newly arrived Arab couple. Omar could sense Soroush was blissfully unaware he was being watched. The man was relaxed, enjoying the view from the restaurant, and evidently waiting for someone.

It was then that a stocky European sporting an atrociously groomed and greying beard walked into the restaurant and indicated to the greeter he was meeting Soroush.

"I recognise him," Omar muttered to Seyadin. "That's the guy who owned the boat that Russian Duma member had his diving accident on a couple of years ago. He's tied in with the Englishman we traded for Oleana, Harry Linley. I can't recall this one's name though."

Seyadin glanced around, and as she did, Graham noticed this Emirati beauty look at him. "It's Graham Tree," she muttered. "He looks a lot older with that beard. And shit, I think he caught me looking."

"That's him," Omar said. "I nearly had it. Soroush was on the boat that day too, so it's interesting they should still be in contact."

"Perhaps we should be listening to Tree's phone?" the sergeant suggested.

"No good," Omar pointed out. "If they go to the trouble of meeting here, then they mustn't be saying anything important on the phone. Also, whatever we actually need to know is probably about to be discussed."

After Graham had sat down and exchanged niceties with Shaheen, he asked, "How long have those Arabs been here?"

Shaheen said they had arrived shortly after him.

"Interesting," Graham said. "The woman just checked me out, and I know I'm good-looking and all that, but it's not often I get eyed up by an Arab woman. I've got a feeling they were talking about us."

"Don't be paranoid," Shaheen told him. "And as long as they can't hear what we're saying, who gives a shit? We're only having lunch. And anyway, Arab women are apparently attracted to bearded men." He smiled, wondering whether Graham would pick up his sarcasm.

They both drank sparkling water and each had some form of salad; Shaheen broached the subject he'd stopped over in Dubai for. "You said Oleana was perhaps a spy – well, you're wrong," he said. "Oleana was my wife's lover at the time of her death."

Graham almost choked on his water – so the rumours were true! His first reaction was to wonder if Harry knew she was bisexual?

Shaheen continued. "You'll recall that, when I was attacked in Dubai last year, I was actually with Oleana and that black-haired Russian friend of hers."

"Maria," Graham interjected.

"Yes, when I was with them and we got in the fight with the men who attacked us, I was trying to retrieve my dead daughter's iPad with all her photos, because Oleana had taken it. I don't know if you remember, but I was injected with something during that scuffle that made me ill for about a week, and I had almost total memory loss."

"I remember," said Graham, concealing the fact he had a lot more knowledge about the attack and its subsequent clean-up since it was he and Harry who'd taken care of it. Of this Shaheen was completely unaware because he'd been unconscious. "After the incident, didn't the girls say they went to Oman or something?" Graham was reminding himself as well as Shaheen.

"They actually went to Singapore." There was a bitter tone in Shaheen's voice. "And while I was stuck here immobilised, they went to my apartment and stole millions of dollars." He took a sip of water. "I don't know how they got the money out, but I do have them entering and leaving on the security cameras, so I know it was them."

Graham was locked on to Shaheen's eyes. "Shit," he said. "What did they steal?"

"Cash, money, diamonds. I kept it in safes in my apartment; they got into them and cleaned me out."

"How could they carry gold, Shaheen, it's bulky stuff?" quizzed Graham. "And what could they possibly do with it once they'd got it out of your house?"

"I don't know, that's one of the bits that doesn't add up. When they left my place, they only had a large handbag each."

"Could you have been robbed twice?" Graham asked.

Shaheen paused uncertainly. "I hadn't thought of that. It's possible, I suppose."

"If they still have the security video, then it could be worth watching it again. I'll take a look at it if you like," Graham offered.

"Okay, but I'll have to send it to you when I get back to Singapore. In the meantime…" Shaheen paused again. "I want Oleana snuffed."

This was the second time Graham choked on his water. "Fuck me, Shaheen! Even if you think it, don't say it. That's not what we do."

"Maybe not, but you must know someone who does," Shaheen countered.

"I might," Graham said in a low voice. "But arranging that kind of stuff is the same as committing it, legally speaking, so I'm not sure I can help."

"Okay, no problem," Shaheen said, matching his low tone. "But if you know anyone in London that does that sort of stuff, then there's $20,000 in it for just the name."

"Let me think about it," said Graham. "But if I give you a name, you must never say where you got it, okay? And I don't want any reference to this conversation ever again, unless it's face to face."

"No problem." Shaheen looked up and smiled broadly as a petite and beautiful Oriental woman entered the restaurant. He stood up, and in a voice clearly audible to the watching detectives said, "Graham, meet the next Mrs Soroush, Lee Lai Xian, the love of my life."

Graham shook hands and was instantly enamoured. Shaheen had no idea that the Englishman had long had a penchant for Far Eastern ladies. He wasn't often lost for words but he was right now. He noticed the firmness of her handshake, and her well-muscled arms and legs. He assumed she must be an athlete of some sort, and he wanted her.

The three sat down to discuss the merits of Dubai and the Emirates, and all agreed that, if one had to live in the Middle East, this was probably the only country to consider.

Omar and Seyadin left the restaurant before their three objects of surveillance; they'd seen all they had to see and Shaheen had inadvertently confirmed identification on all three.

"Run the system on Tree and Soroush's wife to be," Omar instructed as the detectives walked out into the early afternoon sun. "I've got a feeling something significant is going down, because it always is when Oleana and Soroush are in the same city, and he has tickets to London tomorrow. At least whatever they're up to won't be here for now, but I think I need to take a couple of weeks off and go to London. Our GPS tracker in Oleana's bag isn't going to do us any good if we're sat here."

Seyadin looked at him. "Can I come too?"

He laughed, completely ignorant of her reasons for asking. "You're going to get the office talking about us, but sure, if you can get the time off."

CHAPTER SIXTEEN
Brown's Sugar

J ust before Harry left for work in the morning, he'd informed Nazrin he was probably going to have to work overnight. The combination of female intuition and female suspicion was driving Nazrin crazy, but she remained in control of her emotions and was doing her utmost not to seem fazed. She was after all used to Harry's absences abroad whenever his security work took him to Nigeria and Ghana. She was, however, rightly sure that any opportunities of the female variant in those climes would almost certainly be rejected by Harry for reasons of medical risk.

Harry had explained he was tasked to conduct a security review of a West End hotel, and an overnight stay would in all likelihood be needed to fully test their protocols. Nazrin didn't ask him which hotel for two reasons: firstly, she was well aware that in Harry's trade client confidentiality was a primary requirement; and secondly, she didn't need to – she had her own methods. So just before he walked out the door carrying his overnight bag, she simply asked, "Are you taking the train or the tube today?"

"I'll grab the tube," Harry replied. "I've got a meeting in Chelsea before going to the office, so it'll work better." He kissed Charlie goodbye, and then his wife, who watched as he began the walk down Richmond Hill towards the town centre and underground station.

Nazrin checked her watch and left it forty-five minutes before calling Harry's office, judging that by this time his train would actually be underground and his mobile rendered useless. She breathed an undetectable sigh of relief when she heard the Moroccan receptionist's voice announce the name of the firm. She knew that, if Sid Easton had picked up, she would have had to make some lame excuse for calling since he would have almost certainly smelled that a tactic was in play.

"Salma, it's Nazrin, how are you?" she opened and the two women exchanged niceties. "Harry called me to say he'd forgotten his toilet bag and need it dropped off at the hotel where he's working tonight, but Charlie was in the middle of a tantrum when he called, and now I've completely forgotten the hotel's name, and he must be underground because I can't reach him, and I do need to leave to get my train. Can you help me with the name?"

"Sure, no problem," replied Salma as she brought up Harry's calendar on her computer screen. "He's doing a security review at Brown's, the one on Albemarle Street."

"Of course, Brown's, how could I forget that, thank you. But don't let Harry know I called, he'll be irritated I had to call the office just because I forgot; you know what these Special Forces guys are like."

"Tell me about it!" Salma laughed. "I work with their professional perfectionism every day. It drives me nuts!" She smiled to herself to think her boss could have forgotten his toilet bag. The guy was human after all.

The ladies exchanged laughs and said goodbye. No sooner had the call ended than Nazrin dialled her lunch-club friend, who she'd met through the Internations website that linked up Azerbaijani expats living in London. She explained to Tarana that she was having husband trouble and he was supposedly working at Brown's Hotel that evening. "Do you think you could do me a huge favour and pop in there for a drink, just to take a look and see if he's not up to any monkey-business. I'll cover all the cost of your drinks and taxi fare."

Tarana had never met Harry but half-wanted to. Nazrin always spoke so highly of him, but she'd also let her know how little she trusted him where other women were concerned. Tarana knew all women in a relationship had one common enemy – other women. For that reason, she didn't mind helping her fellow countrywoman out of solidarity, nor drinking wine for free in one of the finest bars in London.

"Can you send me a picture?" she asked. "I'll take a friend so that no one starts hitting on me."

"No problem," Nazrin confirmed. "I think if you're there between 7 and 10 pm, that should let you see what he's up to. You can give me the bill when we next do lunch."

Tarana then asked something that shocked Nazrin. "Are you really sure you want to know the answer to this, hun? You know sometimes it's better for a wife never to ask a question she might get the answer she *doesn't* want to?"

"I have to know," Nazrin said. "We've had issues before. I married him because he had a wild side, now it's my job to tame it. I do realise it's like bringing a wild hyena into your living room and expecting it not to piss on the carpet, but it has to be done. I have to know."

Oleana had woken up early that morning and had time to kill, so she decided to take an early morning stroll in the freshness of London's air. The willing receptionist in Chelsea's My Hotel suggested she walk up towards Hyde Park so Oleana did just that.

As she walked up the immaculate street between the grandeur of the Natural History and Victoria & Albert Museums, she reflected just how much her incarceration had made her appreciate life. She recalled a saying that went something along the lines of "you've never lived until you've almost died", and pondered her new respect for freedom and rights.

After about ninety minutes she realised she would be too late for breakfast in the hotel, so decided to call her only friend, then grab a coffee and some toast in Aubaine, which she quickly figured out as one of the most fashionable restaurants of its kind in South Kensington. She need not have felt inferior in her casual Hot Miami Styles jogging suit, which, with the addition of high heels, would have got her into any nightclub in town; but as she viewed the well-kept local wives alongside affluent Qatari women enjoying the liberation of London fashion, she couldn't help but think how much she wanted to get back on her game.

She scrolled through her mobile phone and waited for her order to arrive; there were no texts or messages – her time in prison had made sure of that dearth.

She saw Maria emerge from a taxi outside the restaurant, looking stunning in what Oleana assumed were low-cut diesel jeans and a short white top, purposely designed to provide a glance of her chiselled abs. Heads turned as the black-haired beauty with ice blue eyes entered Aubaine; she'd never stepped into the place before, but already she belonged there.

Oleana stood and smiled, and Maria did what amounted to a girly trot over to her and hugged her tight. They greeted each other so enthusiastically in Russian that they failed to overhear the three English women on the next table curse them out for being so Russian and so damned sexy.

"You look great, Maria," Oleana said. "I'm so envious."

Maria reached across the table and held her hand. "Baby, you need some weight, plenty of protein, calories and water." She looked at the tea and toast on the table and smiled as the trendy waitress came over. "I'll have a coffee, and please bring my friend a large Eggs Benedict."

Oleana was about to protest but Maria spoke over her. "Girl, you need to eat until you're full and then you need to eat some more. If you can combine that regime with gentle exercise, you'll be back to where you need to be in no time."

Oleana enjoyed having someone care about her again. The coffee and food arrived and Maria got down to business.

"I don't know exactly what's going on yet with Ivanna, but she's restless. Maybe she's missing Alexei, I don't know." She took a sip of her coffee. "If she is though, she'd better get used to it; he's got another seven years in prison."

"How's the business?" asked Oleana.

"It's good so far as I know, and what I do know, I know through that slime ball, Isaak." The bitterness in Maria's tone was all too apparent. "He has us over a barrel, Oleana. Me literally. So until we come up with a plan, it's best that he doesn't know you're out; after all, he might try the same on you." She took another sip of coffee. "You name it; he's made me do it. I hate him. We have to get rid of him."

"Is he still in Moscow?" Oleana asked.

"He is, and we can't do anything there; any plan or hit would quickly lead straight back to whoever did it, and I don't want to have to live with that worry."

"So did you figure out how yet?" Oleana asked.

"Well, I can't do it because my 'relationship' with him is common knowledge, given how much he likes showing me off in public, so I'd be an immediate suspect. But I can surely lure Isaak over here. We have to get rid of him or he could destroy both of us." Maria repeated herself to ensure she could win Oleana's support.

Oleana had stopped eating her Eggs Benedict; Maria could see she was thinking. "I'm planning to meet Harry in any case, perhaps I can get him to help us deal with Isaak. It might be crazy but it might just work."

"Go on," urged Maria.

"I've thought for months about my revenge on Harry and his wife, because they almost certainly sacrificed me to keep their own freedom. The one problem is, though, that I don't really know the actual circumstances, or if it was Harry, his wife, or both that planned it. So I'd planned on meeting up with Harry to find out his version. Then I can figure out what to do." She paused to take another bite of her breakfast. "Supposing we assume they are guilty, and supposing Harry thought a bigger plan was in action against him and his wife by our employer rather than us, and the only way out was for him to get rid of the man driving the threat to his family. I could tell him that, unless he gets rid of Isaak, his family's in grave danger, and that I'm helping him out by letting him know. What do you think?"

"Do you really think Harry would dispose of Isaak for us?" Maria asked, working the plan through as she spoke.

"I think he would if the circumstances were right."

"Would he do it himself or get someone else to do it?"

"Who cares as long as that raping blackmailer is gone." The hardness in Oleana's voice was apparent. "In any case, let Isaak know I'm out and in London, that should be enough to lure him here for my money – or sex."

★   ★   ★

The transit into Sinaloa had gone perfectly. Jorge and his boss had flown on the same flight but booked, checked in and sat separately. Jorge in business class, Archivaldo in economy using one of his many false passports with dyed hair and eyebrows, glasses, and in a holiday-maker's attire. Their route ran from Costa Rica to Guatemala, followed by a transfer to a Volaris flight to Cancun. Once they had penetrated the Mexican border, the cartel's aviation assets kicked in, and an apparently chartered Pilatus PC-12 completed the infiltration by flying the two men to Mazatlán, just inside the Free and Sovereign State of Sinaloa, home of the cartel where they ruled with an iron fist or a jagged blade – whichever worked best.

The drive to Los Mochis took four and a half hours, but it was deemed safer than flying into the airport directly. Again the boss and Jorge travelled in separate and inconspicuous vehicles, while the outriders drove ten, five and two kilometres ahead to call in any un-paid-off police check points.

Jorge had arranged for Archivaldo to stay at the safe house belonging to one of their most trusted tunnel engineers; he would surely be safe there, and if discovered, the escape tunnels were already dug.

Upon arrival, the covert minders were already in place and the area was declared secure. Both men changed their clothes, swapped cars into an old Toyota Corolla, and Jorge drove Archivaldo to the installation opposite the International Paper plant.

Sheetal had his back to the door but spun around when he felt the pressure in the room change from the door opening against the overworked air-conditioning.

"It's fucking freezing in here," the boss complained.

"It's the computer," Jorge explained. "It cost fifteen big ones, so we don't want the fucking thing to overheat." He looked at Sheetal and introduced his companion. "This is Archivaldo. He's one of our finance guys, so I thought it would be interesting for him to see what you're doing."

"That is absolutely fine, Mr Jorge, let me show you," Sheetal said after he had shaken the new man's hand. He then went on to explain how the quantum computer and his MIT training had enabled him to crack Shor's algorithm.

The boss didn't have a clue what he was talking about, but let him finish before asking, "So what are your screens telling you?"

"Well, several things," Sheetal explained, and pointed to the screens in turn. "This one is monitoring our accounts and all the accounts through which our monies were transferred by whoever was stealing them. What is interesting is that, until the monies arrived in Djibouti, none of the accounts had any significant amounts in them, so I'm guessing they're being used rather than actually being part of the theft." He moved to another screen. "This screen is strictly tracking VPN activity, and that's what found the commonality to bring it back to the address in the UK." Here Sheetal frowned. "Now this isn't a hundred percent, because I'm very concerned as to why the operator at that end didn't shut his system down straightaway when it was interrogated; that means it could be a surrogate."

"What are the chances?" Jorge asked.

"Ten, maybe fifteen percent," Sheetal replied. "The VPN and IP address is correct; I'm just wondering whether the thieves operate it through a remote terminal that's unaware their system is being used."

Jorge looked at the boss; they could almost read each other's mind. "*Tal vez tenemos que hablar con el ladrón antes de matarlo.*"

He assumed correctly that Sheetal couldn't understand Spanish, and so wouldn't realise they planned to determine the certainty of guilt before they killed the thief.

"*De acuerdo. Hazlo,*" the boss replied, ensuring certain torture and death to the end user in the UK.

Sheetal wished he understood Spanish, not realising it was far more beneficial to his immediate health prospects not to. "There is one more thing," he said, hoping he wasn't interrupting, and pointed to a third screen.

"Go on," Jorge urged.

"Well, it's this." Sheetal pointed to some line items. "Whoever the user is in the UK, they're looking at these bank coordinates in Cyprus. Perhaps it's their next target."

"Okay?" Jorge answered quizzically.

"Well, look at the numbers, there's €610 million in each. But there's something else that's interesting…" he said, now speaking to himself more than anyone.

"What is it?" Jorge wanted to expedite the conclusion.

"Well, the account balances moved from 600 to 610 million, but the €10 million both came from the same account at almost exactly the same time."

"Are you saying you could pull some money out of those accounts?" the boss asked.

"I think so," Sheetal said, but I'll have to select some accounts through which to transit it. "Do you want me to try?"

Jorge and Archivaldo looked at each other and shrugged in unison. "Why not?" said the lawyer, maintaining the façade of being in charge. "Let's give it a go, provided you can't get traced."

"How much?" asked Sheetal.

"Well your computer cost $15 million, so why don't you see if you can reverse those two lots of €10 million. Could you transit it back through the accounts that sent it?"

"That would probably be the easiest option," Sheetal replied. "Because the bank would just think it had bounced back. I could then use some of the other transit accounts to bring it back to one of our deposit-only accounts in Panama or Mexico City."

"Great! Let's do it." The boss sounded excited, then, looking restless, both he and Jorge bid farewell to Sheetal.

"Keep me posted," was Jorge's last order to the Indian, before both men laughed at the idea that, not only were they going to catch these thieves, but now they were also going to make profit from the whole operation.

"Shall we make a business out of this?" Jorge asked.

"I don't think so," Archivaldo replied. "If we can find them, then someone will eventually find us. Let's just recoup our losses, make a bit of profit, then send a message to the bastards that stole from us. We need to stay with the drugs trade; it's what we know."

As they pulled into the driveway of the villa and the metal gates shut behind them, two pivotal events occurred.

Sheetal was working on his side project, which existed solely to relieve his boredom. He woke up two sleeping screens that reflected the direct recording electronic voting systems representing the vote-counting servers for the US States of Wisconsin, Ohio and Pennsylvania, knowing that there would be a back door into all three.

At the same time, Archivaldo ordered Jorge to get to London to close out the *muerte*. "And make sure our signature's all over it."

"I'll leave in the morning," Jorge replied.

Back in the warehouse Sheetal purred to himself, "Shall I be a Republican or a Democrat?"

When Harry's phone rang at about 1.30 pm, he looked at the incoming number and hesitated nervously before answering it.

"Oleana, how are you?" he said before giving her a chance to say hello.

"I'm well, Harry, how are you?" Before giving him a chance to respond, she added, "I'm in London."

"Really?" Harry replied. "My Hotel, right?"

"How the hell did you know that, Harry?" She was genuinely amazed.

"Actually, I guessed like most humans you're a creature of habit, and because you liked that hotel so much the last time you were here, it seemed likely you'd use it again." The rest of it was bluff. Harry chuckled, being careful not to reveal Graham as his source. "How long are you in town?"

"I'm not sure, Harry, but there's something very pressing I need to speak to you about. I'm worried for you and your family." She knew the mention of family would get his undivided attention.

"Okay?" Harry's tone now sounded genuinely concerned. "So how soon can we meet?"

"This evening, Harry. After six preferably." She wanted to get her hair and nails done before she met him to ensure maximum allure.

"Well, I'm actually doing some work for a hotel in town tonight, so I could maybe meet you there after about seven. Would that work?"

"Perfect, let's say 7.30 pm, where?" She grabbed the pen and little notepad on her room's cabinet.

"Brown's Hotel, Albemarle Street. Just go into the bar and I'll meet you there. Harry grinned as he heard her say she looked forward to it. The call ended.

Harry felt a wave of satisfaction – what a stroke of luck he was booked into Brown's tonight.

CHAPTER SEVENTEEN
Boss Out, Spy In

S haheen was pleased to be in London; he'd been there many times before but never with Lai Xian. He decided to book into the same hotel as Oleana, figuring he could intercept her at breakfast and confront her over the theft. Whether she stayed or fled would pretty much confirm whether she was guilty or not.

No sooner had they settled into their room than he persuaded Lai Xian to change clothes and sample the shopping delights of Harrods, which the hotel receptionist advised was a refreshing walk along Walton Street. Shaheen had already decided to touch base with Harry and called him up on their way down to Knightsbridge.

At the other end, Harry was gobsmacked to see Shaheen's number come up on his screen, and he hesitated before answering.

"Hello?" he said, trying to give Shaheen the impression he hadn't saved his number.

"Harry, it's Shaheen!" announced an excited Shaheen. "I'm in London. How are you?"

Jesus Christ, thought Harry, choosing instead to say, "Shaheen, so this is a pleasant surprise! I'm fine, thanks. Where are you staying?"

"With friends in South Kensington," Shaheen partially lied; he didn't want to give anyone the chance to warn off Oleana. "We're just staying a few days before heading home. We'd like to see you and catch up."

"We?" asked Harry.

"Yes, I'm with my partner, my new love from Singapore." The pride in Shaheen's voice was apparent.

"Well, I'm tied up tonight." Harry was still in shock over the call. "But if it suits you, I can check with the wife to see if we can get a sitter for tomorrow night?"

"That's perfect, Harry. I'll get the hotel to book somewhere about eight." The words were hardly out of Shaheen's mouth than he knew he'd fucked up – but would Harry notice?

Harry of course picked up the error straightaway. The little shit wasn't staying with friends at all; so why would he lie? But he let it pass to see where it would lead. "Sounds good, Shaheen, is this a good number to reach you on?"

Shaheen confirmed it was and they said their goodbyes.

"Thank God!" he told Lai Xian.

"What for?" she asked.

"I didn't want him to know we were staying at a hotel, so I told him we were with friends, and then like an idiot I blurted out that I'd get the hotel to book dinner for us. But I don't think he noticed."

"Would it make any difference if he knew we were at the hotel?" asked Lai Xian.

"I'm not sure, but thank God Harry's never been the sharpest tool in the box." He smiled at his Oriental beauty and took her hand affectionately in his as they continued their walk down the loveliness of Walton Street towards Harrods.

Ivanna was not happy and Maria knew it; she just didn't know why. It had become perfectly obvious to her that, rather than simply being Ivanna's executive assistant, she was in fact expected to be much more of a companion. She assumed it helped that Ivanna knew Maria to be lethal and a cold-blooded killer, and perhaps this protection element was why she'd asked her to come to London.

They were sitting together in the Antelope pub while Ivanna silently reminisced that this was the very place where she'd met her Harry.

Since their row she'd wanted to call him, but her Russian stubbornness and genetic inability to say she was sorry had prevented her from doing so. She'd wrongly presumed Harry would call, and it was killing her inside. She knew she needed to be tougher than this, otherwise the distraction would start to show, but she still had to figure out a way to get Harry back to her.

"Have you ever been in love?" she asked Maria.

"I'm not sure." Maria surprised her with her answer. "I suppose I was a long time ago when I was in the military. I met a guy, also Spetsnaz, but navy. We had a passionate affair for about a year, but then we were posted away from each other, and because we were young we drifted apart. He's married now with two daughters, but there's hardly a day when I don't think of him."

"And nothing since then?" Ivanna asked.

"Actually yes," Maria replied. "Someone recently introduced me to an Englishman; we met, and like a slut I let him sleep with me on the first night. I've not seen him since, but I also think of him more than I've thought about anyone for a long time." She took a sip of her wine. "Perhaps it's because I can't see him that I want to see him – or maybe it's because he never called me since. I don't know; forbidden fruits and all that."

"Is he in London?" Ivanna asked.

"I think he's in Dubai actually. I haven't really checked, perhaps I ought to."

"I think you should; I hear Englishmen make good partners." Ivanna was prompting.

"They are gentlemen compared to what we're used to, but there's something about this guy, and his friend actually – a sort of soft exterior but very hard inside." She reflected.

"It sounds like he was hard inside of someone!" Ivanna laughed as she sipped her wine, and Maria emerged from her thoughts to laugh with her.

Then, almost in an instant, Ivanna's mood changed. "I've been very lonely since Alexei went away; it's been very difficult holding it together."

"You're joking," Maria told her. "Everyone in the organisation thinks you're doing a great job!"

"Sometimes I feel like I'm clinging on by the skin of my teeth," Ivanna confessed. "We're going to have to change a lot in the organisation. It's the only way we can stay ahead of those who would close us down. And there's one more thing." She could feel herself not wanting to continue with what she wanted to say, but she said it anyway. "I met someone, Maria. Nothing's happened!" she quickly lied as she saw Maria's reaction. "But I am very attracted to this man. Is that wrong?"

"It's understandable," Maria consoled her. "Your husband's away in jail for ten years, and you're in your forties, a beautiful and wealthy woman. I think you could be excused for having temptation." She'd unwittingly opened the door for Ivanna.

"Do you think I could be forgiven if I went a little further?" Ivanna asked.

"It depends by who," Maria reasoned. "If it's just to fulfil your lust, maybe so. If it's a love replacement, then you have to be careful not to lose control of your feelings. Who is the guy anyway?"

"I have a high-end security company looking after my needs, he works for them and advises me on my security protocols. I feel very safe when I'm with him," she confessed.

"Of course you do," Maria said. "We're women, we're hardwired to be attracted to strength, we can't help it." She paused sympathetically. "Do you want me to call the security company and fabricate some pretext so you can spend some time with him?"

Maria had laid down the temptation and the excuse Ivanna needed to reel her Harry back in. She smiled with a naughtiness Maria hadn't seen before. "No, I think I need to be the one do it." She looked at her near empty glass of wine. "Fuck it – let's share a bottle."

"Good idea," Maria agreed.

They were halfway through their bottle of Bichot Puligny-Montrachet Chardonnay when Maria suggested Isaak was well overdue for a visit to London.

Ivanna laughed. "Shall I tell the skinny bean-counter you said that?"

"Actually, you do know he fancies the shit out of me, right?" Maria confided.

"No kidding!" Ivanna continued to laugh.

"No chance," said Maria, concealing her bitterness.

"But you're right," Ivanna thought out loud. "It's time I got his skinny arse over here for a catch-up."

★   ★   ★

Isaak sat in his Voentorg Building office, reconciling the cartel's multiple accounts across a dozen countries. The two wire transfers of €10 million to each of the Cyprus accounts had gone off without a hitch, and now he was trying to recall with some satisfaction if they actually had an account in any bank that didn't have a corrupt official working for them.

He smiled to think that, while he and his organisation went to so much trouble to conceal their theft and laundering, banks did the equivalent in plain sight every single working day, by fixing LIBOR, by front-running exchange rates, and by churning and even laundering for drug cartels. There was one big difference between bankers and gangsters, however – only the latter ended up in jail. His thoughts were broken by his phone ringing; he didn't recognise the number.

"Isaak, it's Artur." The caller spoke in Russian.

"Artur who?" Isaak had no clue who was calling.

"Artur Kiselev, you forgetful prick, your fellow employee."

Isaak suddenly remembered the ex-convict scumbag from Krasnoyarsk prison.

The voice continued. "I've got someone who wants to speak to you; hang on." Artur cut off, though Isaak could still hear some muffled sounds in the background before a different voice picked up.

"Isaak, how are you?"

"Alexei?" There was incredulity in Isaak's voice.

"I'm out, Isaak, the payoff worked, you efficient son of a bitch!" Alexei laughed.

"My God!" Isaak was now feigning his excitement and concealing his dread that this day had come. "This is brilliant, where are you?"

"I'm with Artur for now, Isaak, I've been told I need to keep a low profile. The lawyer's going through the motions to get my passport ready and I'm told I'll have it in a day. I'm hoping to get out of the country for a few weeks, just so the favour we bought isn't advertised. Where's Ivanna?"

"She's in London, Alexei, she's pretty much been running things from there for the past year or so, it was getting too awkward here." Isaak made the only excuse he could think for her.

"I understand, she's a smart girl. How's the business?" he asked.

"It's as good as ever, Alexei, you married wisely. She's controlled everything, closed down a lot, opened up other stuff and cleaned house. I can explain when I see you."

"Call the lawyer," Alexei instructed. "Tell him to sort out a UK visa for me, pay off whoever he needs to. You and I are going to London – and by the way…" Alexei paused emphatically. "Don't tell Ivanna I'm out or coming to London; I want to see the beautiful look on her face when I walk through that door."

Isaak has already concluded that it would literally be more than his life was worth to betray Alexei's confidence on this one. "Consider it done."

Alexei's joy was palpable. "Hopefully she and I will be enjoying some of that fucked-up English rain and warm beer by the end of the week."

The call ended and Isaak sat in his office shell-shocked. His easy ride with Ivanna in charge was over. Even after having sent the payoffs to Cyprus, he never thought the Cellist and his boss would act so quickly. He picked up his phone and called Maria; he could at least hint at an impending event that would put Ivanna on her guard.

Maria looked at the number flashing and cringed; she didn't want to take the call but knew she had to in order to lure Isaak over.

After exchanging false niceties Maria disclosed, "Isaak, I think you're going to need to get over here soon, Ivanna's mentioned it. And there's one more thing – Oleana's here, and she says she's willing to do a deal with you over her part regarding the funds in our accounts."

Isaak smiled triumphantly. "I knew she'd surface eventually, and as ever her timing is perfect. I was planning on coming over very soon in any case. Do you think the end of the week would work?"

Maria assumed he was mentioning the timing because he wanted to violate her body, but in actual fact he was trying to warn her off for Ivanna's sake.

"How's Ivanna's security?" he asked.

"I think it's okay now I'm here," Maria told him.

"Well, I've heard some of her old friends might be coming to town, so you should just make sure she's ready for any surprise visits. He put down the phone.

Maria had got the message loud and clear. Clearly one of the opposing mobs were in town and Ivanna might be under threat. She would be ready to react in the only way she knew how.

Omar and Sergeant Seyadin had just completed a long discussion over coffee in Starbucks in Emirates Towers. They'd coordinated their time off and could travel within two days but both were aware how off their turf they would be once they set foot in London, and finding Oleana *and* Soroush was going to be no cake walk.

"Do you think we'll stick out in London?" Maryam asked. "It's Hajj after all, do you think there'll be any Arabs over there?"

"You must be joking!" Omar replied in his typically calm tone. "This time of year, millions of Muslims go to Hajj, but what you'll soon learn is that it's the Muslims with millions who go to Knightsbridge." With a wry chuckle, he took a triumphant sip of coffee, clearly pleased with his own joke. "It's time to call in a favour." He picked up his phone and started scrolling through his contacts. Maryam watched on, filled with the curiosity Omar had purposely provoked.

"Mr Sotheby," Omar said, "It's Omar Shamoon from Dubai CID. How are you?" He waited as his interlocutor's mind raced to connect the dots as to who the hell the caller could be.

"Warrant Officer Shamoon, how nice to hear from you," the voice lied. "To what do I owe this pleasure?"

"I'm coming to London, Mr Sotheby; mostly pleasure but a bit of business, and there are some people in your town I think could be of interest. So consider this a tip-off."

Toby Sotheby, MI6 Regional Head for the Middle East, was thrilled. This was free, unsolicited intelligence, so, whatever it was, he would happily claim full credit for it and put it down to meticulous spy craft. "Go on," he urged modestly.

"Shaheen Soroush and Oleana Katayeva are in your capital, and in my experience, whenever the two of them are in the same town, somebody ends up seriously hurt – or dead."

"Is that why you're coming?" Toby asked.

"Not directly, but I would like to know where they're staying, just to be on the safe side; and as we've helped you many times in the past, I thought I'd ask for your help." Omar knew full well this man would recognise that, in the shadowy world of intelligence-gathering, the ongoing value of a favour asked was that a favour must one day be repaid.

"Well, as you know, Warrant Officer," Toby said, his Eton-schooled accent shining through, "my mandate is not domestic operations; that falls to the police and my colleagues in the Security Service. But in this case I'll make an exception for you. However, we must meet when you arrive – when will that be?"

"In two days," Omar replied. "Would you recommend a place to stay?"

"Your countrymen typically stay at one of the Jumeirah hotels, so I'd recommend the Jumeirah Lowndes. You'll blend in there, and it's more discreet than the Jumeirah Carlton Tower. Call me when you arrive, and I'll get you the information you need."

As he put the phone down, Toby revelled to think there might be yet another international operation in play from which he might seize a spot of tradecraft glory.

At his end, Omar explained to his sergeant how, although they didn't need Toby Sotheby to find their marks, Toby Sotheby had been MI6's most successful agent in the UAE to date, and having such a senior officer on their side in the UK could give them top cover if the need arose. He pulled his iPad Pro from its sleeve and booked separate hotel rooms for him and Seyadin. Once they arrived in London, they would only have a week to find out what the hell was going on.

CHAPTER EIGHTEEN
Mexit

Jorge González's route to London was protracted; necessarily so. He'd flown KLM out of Mexico City and transferred to an Aer Lingus flight to Dublin. Entering Ireland had been a breeze, and here he hired a limo from the airport to drive him to Aldergrove Airport, in Northern Ireland, and more importantly the United Kingdom. While boarding there for the journey to London, his passport and UK visa were checked, but once on the plane his entry into the UK was complete, and his arrival aboard a domestic flight bore the low levels of scrutiny he desired.

He took a London cab to White Horse Street, which led to the Shepherd's Market area of London, where he asked the driver to drop him off at the Kings Arms pub. As the taxi disappeared down Shepherd Street, he pulled a handwritten note from his pocket and walked across the road to enter L'Autre, which he assumed had to be London's only Polish–Mexican restaurant. The polite young waitress greeted him in English from behind the small bar and he said, "I'm Mr Jorge, you have a table reserved for me?"

She pointed him to a table over his right shoulder. There sat an unmistakably Mexican woman who could have come right out of the 1950s. Her wavy, shoulder-length hair was a deep brown and parted at the side. Her eyes were black, her lips garnished with deep red lipstick, the top half of her dress was figure hugging and the lower half under the table was calf-length and flared. She didn't stand up, but smiled at him in greeting.

"Alejandra?" he asked.

"Sí," was her simple reply, as she beckoned him to sit.

"¿Dónde está el señor G?" he asked.

"Not here for sure," she replied in Spanish. "I'll take you to him, but let's talk and have a drink before I do." She picked up the bottle of Rioja on the table and poured it without asking him if he wanted any.

He already loved this woman's confidence.

"We've never met, Mr Jorge, but I've heard all about you." She pushed the wine glass towards him. "I'm told we have a problem with a certain individual here; but I don't want to know who it is or your plans for him. Salud." She raised her glass to him. They clinked glasses and Alejandra continued. "The police are very effective in London. There are cameras covering just about every square foot of this place. So we'll finish this wine and then I'll take you somewhere else. There you'll meet Mr G."

"Answer me this," Jorge demanded. "Why are we using the Italians to sort out our dirty work?"

"The Italians are part of the EU," she explained, "so they can move their men in and out of the country with minimum fuss and no visas. Whatever you're asking of Mr G, I'd bet he'll bring in an unknown from Italy, have him do the job, and then he can disappear back to Sicily without any fanfare. Whereas we Mexicans have to have residency visas, work, and so on, just to remain here. So it's better that we should…" She sipped her wine while she searched for the right phrase. "…stand off and subcontract to our Latin brethren. A different kind of Mexican standoff, you could say," she added with a playful look.

Jorge nodded. "It makes sense. When do I meet him?"

"After we've eaten. I've ordered Polish wild boar sausages and a chicken fajita, so take your pick."

For the first time in his life Jorge ate wild pig from northern Europe, and afterwards they walked out into the cooling air of an early evening in London's Shepherd's Market. Alejandra hailed a taxi.

"Take us to the other side of Chelsea Bridge," she ordered the driver. "I'll tell you where to drop us."

As the taxi manoeuvred its way towards the River Thames, she instructed Jorge in a low voice, "I'll get the cab to drop us and then you'll go to a restaurant. I'll show you where but I won't come in. When you've finished your meeting you should get a taxi to Knightsbridge station; use this card to get on the underground." She handed him an Oyster Card, topped up with his fare. "Then go to Heathrow Terminal 3, and book the first available KLM flight to Amsterdam; you can arrange wherever you need to go from there. If you have to stay overnight, you can organise that at Schiphol Airport."

"So I won't see you again?" Jorge asked – there was obvious disappointment in his tone.

Alejandra laughed enchantingly. "Not unless you fuck up these instructions! Perhaps next time when you're not busy conducting business…" she teased.

He nodded in reflection. "Yes, perhaps."

She told the taxi to drop them just short of Battersea Park Road, and as they stood at the junction she said, "I'm going this way to the train. You're going that way to a little Italian restaurant with a red front. It's called San Gennaro, although everyone who knows it calls it the 'Canteen'. It's actually the very best Italian in London as far as food is concerned. When you go in, ask for 'table one'. It's at the back and…" She looked at her watch. "Mr G will be eating there right now." She turned to face him. "*Suerte, señor Jorge. Hasta la próxima vez.*"

"Until next time," he echoed in English, and she was gone. He was immediately left to cope on his own crossing a busy London road with traffic driving on the 'wrong' side.

He entered San Gennaro where the polite owner greeted him and responded to his request. He showed him to the back of the restaurant where there was a small set of steps leading down to a table on the left and a small bar on the right. The table was out of sight from passers-by on the pavement outside.

Sitting there was an immaculately groomed, lean man of small stature who sported a deep suntan, which contrasted strongly with his thinning but distinguished silver hair. Jorge guessed the man to be in his late fifties, perhaps early sixties. He was reading an *Evening Standard* and eating pasta. He looked up as Jorge walked down the steps towards him.

"Jorge, take a seat here," said the man, indicating to Jorge to sit at a right angle to him, not bothering with any form of introduction. "Did you have a good trip?"

Jorge almost got to answer, but was cut off when his host told the Canteen's owner, "Get him a glass of the best house red."

What was it with people in Britain? thought Jorge. They all seemed to give you red without even asking if you liked it!"

The wine came quickly and Mr G looked at Jorge with a smile. "Have you eaten?"

Jorge told him he had, but once more his situation was ignored.

"Get some of those pizza bits you do," the man instructed the owner before turning back to Jorge. "You'll fucking love them."

As the owner pushed the order into the kitchen Mr G got serious and lowered his tone. "So you guys have a problem on my patch?" He chuckled. "Fucking criminals everywhere."

"There's a cyber-dude," Jorge replied. "He's stolen millions from us by hacking our accounts. We've tracked him down to about eighty kilometres south-west of here. We need retribution and to find out if he's working alone or, if he's working for an organisation, then we need to send a message to his bosses."

"If he is working for another organisation on my patch, there'll be more than a fucking message sent out, Jorge. I don't like competition and that is well known in these parts," Mr G explained. "Either I get a cut or people get cut, simple as that. What exactly do you need?"

"Two things," Jorge said. "We want him to know why he's going to die, and we want to know who he works for."

Mr G nodded gently. "We can oblige Jorge, but on two conditions."

Neither man said a word for a few seconds.

"First, any information we get out of him is jointly ours, and I'm allowed to act independently on it without recourse from your boss?"

"That's fine," Jorge responded. "But we want the actual computers."

Mr G continued as if Jorge hadn't replied. "And secondly, I have a cousin in New Jersey. We'll do this for $5 million wholesale worth of your Mexican product shipped to him at wholesale price."

"Mr G…" Jorge's tone rose slightly. "$5 million could sell at five times that on the streets of New Jersey."

"I know that, Jorge, but you can't ship it in this country without going to war with the fucking Afghans and Pakistanis; and it probably cost you less than $100,000 to produce in Mexico – so I'd say you're getting a hell of a deal...and a fair one too, I think."

Jorge could see the win–win in what Mr G was proposing. "Okay," he said. "I agree, but what about the timing, it might take a few weeks for us to get it to your cousin."

"Jorge, Jorge, Jorge." Mr G spoke in a resigned tone. "If we can't trust each other, then what has the world come to?"

Jorge knew they would deliver but was surprised at the level of Mr G's trust. He liked this guy, and could now see how he'd come to reach the pinnacle of criminality by adhering to a code of honour amongst thieves.

"Here are the details of the target as best as we can figure out." Jorge handed him a piece of paper. "The target lives in one of these houses. It surely can't be difficult to figure out who the IT guy is from these."

Mr G looked down at the paper. "I know this village," he said. "I used to know a guy who lived in the next town. These places are tiny; it won't take much to figure out who it is just by trawling the local pubs."

Jorge was about to commence his goodbyes when Mr G said, "One more thing, Jorge." A pause. "Once I set this in motion, this guy is going to die a miserable death. So if you have any doubts, say so now, because once you walk out of the door, you owe me product – and I owe you a result. No refunds, no returns."

Jorge held his hand out across the table. "No refunds, no returns."

Within two minutes Jorge was in a London cab heading towards Knightsbridge tube station, wishing he was checking into a hotel with Alejandra.

Mr G, meanwhile, headed back to his apartment in Battersea. He would call his cousin in the USA later that evening to let him know of the impending windfall.

The very next day, two Italian-looking men in their twenties sat at the bar in the Whistle Stop pub in Liss, loudly discussing their need to find a really smart IT guy for some local commercial work. By the time they'd left the pub, a pensioner calling himself Ray, had told them two names. One lived in Liss Forest, the other in St Mary's Road near the church – fourth house down on the left.

CHAPTER NINETEEN
The Good, The Bad And The Innocent

Harry arrived at Brown's at just after 4 pm. He entered through the Albemarle Street entrance and made his way across the mosaic entrance hall to the reception desk. He spent the next two hours with the manager and assistant manager covering aspects of the hotel's security and crisis response protocols. Both men were keen to show him the contact lists for all key staff, and the 'go-team' backup along with their procedures and checklists. Harry was left in no doubt that the security and response to a breach or incident had been well thought out. He quipped to the two men that, given Brown's history as London's first hotel, they'd certainly had enough time to figure out what they were doing wrong.

By 7 pm, Harry was being shown the hotel's technical surveillance system integration, covering basically every inch of the public areas. The on–duty security guard had all but completed his demonstration when the assistant manager reappeared.

"We assumed you'd be staying the night, so here's your room key. Feel free to have the run of the place, and if you need anything, just ask." Having handed Harry the key, he began to leave the room, before turning back to ask. "Will you be letting us know how we did tomorrow before you leave?"

"Of course," Harry confirmed. "Nobody likes negative surprises, right?" He checked his watch. "I'm actually meeting someone in the Donovan Bar in about twenty minutes, so I'll do my walkabout after that."

It was closer to forty minutes later when Oleana walked tentatively into the Donovan Bar, having been directed there by one of the door staff.

Harry was sat almost opposite the door so he could see her coming. She beamed as she spotted him and he stood up and kissed her on both cheeks. A dozen of the twenty-odd people in the bar turned to check out this obviously Russian blonde, among them a pair of Persian-looking women Oleana walked past to get to Harry.

"You look well," Harry said, trying to inject a positive spin from the outset.

"You should have seen me three weeks ago, Harry. I think I've put on about three kilos since I got out of jail, but at least it gives me a good excuse to buy new clothes every week." She gave a half-bitter laugh and ordered a passion fruit martini from the waiter.

Over the next half an hour she described the experience and trauma of her jail time, carefully avoiding the fact that she knew either Harry or his wife had stitched her up.

Harry, meanwhile, waited tensely for the 'you bastard' bomb to drop, but it never did. Perhaps Oleana didn't know it had been Nazrin who sacrificed her for Harry.

He was about to ask her why she'd wanted to meet when he found himself distracted by the two Persian women taking selfies together. By now they were standing at right angles to them trying to get a photo of themselves with the George and the Dragon stained-glass window behind the bar in the back-ground.

"You have to love this place," he chuckled, "It's a five-star tourist's dream!"

Oleana laughed. "I think you love this place because I know how much you love women's legs and stockings, Harry." She nodded around at the black and white photos of shapely women adorning the walls. Meanwhile the Persians, who now had their backs to the two of them once more, took their last selfie. Oleana turned to face Harry square-on. "Harry, your family may be in great danger. That's why I had to see you."

A little piece of Harry was disappointed to hear she wasn't seeing him for him, but he simply said, "What? From whom?"

Oleana had spent all night rehearsing the lie; she'd decided her need to use Harry outweighed her need for revenge. "You once told me Shaheen Soroush paid you quite a bit of money."

"I did?" Harry honestly couldn't recall.

"Yes, you did, Harry – how much was it?" she asked pointedly.

Harry shrugged his shoulders. "Firstly, he didn't give it to me, Oleana; it was part of a business deal. And I can't recall exactly but let's say in the region of $9 million."

"Do you still have it?" Again pointedly.

"I have a wife, a kid and a place in Richmond," Harry sighed. "Take a wild-arse guess."

"Can you get it?" she asked.

"No way!" he replied.

She nodded thoughtfully and put on her most knowing expression. "Then that shortens the options." The conversation was going exactly how she'd predicted. She leaned forward and spoke in a low voice. "That money wasn't his, Harry – it belonged to a Russian cartel. They want it back, and they'll kill your family if they don't get it."

"How do you know?" Harry asked.

"Two sources," she replied. "One's Maria, the girl you met in Dubai when Shaheen was attacked by those guys in the car park. The second is Shaheen himself, because apparently he was robbed of millions from his apartment in Singapore while he was in Dubai." She omitted to tell Harry that she knew the latter because she happened to be one of the robbers!

"And they've said the Russians are coming after me?" Harry was seeking confirmation.

"That's what I'm fucking telling you, Harry!" She was trying not to raise her voice. "For fuck's sake, hear me on this one." She sipped the last of her martini, then indicated straight away to the waiter for another. "There's an accountant, Harry, running the cartel's finances. He has your name as one of the recipients of their money. He's coming to London, and you'll be asked to repay the money or they'll harm your family. These are not nice people, Harry." She stopped talking as the good-looking waiter replaced her passion fruit martini.

"It's nice to see you in here again, Miss Elena," the waiter told her.

She looked at him perplexed. "I've never been here before," she replied. "You must be confusing me with someone else."

"Oh, I'm so sorry, madam," the waiter responded. "Then I can only say that she was very beautiful too."

"Well, that's okay then," she flirted back. "And I suppose you were quite close with the name – it's *Oleana*, not Elena."

"Once again I apologise," he said with a little deferent bow. "Please enjoy your martini, Miss Oleana." And he left them to take his next order.

"Some bloody waiters…" Harry was clearly irritated. "They think they have a God-given right to interrupt."

"If I didn't know you better, Harry Linley, I'd think you're bit jealous of that good-looking man," she teased.

"Not really," Harry told her, "because I still get to be here with you while he's over these serving those Persian girls. Now, what about this accountant?"

"His boss is in London; he's coming here to brief him," she said, concealing the person in question's real gender. "You have two choices, Harry." She was leaning forward again. "Either give them the nine million when they confront you, or you need to silence the accountant before he passes your name to anyone who can really do you proper harm."

Harry knew he wasn't in any position to repay these people. "When does he arrive?"

"In a day or two. I can deliver him to you, but then it's up to you how you silence him."

"Why are you doing this for me, Oleana?" Harry was feeling very guilty about her taking the fall in jail.

"Harry, we were lovers." She sipped her martini. "And quite good ones too if I remember correctly. But our timing was always awful; in another reality it could have been me they were coming for, who knows, I could have been your wife!" She knew all men were suckers for such sentiment, and Harry was certainly no exception.

"I've always adored you, Oleana, you know that." He was perfectly serious. "Thank you for this." He reached over and put his hand on hers. There was a flash of a camera and the mood was broken. "Do Persians ever stop taking photos of each other? I bet the snaps are already on Instagram. Anyway, thank you Oleana, I really appreciate this." He stood up. "I'll walk you out, through the back exit, it's easier for taxis there."

He escorted her out of the bar, guiding her to the right to the Dover Street entrance at the back of the hotel instead of left to the main entrance.

At the same time the two Persian women also left the bar, but without following Harry and Oleana. Instead they left through the front and hailed a cab. No sooner were they in the cab than Tarana made a call on her mobile. "Nazrin," she said. "I'm sorry to have to tell you this but your husband met a blonde – thin, in her thirties. We asked the waiter to find out her name, it was Oleana." Tarana would have paused if she could have seen the look on Nazrin's face, but she continued. "We got a load of photos pretending to take selfies, I'll send them to you."

Nazrin was seething. "Where are they now?" she asked. "Well, that's the worst bit, and I hate to be the one to tell you, but when they left the bar they didn't leave the hotel; they went further in, it looked like towards the lifts." She paused. "I'm so sorry, Nazrin, but you did want to know."

"It's okay, Tarana. Thank you for doing this for me, at least I know what they're up to. That woman's paying me back for something I once did to her, and Harry's clearly all too happy to be her willing pawn."

At the Dover Street entrance Oleana was just about to say goodbye to Harry when he said, "Oleana, I have to tell you something – Shaheen Soroush is in town."

"What?" she said in shock.

"I'm having dinner with him tomorrow night, but now you have me wondering, because him being in town must have something to do with money." Harry was thinking out loud.

Oleana was now scared. If Shaheen was in town for the money, it would be because of the money she and Maria had stolen from him, and certainly not the fabrication she'd just made up for Harry.

"Where's he staying?" she asked.

"Not sure," Harry replied. "He told me with friends but I think he was lying. I can't imagine he's visiting for anything else but business." He'd just inadvertently fuelled the fire of Oleana's panic.

She jumped into a taxi, pledging to call Harry as soon as the accountant arrived in town. Inside the cab she immediately called Maria to tell her the Isaak plan was in play, but now they had another problem.

Harry walked back into Brown's and his phone rang. "Hey sweetie," he said.

"Where are you?" Her tone was stern.

"Brown's Hotel."

"Are you alone?"

"Of course, I'm working."

"And staying the night?"

"Yes. It's part of the security survey."

"Okay, Skype me from your room now – right now!" She did everything she could to sound calm.

"What?" Harry was confused

"Right now, Harry, I need to speak to you about something, please, quickly!" She abruptly hung up.

Five minutes later she made up a story involving a thumping noise coming from next door and attempted to let him hear it over Skype. Of course he couldn't make it out, but told her if it continued past midnight, then it might be an idea to call the police. Feigning reassurance, Nazrin then asked Harry to show her his room in Brown's in the nicest tone she could muster, including the bathroom, the size of the wardrobes and the view outside behind the curtains. The call ended with Harry suspecting nothing, and with Nazrin calling Brown's and asking to speak to Mrs Linley in Mr Linley's room.

"I'm sorry, ma'am," the polite receptionist told her. "Mr Linley is single occupancy."

Nazrin put down the phone. "Fuck!" she said out loud to herself. Her bastard husband had clearly got Oleana out of the room while he was on Skype and obviously bribed the staff to say he was alone too. Her decision now was to wait for the photos from the bar – or should she wake up her little boy now and go straight to the hotel and confront the two fuckers?

Maria was sitting in the Surprise pub in Chelsea with Ivanna and Willie, the London fixer. Ivanna was explaining how, if Maria needed anything done in London, then Willie was her man.

"Everything from arranging a plumber to getting a last-minute table at Zuma," Willie pronounced.

The conversation was interrupted when Maria's phone rang – it was Oleana. Her two companions could see her demeanour change from relaxed to serious and alert.

"Is everything okay?" Ivanna asked when Maria had put down the phone.

"I have some news you may or may not like," Maria told her. "That call was from Oleana, our previous fixer in Dubai; she's in London, and she's tracked Shaheen Soroush down here too."

Ivanna remained calm and looked at Willie.

Willie, polite as ever, wrongly assumed he needed to be excluded from the conversation, so he smiled and stood up. "Top-up, ladies? Same again?" Both women replied in the affirmative and Willie took three short steps to the bar.

"Maria, you know what you have to do. I wanted Soroush dead when he was in Dubai, and now he's come for us. This is the man who got my husband thrown in jail and made us have to change everything about the way we operate. I don't care how you do it, but get it done. Does Oleana know how long he's staying?"

"Not a clue," answered Maria. "I don't where he's staying either; I'll make a few calls right now to find out."

Maria walked out of the pub and walked slowly past the smokers, who nudged each other in admiration of her jeans and perfectly contoured ensconced bottom.

By the time her phone connected, she was out of earshot. "Isaak, baby, I miss you," she said, summoning all her anti-cringing power. "Please come over and see me."

"My darling, I'm all but on my way, I'll be there today or tomorrow." He paused hesitantly. "I'm coming alone, but there's a business associate coming as well. He'll want to meet with Ivanna – is she there and okay?"

"She is, I'm with her now, although she doesn't know about us or that I'm talking to you right now of course. Come soon, please." She knew she needed to work on her begging tone. "I've also told Oleana she has to meet you, to sort out a deal."

"That's super," he told her. "I'll come very soon, my darling." His double entendre sickened her, but his tone suddenly shifted. "Tell me, is Ivanna alone? I mean completely alone."

"Well, not right now, Isaak, she's in a pub with Willie," Maria said, taking him literally.

"No, no, I mean there's no one else in her life – apart from those we know?" He was skirting the reason for his question.

"Not that I know of," Maria answered half-truthfully. "In fact, she actually seems quite lonely these days."

"That's good," Isaak blurted. "Well, not good, but you know what I mean."

"I have no idea what you mean," Maria told him. Her mind was already racing back to Ivanna's confession regarding the security company man she fancied.

"Well, I'm just worried about business and I don't want her distracted." It was a bumbled lie, but he hoped it was enough to ensure that, whenever Alexei arrived, Ivanna would be the only one surprised.

"She's fine," Maria reassured. "Just get yourself over here and see for yourself."

"Where are you staying?" he asked. "My favourite Cadogan Hotel is closed for refurbishment…"

"Don't even think about it, Isaak," she cut in quickly. "You can't stay in the same hotel as me; no one in the company knows about this and it could be very dangerous for us if they did." She was right and he knew it.

"No problem," he told her. "I'll find a place close-by. He was already thinking of the Millennium Hotel on the same street; that would certainly do for a few days. The call ended with Maria telling him again to come soon. In his Moscow apartment he looked at the bed on which he'd so often had his way with her and chuckled to think there was no part of her body he hadn't explored. He walked to his bathroom to check he had an ample supply of Viagra for the trip. He would call Alexei to let him know he was going to

London ahead of him to ensure Ivanna would know nothing of his pending arrival.

Back outside the Surprise Maria made a second call, this time to Oleana. "Isaak will be here in a day or two, he knows you're in town, so we need to be ready. In the meantime, find out where Soroush is staying and how long."

"We'll be ready," Oleana told her. "I know he's having dinner with Harry and his wife tomorrow, so let me work on it."

"Good. Find out where and what time. Ivanna wants him dealt with." Maria was already formulating her plan. She put the phone down before once more giving the smokers outside the pub a tight jeans show. Willie was already sitting back with Ivanna and recounting a humorous anecdote from his military days.

Maria sat down, picked up her red wine. "It's in play."

CHAPTER TWENTY
Mac's Home

The innocuous rental van parked at the top of Saint Mary's Road in Liss had not brought itself any undue attention. Of course, in reality, the van was not rented at all. The ultimate – untraceable – owner was Mr G, and the van was a precise ringer for an actual and identical rental van in all likelihood being used somewhere in Wales.

However, as innocent as the vehicle looked on the outside, inside, to an educated eye, it was anything but. The lining was made of professionally installed plywood laid over three inches of sound insulation material. This easily removable liner had then been sprayed with Line-X protective coating. To an unwitting onlooker the installation was to protect the interior of the van; to anyone who worked for Mr G, it was a sound-suppressing interior that enabled efficient and thorough DNA-removal.

The tool racks were equally deceptive, and if, by chance, an inquisitive policeman were to ask to look in the back of the van, he would believe the array of neatly racked saws and knives were simply the necessary implements related to tree surgery. The chemical protection suits and masks had to be for the purpose of protecting the wearer against the tree chemical treatment seemingly contained in canisters bungee-corded alongside the wheel wells.

The two men sitting in the rear of the van were not visible from the outside or indeed from the front seats, due to the full-length screen and liner. The rear was, however, accessible from the front, thanks to a fall-away panel, which both men had used to enter to alternate shifts every hour observing the gateway of 7 St Mary's Road through the heavily tinted back windows of the van.

Both men had been trained by the best in their craft in Sicily, and both spoke decent English. They had figured that the occupant of Number 7 probably worked in local offices. They'd therefore parked the van for a surveillance 'soak' between 6 am and 10 am, which would surely establish what time the occupant went to work. It didn't.

So they returned the following day, soaking between 4 pm and 8 pm, which would surely catch the target returning from work, assuming he worked anything like normal hours. Unfortunately again for them, the target didn't show himself.

They had all but given up by 7.20 pm, thinking they were going to have to rework the plan, when a tall, elegant woman in her fifties emerged from the gateway of Number 7 with a springer spaniel on a lead walking gently alongside her.

"*Andiamo*." The watching Italian told his colleague, who'd covered the previous hour, and the man moved over gently to look out of the rear window alongside him.

"*La donna di casa?*" said the second Italian, identifying the woman as probably being the target's wife. "*Dev' essere stata bellissima ai suoi tempi*," he continued in typical Italian style.

"But now she wears a wax jacket and rubber boots," said his watching colleague. "As soon as she's gone past, do your thing."

The woman turned right up Station Road and, as she did so, the previously admiring Italian slipped through the fall-away panel and exited the van via its passenger door. He then crossed over to get a clear view of the woman and dog walking up the road facing oncoming traffic.

He watched as the springer spaniel tried to increase their pace as they approached the nearby park, and the woman released the dog as they came to the entrance of the field. He temporarily lost sight of them behind some trees, but quickly regained it and casually glanced over as the woman meandered slowly away from the road, the dog running frantically to and fro with head down, giving the impression it wanted to vacuum the grass up with its nose.

About halfway along the edge of the park was another entrance through the low hedge that separated the green space from the road. The Italian crossed the road and lit up a cigarette, then started to walk slowly back in the direction he'd just come, having just executed a subtle and unnoticed U-turn. He continued to observe as he walked and saw the woman call the dog, only to disappear through a gap at the bottom corner of the park. He altered course and headed in that direction.

When he reached the gap, there was no sign of either the woman or the dog. He quickly peered down the track on the other side of the hedge, and then back up towards the road. They had vanished.

He made one last sweep up the road, then abruptly stopped and followed the track back to the van, where his colleague was already sitting in the driver's seat.

"They have a back gate," he said as he climbed in. "If this guy doesn't work, then maybe they take turns walking their dog. Maybe, for whatever reason, she walks it this way and he walks another way using the gate at the back."

"If he does, then that'll work," said the driver. "Call the boss, tell him we need Nicco *il Toro* down here. We can pick him up from the station in Petersfield."

The next day the van was back in Liss at 6 am, only this time parked alongside the recreation ground, the two Italians in the front seats drinking coffee and looking like workmen waiting to start their day.

Just past 7.30 am, the first movement they saw was the flash of the excited spaniel dashing into the park to soak up the fresh scents of the morning dew.

A few moments later a slightly built man dressed similarly to the woman they'd seen the previous evening emerged onto the park and started to walk along the bottom of the treeline.

"*Eccolo qui*," said the passenger, and as the driver put the van in motion he tapped the partition to the rear of the van, telling the new occupant, "*Questo è.*"

The van moved slowly along the road before pulling into a small car park sandwiched between the park and the rear of the back gardens belonging to the houses on Saint Mary's Road.

There were two empty cars parked close to the road but the van took the space furthest from the road, which was shielded from view in two directions by high unkempt hedges designed to give the houses' occupiers some privacy.

No sooner was the van stationary than Nicco 'il Toro' was out the rear door walking down the track that led away from the road towards Number 7's back gate. He realised the dog's owner would have to come from the park and turn right to get home, so he continued down the track to the corner of the park and loitered.

As the man reached the gap in the fence Nicco started up the lane. The dog then came bursting though the gap in the hedge and immediately came to a halt in front of Nicco.

"*Il mio bambino!*" Nicco said as he went down on one knee, and the dog instantly went over to him, tail wagging, looking for a good stroke.

Mac spun around, totally shocked to see a fellow human being not ten metres away from him.

"What a beautiful dog," this stranger said to Mac, exposing his Italian accent. "And it's a beautiful morning in your English countryside. This dog is a shooting dog, yes?" He made a huge fuss of the appreciative dog. "What's his name?"

"His name's Hardy, and yes, he is a shooting dog," Mac told him with noticeable pride in his voice. "Do you shoot?"

"I do," the stranger said, his eyes fixed on the dog. "For a living, in fact, but not here."

Mac was about to ask what the hell he meant by that, when suddenly he sensed a presence behind him, just a moment before the force of a rubber nunchuck in full swing hit him across the side the head. The blow was practically silent but was enough to utterly poleaxe Mac, and the force instantly felled him into the thick hedge.

Nicco was immediately on him and grabbed his throat to ensure he couldn't regain consciousness in any great hurry. He then lifted him vertically as the driver reversed the van out of its parking space, completely obscuring the view from the road. The men rushed the limp body the ten or so metres to the van and threw it in the back.

Nicco then turned to the spaniel, who, without a cell of aggression in its body, and having had the bark bred out of his line for the sake of being a good shooting spaniel, stood, little understanding what was going on. It then vaguely wagged its tail in a submissive gesture towards any trouble.

"Hardy," Nicco said in his kindest voice. "Here boy."

And the spaniel, figuring out that his master was already in the van, trotted up and jumped into the van. Nicco and the other Italian followed him in and gently closed the doors. The driver then pulled out of the parking area and turned right to drive sedately away from the awakening village.

Within half an hour the van had skirted Liss and emerged at the top of Hill Brow. Here it took the road towards Rogate, and after approximately 1.5 kilometres it turned right up a track into a deeply wooded forest, stopping approximately two hundred metres from the road. All had been reconnoitred by the Italians the previous day.

Nicco pulled some rope from one of the racks in the van and made a loop to act as a leash for the dog. He took the dog to the front of the van and tied it to the van's towing ring.

The driver went around the back of the van and took out a spade, before walking some twenty-five meters into the woods away from the van. He selected a small hollow in the ground and started digging. The third Italian had placed plasti-cuffs around Mac's hands and feet.

Mac's first sense of consciousness was that his hands and feet were tied. He opened his eyes and realised he was lying in the back of a van with two other men, including the big man who'd been petting Hardy.

"So you're Mr Harris, the well-known local IT expert?" the big man asked.

Mac's head hurt, he was still dazed. "Well yes, you could say that, but I think you've made a mistake."

"I don't think so, you see we know there's significant computer power coming from your address, and we want you to help us." Nicco's accent was rich Sicilian.

"I'm sure I can help," Mac's tone was pleading, "but there's no need for this kind of treatment."

"I'll tell you what," said Nicco. "Here's a pen."

Mac reached for the pen with his bound hands. It was then he noticed the man was wearing surgical gloves and industrial overalls.

"Now write down the passwords to your computers," Nicco ordered.

Mac was overcome by panic as he quickly reasoned they would only need these if they planned to separate him from his computers, and if this was the case, it meant these men would go to his house and possibly hurt his wife.

"I'll give you them," he told them, "but you'll need me to access them if that's what you want." He wrote down 'q1w2e3R$T%%'. Nicco looked at it thinking it was nonsense, not realising it was a basic keyboard pattern password with a shift.

"Okay, no problem, but we need to spend some time with you, Mr Harris, so write down this message for your wife." He then dictated, "*Dear* your wife's name, *I've gone away for a few days and will be back in a week or so. Don't worry.* Then sign it."

Mac scribbled his Rebecca's name and completed the letter according to the instructions, signing off '*Love Mac*'. Nicco took it, glanced at it, folded it gently and placed it on one of the racks in the van.

"Good. Now we're getting somewhere."

The man had hardly completed the sentence when he punched Mac squarely on the nose, causing it to immediately spurt blood.

Mac tried to let out a scream, but as soon as he'd opened his mouth a rag tasting of a vile chemical was thrust into his mouth.

"We know you stole our money, motherfucker," Nicco told him. "So we can do this the easy way or the hard way; it's up to you. The rag in your mouth is laced with carbon tetrachloride, which causes liver failure. If you scream, it stays in your mouth and the poison permeates; if you talk, it can stay out. Do you understand?"

Mac nodded and the rag was removed. He remained silent.

"Mr Harris, we know you're the IT guy who's been stealing our money from Mexico, we were able to track you to your house, you stupid bastard. We represent the Sinaloa cartel and want to know why you stole it – and of course we want it back. So let's start with 'the why', otherwise we'll need to make sure you can't ever steal from us again. *Comprendi?*"

"I don't know what you're talking about," Mac pleaded. "You've got the wrong man! Please, for God's sake, believe me!"

Nicco shoved the rag back into Mac's mouth, gripped his captive's bound hand, which was still holding the pen, and grabbed the little finger on the same hand. He then snapped the finger back more easily than if it had been a pencil.

Mac's muffled scream could not be heard outside of the van.

Nicco's continued. "You've stolen a lot of money, Mr Harris, and the only way you'll live through this is if you fully cooperate. Anything I don't believe will result in a lot of pain for you, so I need you to understand that I will break every fucking finger on your hands, I will chop off your toes with bolt croppers, then slit your nose, and then we sever your balls. So please understand this, we know it's you and we want our money back. So either you start talking, or be prepared to lose all your extremities – what's it going to be?"

Mac looked at his dangling little finger. He didn't know what hurt more: his head, his nose or his finger; he'd never been in such agony. Nicco removed the rag and simply said, "Speak."

"You've got the wrong guy, I'm telling you." He hoped to hell his lie would work; he knew he was close to caving.

He hadn't noticed the other Italian take the dead-blow hammer from the rack, nor did he know that such a hammer was described in the trade as being an 'iron fist in a velvet glove', known to be non-marring but able to deliver hits with tremendous force.

Nicco placed the palm of his hand across Mac's rag-gagged mouth. The other Italian swung the dead-blow and brought it down squarely on Mac's right patella. In that instant, Mac somehow recalled from a distant biology class that the kneecap was the hardest bone in the body as he felt it shatter, combined with the unbearable pain shooting up and down his entire body. He screamed to no avail and felt himself gagging on the chemical that had by now permeated every taste bud in his mouth, before it went to work destroying his vital organs. He was now crying like a baby.

"I forgot to mention the kneecaps," Nicco spoke quietly into his ear. "Sorry about that. We'll do the other one and then we can start cutting bits off. *Capisci*?"

Mac nodded and Nicco removed the gag; however, even he was now wondering if the man really was guilty. He'd give it one more kneecap, and if Mac didn't talk, he'd have to call Mr G and tell him they may have picked up have the wrong guy.

Mac sobbed. He just wanted the pain to stop and had realised these guys were just going to keep going. "Okay," he said, "if I tell you what I know, will you stop?"

The back door of the van opened. There was an Italian with a spade standing there Mac hadn't seen before. He threw the spade into the van and said, "*E tutto pronto al di fuori.*" And then in English, "What do you want me to do with the dog?"

"Nothing yet," Nicco told him, "he's starting to talk, but if he screws around, bring it round the back and we'll slit its throat in front of him."

Mac felt as if he was on the downward plunge of a rollercoaster; he was in abject agony, and it was clear to him these guys were going to stop at nothing. He wondered if they'd let him go if he told them everything – he had to barter somehow.

"I'm just the IT guy," he sobbed. "I don't make any decisions." He was lying. "I'm just told to hack an account and then transfer the money. None of it goes to me." He was telling the truth. "You have to believe me, please."

"Okay," Nicco told him, "so where does the money go, where is it now?"

"They give me the account numbers; I have a record of them. I can give them to you?" Here was his lifeline, or so he thought.

Nicco nodded; he knew these could be useful. "Okay, so who's your boss, what's the name on the accounts?"

"I only know first names, and the accounts are all foreign, complicated names," Mac explained. "I'll give you all the account numbers I have. Please!" he begged again.

"And the first name of your boss?" Nicco asked.

Mac wondered what he should do. Should he cover for the cartel or try to stick to first names only? He recalled hearing the golden rule of interrogation; make it believable, stay as close to the truth as you can but not completely. "Isaak," he blurted. "He's an accountant."

"Second name and where does he live?" Nicco asked.

Mac had not even got the words 'I don't know' beyond his lips when the rag came back in and he saw the flash of the dead-blow hammer just before it smashed down on his left kneecap. He squealed like a stuck pig.

Nicco ripped the rag out of his mouth and grabbed him by the throat, almost spitting as he talked, this time with pure venom in his tone. "You lied to me? You think you can fuck with me? Last fucking chance. Your dog goes next."

"He lives in fucking Russia! His name is Rabinovich or something. Honestly, that's all I know!"

"Get the fucking dog." Nicco ordered his colleague.

"No wait – wait!" Mac had just had another idea that could save both him and the dog. "The accountant works for a Russian woman; she's the boss, she lives in London. I swear to God, if you take her on, she'll kill you all. You have no idea. She rules Russia's underworld or something."

"Name and where does she live?" Nicco seethed.

"I don't know," Mac insisted, "please believe me."

A few seconds later the van doors opened and there was one of the Italians holding Hardy by the scruff of his neck with a knife at his throat.

"What's it going to be?" Nicco asked.

Mac knew they were going to kill Hardy. This dog who'd always been so loyal to him; how could he possibly betray his best friend in the whole world. "Her name's Ivanna, that's truly all I know. I've only met her in Sloane Square and St James's, I think she lives near Sloane Square, I met her in the Botanist restaurant there." He paused; his tormentors seemed to be waiting for more. "Do you honestly think they'd let me know more?"

Nicco reasoned with himself that now this guy was probably telling the truth; after all, he did have two smashed kneecaps, a broken finger, a broken nose, and what must be a very sore head; and hell, even he didn't know Mr G's real name, or where he lived. "Okay," he said in the friendliest tone Mac had heard since gaining consciousness. "For this we let the dog live, but you need to give me any more names and locations you know. If you tell me this, we'll let you go. Let's face it, what's the point of holding back now and just getting more pain and injury?"

Mac understood the guy was making sense. There really was no point in retrograding what was his obvious escape route. "There's a guy called Willie, he's a big former military guy. He's with the woman whenever I see her. That really is all I know."

Nicco looked at him and smiled. "You could have saved us a lot of energy, Mr Harris." He suddenly realised he hadn't once used Mac's first name as had been passed to them by the village's pub-gossip. "Relax now, it's is over." He tapped him reassuringly on the shoulder and exited the van.

Outside, he dialled a number and heard Mr G pick up. "I think I've got everything the guy knows. It's not complete yet, but he's gone from pain to Stockholm Syndrome pretty quickly. So, with the exception of going to his house and picking up his computers and account details, which you need to organise, how do you want to play it?" He listened to his boss's response and hung up.

He opened the doors of the van and smiled at Mac. "Okay, my friend," he said. "It's over, let's get you home." Nicco then smiled and nodded to the Italian standing over Mac.

The relief that washed over Mac at those few words and the mention of home gave him solace beyond anything he'd ever experienced. He swore to himself right there and then that he would never do anything like this again, never commit another dubious BARF transaction. He'd simply breed spaniels until he died.

Mac was correct on the first two points, but wrong on the last. The gestation period of a springer spaniel was sixty-three days. Mac had closer to sixty-three seconds to live.

The heavy duty plastic bag went over his head in a flash; Nicco leapt into the van to hold it firmly around Mac's neck while his Italian colleague wrapped duct tape around his head and worked it down around his neck. Both men held Mac as the latter squirmed and gasped for air that didn't exist inside the tight bag that was now his whole and very short-lived world. He could feel the life draining from him; he thought of his mother and father, he could see their faces. He wished he'd been more attentive to his wife; he saw her face and hoped they wouldn't kill Hardy. Mac felt the pain in his legs fade, and his last conscious sense was hearing an Italian accent saying, "He's gone. Poor patsy bastard."

The men dragged Mac's body from the van and carried it to the grave that had been dug. Before they buried him, they smashed his face to a pulp and hammered his teeth to pieces, they then cut off an ear and axed off his hands and feet. It was the Sicilian signature that had been developed before the days of DNA. All men knew, however, that it would certainly slow down the identification process whenever the body was discovered. The grave was levelled off, and they used ferns and dead foliage to make it indistinguishable from its surroundings.

They then went back to the van and placed Mac's hands and feet in one of the chemical canisters. They sprayed the tools and the inside of the van with disinfectant and removed their overalls and rubber gloves to seal them in a plastic bag, along with the bag and tape they'd used to kill him. They also added one of the larger, unused hammers to the bag for weight in case they had to ditch the contents in a river.

The driver put Hardy in the back of the van and together the three men drove to Hill Brow, where they mailed the letter from Mac to his wife. It would bear a local postmark and be delivered that afternoon.

From there they drove back towards London, joining the A3 near Bramshot. Just short of the M25 they pulled in to a layby at Wisley Common.

The Italian passenger got out and walked Hardy into the woods. About fifty metres in he let the dog off his makeshift leash and watched it dash off to explore the new smells. He then turned and walked briskly back to the van, which resumed its journey to Davis Road Industrial Park in Chessington.

Safely inside their industrial unit, the van's rental logos were removed, the inside was stripped and re-disinfected. Once darkness had fallen, the overalls and men's clothes were incinerated along with all of the dead man's extremities, with the exception of his ear, which was placed inside a frozen chicken and put in a freezer.

The men left the unit and walked individually to the Chessington North train station, where they each caught separate trains to Waterloo. The driver and passenger made their ways to Heathrow and returned home to Naples via Rome; Nicco, meanwhile, went to meet with Mr G in the Prince Albert pub in Battersea to provide him with all the information Mac had given them and the whereabouts of his ears.

Mr G sent a text to the London contact number for the Mexicans, simply stating: *'Job done, have the info, send your person to table 1, usual time'*.

Nicco found himself at Gatwick later and boarded the Easy-Jet flight to Naples, not giving a second thought to the fact he'd neglected to mention the dog; he wouldn't find out that all dogs in the UK were microchipped until it was far too late.

CHAPTER TWENTY-ONE
Wrong Tree

Shaheen had it all planned out, but already things weren't quite working out the right way.

He'd decided that he should pop down to the My Hotel's breakfast room every thirty minutes to see if Oleana showed up. The energetic, insatiable Lai Xian had other ideas, however, and his first rise at 7 am didn't exactly have him getting out of bed. Her extraordinary passion was something he'd been taken with from the very outset of their pay-and-play relationship, and he got a considerable thrill from the fact she was now happy to arouse him at every opportunity for free. He couldn't care less about her bygone days as an escort; in fact, given her prowess in bed, it had turned out to be a significant advantage.

As he lay on his back, she used all her expertise to bring him to the verge of orgasm, before carefully backing off again. She climbed on top of him and looked down at this man who'd been so kind to her, determined to please him for the rest of her life, or at least until he no longer wanted her – which she'd make sure was never.

The feeling of his warm fluids flowing into her was enough to put her over the edge, and she gripped his body between her legs, shuddering in ecstasy. Spent, she rolled over to his side and nuzzled into him. Within a minute the natural chemistry in Shaheen's body had gone to work, and the prolactin hormone, released in droves as he'd ejaculated, supressed the stimulation of his neuro-transmitter – he was sleeping like a baby.

Hence, it wasn't until about 8.30 am that he actually made it to the breakfast room for the first time. He cursed his lack of discipline, worried that Oleana might be an early riser when he returned thirty minutes later and there was still no sign of her.

At 9.30, however, his luck changed, and he was very glad to have chosen the early orgasm option with Lai Xian, because there, sitting on the small veranda outside, was a woman who looked a lot like Oleana; he needed to get closer. He walked over to the bar and helped himself to a grapefruit juice. As he turned, he had a full view of her. She had shorter hair now, and was noticeably thinner; however, Shaheen had learned long ago that, if you thought you recognised someone, then it probably was them. He tried to sub-due his nerves as he walked to the single French window which gave him a direct route to her table.

"Oleana, how are you?"

She looked up and instantly realised that, if Harry hadn't warned her Shaheen was in town, this moment would have caught her totally off guard, and caused her in all likelihood to shit herself.

"Well hello, Shaheen," she said, neither standing up nor offer-ing her hand. "I'd heard you were in town."

"From who?" The incredulous tone in Shaheen's voice was a clear indication his calm façade had been instantly shattered.

"I have my sources." She looked up at him smugly. "And by all accounts, it seems they're pretty good."

Shaheen wondered who the hell could have told her. Only Harry and Graham Tree knew he was in London, and only the latter knew his hotel location. He cursed Tree under his breath and pledged never to pay the bastard another penny, nor, clearly, could he use the man's sources to kill this woman.

"We need to talk," he told her.

"It looks like we already are, so you might as well sit down." She gestured to the chair opposite her.

He took his seat and the polite young waitress came straight over and took his double espresso order. "Same room number?" she asked, when she returned with it.

"No, no," Shaheen answered subconsciously, mistakenly wanting to distance himself from Oleana. "It's 302."

The waitress thanked him and left.

Shaheen dived right in. "I want my money back, Oleana, I know you took it."

"You know no such thing," Oleana replied defiantly, not knowing if he was referring to the fact she'd maxed out all his dead wife's credit cards after her death, or that she and Maria had robbed his apartment of nearly $6 million in cash, gold and diamonds.

Shaheen had long forgotten the credit card fiasco, because he'd been bitterly aware Oleana had been his wife's lover after their separation until her death; so a few hundred thousand dollars had been worth it, just to get Oleana out of his life. "I do know such things," he told her, trying to suppress his anger. "Because you're on film entering and leaving Ascott Towers in Singapore while I was injured and stuck in Dubai." He had her by the figurative balls, or so he thought.

"I don't see how you can have me on film, Shaheen, but let's face it," she said firmly. "Even if you do, does that mean we stole from you? How many people went in and out of Ascott Towers when you were away? How many are going in and out right now, Shaheen? Come on, get real."

"So why were you there?" he persisted, knowing this was not going at all according to the script he'd rehearsed with himself.

"Look, Shaheen, you and I both know I have a social scene in Singapore, and because of your marriage to Farah and my relationship with her after you separated, we do have some friends in common. I can't remember precisely when I was last in Singapore, but it was before I was in fucking prison." She'd reminded him she had an alibi spanning several months. "Do you remember that, Shaheen?" she said, leaning forward intimidatingly. "Remember how I'm the one who got thrown in fucking jail over all *your* mess?"

"The film shows you with another woman, I think it's that other Russian woman you were with in Dubai." He sounded nervous, and now he'd just revealed his doubt over her identity.

"I think you're mistaken." Oleana leaned back in her chair, quick to capitalise on this hesitation. "Anyway, how much was stolen?" she asked.

"You should know," he countered, trying to regain his composure, before spitting, "About $30 million!"

Oleana nearly spat out her coffee. "What?" she said, showing genuine surprise. "In what form?"

"Again, you know, Oleana. Gold, cash, diamonds. Where is it? I want it back!"

The epiphany going on in Oleana's mind was almost overwhelming. "The two women on your film. What were they wearing?" she asked.

"Summer dresses, hats, sunglasses – why?"

"Any bags?" she asked.

"Quite large handbags," he replied, sensing he knew where this was going.

"So how the fuck do you think two women of my stature could fit all that loot in two fucking handbags, Shaheen? Are you out of your tiny mind?" She was on a roll.

Shaheen knew this was the flaw in his accusation; he had no clue how they'd got the cash and gold out the building. "I know you have it, Oleana, and I want it back." He was clutching at straws right now, and both of them knew it.

"Shaheen, my dear." The tone was condescending. "I don't have it, and even if I did, what could you do to me?"

His mind raced, and his Persian instinct for bluff kicked in. "Why the fuck do you think you went to prison last time? Who do you think was behind that? You stole from me before and I made sure you paid. Now you steal from me again, so just you wait and see. The Dubai policeman, Shamoon? He's *my* man." This was all fabrication, but he could see she'd lost the cocky expression on her fact. "Fuck, even his last name is Iranian!" By this point, Shaheen was seriously impressing himself with his own innovative creativity.

"*You* set me up in Dubai?" Oleana almost hissed, realising she'd blamed Harry and Nazrin for everything when they'd clearly done nothing.

"Yes, Oleana, it was me," he lied boastfully, in the hope it would give him some leverage. "And it'll happen again if I don't get my fucking money. Do you understand?"

Oleana was on the back foot now. "It wasn't me. You're making a mistake."

"I think it was you, so you'd better get me my money. You have until Monday. The Dubai police have reach, you'd better believe me." Shaheen swigged his espresso, stood up and walked away.

Oleana picked up her mobile and called Maria. "I've just been ambushed by Shaheen Soroush. He's staying in this fucking hotel, so somebody must have grassed me out. I need to figure out who, but worse, he knows we stole his money, and worse still, someone stole even more from him than we took!"

"What? How does he know? How do you know?"

"He has us on film, apparently." Oleana was careful not to let Maria know there was any doubt over her identity. "And he says he was robbed of $30 million in cash, gold and diamonds. If that's true, someone else robbed him as well, and we're going to take the blame. He's given us until Monday to respond. And he says he has that Dubai policeman on his side."

"So what to do?" Maria asked.

"I think we both know what we have to do." Oleana was now confirming to Maria something she'd already assimilated.

"Do you have his room number?" Maria asked.

"The clown gave it to the waitress; it's 302, he's only four fucking rooms down from me!"

"Perfect," Maria replied, and cut the call.

Shaheen walked back into room 302 feeling mildly victorious. He admired his exotic Lai Xian who was clearly ready for their day out dressed in a short summer dress with a low back, revealing an ample glimpse of her all too exotic dragon and flower back tattoo. She wore wedge shoes to complete the summer look. He just loved the fact he'd been between those legs just an hour ago and planted his seed. She was small but so beautifully put together.

"Everything okay?" she asked.

"Everything is fine." He walked over to kiss her. "What do you want to do today?"

"Can we do the Big Bus tour?" She stood on tiptoes to kiss him.

"Of course, baby," he replied, happy to kill time over the next few days. "For you, anything."

★   ★   ★

Downstairs Oleana was toying with her coffee cup, thinking about her next steps regarding Isaak and Shaheen. Things were very necessarily about to get messy, but she couldn't think of two men who more deserved what they were about to get. This time, however, she would be damn sure to plan her exit route.

The view from her slightly elevated breakfast table looked out onto the junction of Elystan Street and Ixworth Place, less than twenty metres from where she sat. She noticed three people walking towards the crossing, and it gradually dawned on her that she recognised two of them – the realisation made her physically shudder. She lowered herself in her seat so she wouldn't be seen by them, knowing her problems had just multiplied several times over.

Jesus Christ, Shaheen had not been bluffing.

Harry's night at Brown's after Oleana's departure had been uneventful but busy. He hadn't really thought any more about Nazrin's urgency for a Skype call in his room. He just figured she'd wanted to see what the room was like. At 2 am Harry had gone downstairs to check the night manager's procedures; he saw there were no anticipated guests before the Heathrow arrivals who would start rolling in from around 7.30 am onwards, all begging for early check-in. The bar restaurants were secure, the rear door onto Dover Street had been locked, and the only point of entry was manned. Harry noted that all the security checks were in order, so went to bed about 3 am. His alarm went off at 7 am, whereupon he groggily conducted the three 'S's' of every man's morning routine. Feeling more awake, he proceeded to complete the security review report as he drank his tea. By 8.30 he was sitting with the hotel manager and had only minor comments; Harry informed him the report would be glowing. Before leaving he went to the reception to pay for a sparkling water and the two passion fruit martinis his friend had consumed in the bar the previous evening.

"I think we can cover the water, Harry," the assistant manager told him as he processed Harry's debit card and handed him the itemised bill.

By 10 am Harry was back in the security company's office on Broad Street, where he completed the Brown's report and sent it to head office. Knackered from his long night, he told Sid he was calling it a day and heading home.

Sid surprised him, however. "Oh, I forgot to tell you. We got a call on the Delimkova account, they want an update on their security. That's your account, can you give them a call back to check on the requirement?"

Harry half-smiled to himself. Ivanna had obviously blinked and wanted to see him again. He had to admit he had missed her. There was something about these Russian women that was so attracting, if not always attractive. He made his way to Sloane Square with the intention of jumping onto the District Line home to Richmond, but before he went into the station he decided to make the call. He wondered if she'd pick up; he had to make sure not to let the phone ring more than four times. He was just about to hang up when the line clicked and he heard her voice say, "Hello?"

"Ivanna, it's Harry. Someone from your staff called the office, is everything okay?" He sounded business-like.

"I shouldn't have shouted at you, Harry, I was wrong to do that. Can you forgive me?" she asked, using her most sultry tone.

"That depends on how you want to make up," Harry suggested cheekily.

"I think you know how – where are you now?"

Within five minutes Harry was inside her mews house, and they hadn't even made it further than the living room before he was inside her. As they made vigorous love on the sofa, Harry couldn't help but glance over towards the window a few times, minded that perhaps they should have closed the curtains; but the thought was quickly flushed away by the onset of her ever-increasing Russian passion.

For Ivanna's part it seemed obvious to her Harry had not been with any woman since they'd had their argument, her conclusion confirmed as she felt him fill her completely. She was so pleased to have him back in her arms, satisfied in more ways than one that Harry was certainly hers in passion, even if not in partnership. That, she resolved, would have to do for now.

Harry left the house shortly after and resumed his route home. The welcome he received as he walked into his Richmond house from Charlie and Bunny could not have been nicer. The same could not be said, however, of his welcome from Nazrin.

He went to kiss her and she turned her head away. "What's the matter?" he asked, dreading the answer.

"What do you think the answer is?" She glared at him.

"I honestly have no idea," he sighed. "What is it this time?"

"Harry, I know everything, I just want you to know that." She was clearly irritated.

"Nazrin there's nothing to know, so I don't know what you're talking about. Is there anything to eat?" He hoped her Azerbaijani cultural instinct to feed her man would overcome any impending tantrum.

"There's no fucking food, Harry, not for a cheater!" she shouted.

Harry kept his cool, but his mind raced to a possible compromise situation, in which case there were just three rules to stick to: deny, deny, deny.

"Steady with the language there, Nazrin," he said calmly. "We wouldn't want Charlie's first word to be the F-bomb."

She went berserk. "I know about that Russian whore, Harry! I know you're seeing her again."

Jesus Christ – again? Had she known about Ivanna before, and how the fuck could she know he'd just been with her an hour ago? He stayed calm as he answered her carefully. "Baby, I have no idea what you're talking about."

"I have friends, Harry, and you've been seen, you bastard. How could you?" Now she was crying.

Harry knew he should have drawn the curtains in Ivanna's lounge; surely that was the only way he could have been compromised. After all, he reasoned, no one knew about their affair.

"I don't know what to say," he insisted. "I worked at the hotel all night and then came home. You even Skyped me for Christ's sake."

"You probably hid her, or told her to leave until the call was over," Nazrin fought back.

"Go to the hotel, Nazrin − ask them if anyone was with me." Harry could feel a wave of relief come over him. Nazrin was barking up the wrong tree. She had her facts muddled.

"I'm not going to the fucking hotel, Harry. You just know this − I know all about this Russian bitch and, believe me, I know how to fix her little game. If you ever see her again, I'll be fixing your little game too, and I'll be taking our son to Azerbaijan. Those are the stakes here, Harry, and that's what you've got to lose." She pointed at Charlie who'd started to cry at the melee.

"I'm not seeing anyone!" Harry told her again as he picked up his son to comfort him.

"I swear to God, Harry, I have proof, so don't make me use it." She calmed herself for the sake of their child. "If you're truthful with me, I'll forgive you. If you lie, then life's about to become very difficult for you."

"I *am* telling the truth, I didn't have any woman in my room last night, let alone a Russian," he said honestly. "So if you can prove any different, then you show me."

Nazrin glared in disbelief at his gall. "You can get your own dinner tonight, Harry, and Charlie's too. I'm going out to the Ivy with some friends."

Harry knew better than to contest this one. "Okay," he said, looking down at a now placated Charlie as he rocked him back and forth. "We'll survive, won't we, buddy?"

Nazrin didn't say a word. She went upstairs, got changed and came back down in a figure-hugging Bebe sleeveless wrap jumpsuit. As he looked up from spooning some gungy baby food into Charlie, Harry wanted to tell her she looked hot, but instead settled for a meek "You look nice."

"Thanks," she said abruptly, and walked towards the front door without kissing him goodbye.

"Don't forget we're having dinner with Shaheen tomorrow evening," he shouted after her in a conciliatory tone. He heard the door slam without any acknowledgment.

Forty-five minutes later Nazrin was sitting in the Ivy with Tarana looking at the photos of Harry and Oleana. The woman looked different but it was definitely her. "That fucking bitch," Nazrin spat at the picture, then turned to Tarana. "Did he kiss her in the bar?"

"No."

"Was the handhold long or short?"

"Short."

"Did you actually see them go into the lifts to the room?"

"Well, no, not actually." Tarana's reply was sheepish. "But they didn't leave by the main entrance, that's for sure."

Nazrin handed back the phone. "This woman went to jail because of me and she knows it. She also knows Harry probably had something to do with it too. I'd love to know where she's staying, I'd like to finish this bitch once and for all. But God knows how I can find out." She looked down at her near empty glass. "Fuck it," she said. "Let's have another dirty martini; the world always seems a better place when you mix vodka and olive brine."

Harry had put Charlie to bed and consumed his Hawaiian pizza from Domino's. He sipped from his bottle of Corona and picked up his phone.

Ivanna picked up after three rings; he could hear noise in the background. "Where are you?" he asked.

"I'm at the Ivy on the Kings Road with a friend," she answered loudly.

Harry's panic button was now firmly pressed. "Jesus, this is getting tricky," he said. "When I got home after seeing you Nazrin accused me of seeing you 'again'. Of course I denied it, and I have no idea how she could have found out, but we had a big row and now she's gone out."

"She couldn't know," was Ivanna's simple response, though she was of course quite pleased to hear about the rift.

"Well, it gets worse," Harry continued. "She's in the Ivy right now, no doubt scoping you out. Is there anyone you know who could possibly know Nazrin – or would have recognised me if they saw me going into or leaving your house?"

"Nobody." Ivanna was, as ever, straight to the point.

"Okay, who knew you were going to the Ivy?" he asked.

"Just one person." Ivanna lowered her voice as she glanced at Maria across the table. She then subtly shielded her mouth with her hand so Maria wouldn't be able to hear or lip-read. "And she's with me right now. What does your wife look like, what's she wearing?"

"She has highlighted chestnut hair and she's wearing a blue jumpsuit-type outfit." As Harry talked Ivanna scanned the room.

"I've got her. She's a looker, well done you," she teased. "She's at the bar surrounded by twelve muscular men."

"What!" The shock in Harry's voice was completely apparent.

"Only joking, my dear, calm down." Ivanna was giggling at his discomfort. "She's at the bar, but with a woman I'm guessing is either Azerbaijani or Iranian. She's drinking what looks like a martini, and she *is* behaving herself. Not even looking around or anything. If she is looking for me, she must have eyes in the back of her head."

"She's a woman, trust me, she does," Harry quipped back.

"There's only one way she could know I'm here," Ivanna told him, "so leave this with me." She hung up without another word.

Ivanna smiled at Maria sitting across the table from her, who could not have heard the content of the call over the noise of the restaurant. "Business never sleeps," Ivanna said with a sigh. "Did Willie book this or did you? Was it difficult?"

Maria told Ivanna she had booked it without any difficulty.

"Great, so Willie doesn't know we're here?" she confirmed.

"I can't see how he could. Is there a problem?" Maria wondered what Willie could have been up to; the call had obviously been about him.

"No problem," Ivanna shrugged, placing her knife and fork together on the plate. "I'm all done here, why don't we go over to the bar and have a few drinks?"

Toby Sotheby sat outside the Jumeirah Lowndes Hotel in the *al fresco* café area overlooking Lowndes Square. As he sipped his Belgravia-priced Americano coffee, he looked in the direction of the Pakistani Embassy and smiled to think of its British equivalent in Islamabad. It was quite clear whichever Pakistani had arranged their embassy deal in 1947 must have been quite the negotiator; the London location was beyond five-star.

His thoughts were interrupted by a familiar voice. "Mr Sotheby, how are you?" He turned to see Omar Shamoon dressed in a smart jacket and jeans. He was with an Arab woman, who was slim and elegant, wearing jeans and loose top, but with a cream silk scarf draped casually across her hair. "This is Sergeant Maryam Seyadin." Omar beamed as he made the introduction.

"Call me Maryam, please," she insisted, holding her hand out to Toby, who had known not to offer his before she had.

"Please, sit down." Toby exuded politeness. "How was your flight? I hope you're not too exhausted."

"Not at all," Omar answered. "Business class on an Emirates Airbus 380 is not exactly conducive to exhaustion."

"Unless you spent the whole flight in the bar!" Toby laughed.

"Not this time for me," Omar laughed with him. "And I don't think ever for Maryam," he added with a wry glance at his colleague.

They ordered coffees. Once the waiter had served them and left, Toby said, "Your people are staying at the My Hotel nestled between Chelsea and South Kensington."

"Is that far from here?" Omar asked.

"You could actually walk there in about ten or fifteen minutes, so not that far," Toby replied. "We do a lot more walking here than you do in Dubai. I'll show you the place after this if you like."

"Yes please," Omar said appreciatively.

"So why do you think they're here?" Toby asked.

"To be honest, I don't know," Omar replied. "But in my experience with these two, whenever they're in the same town, bad things happen. Inexplicable attacks, deaths, monumentally negative events."

"Who do they work for?" Toby asked.

"Again, this isn't clear," Omar explained. "Soroush is wanted by the Iranian regime, and yet his undeclared activities seem to work out in their favour, so he could be some sort of plant by them. He's a very clever man and always on the periphery. We also think he's a fighter of some skill – when he was attacked by two men in Dubai earlier this year, he felled them both, even while getting injured in the process."

Omar sipped his coffee; it felt particularly good in London's cool morning air. "As for the woman, Oleana Katayeva, we held her for six months on suspicion she was some sort of agent. If she is though, then she's bloody good at it. In the end we let her go in the hope she'd lead us to some answers, and here we are, and there she is, with Shaheen Soroush of all people." He leaned forward and lowered his voice. "As you know Mr Sotheby, the Iranians and the Russian are in cahoots over Syria, something that's not in my country's best interest. If these two are working for their countries and collaborating, then it's serious for everyone concerned, and we do need to bring them down."

"Please do call me, Toby," said Toby before he continued. "Clearly your own country is concerned otherwise you wouldn't be here. Have you contacted any other authorities over here?" Toby asked.

"We're here on 'unofficial' business, Toby," Omar confided. "You're the only person in your country who knows why."

"That's perfect," Toby responded, and it really was. He was now essentially running two foreign sources on MI5's home turf; he knew he'd be in deep shit if it all went pear-shaped. However, he also recognised that this could work out very nicely if anything did come of it and, if not, he could always claim to know nothing. He stood up. "Let's get a taxi, I'll show you the place."

About five minutes later the three of them exited a London cab outside of the old Michelin Tyre building on Brompton Road, where the first thing Maryam noticed was the Carolina Herrera shop across the road. Toby walked them down the road and turned left onto Elystan Street; Maryam spied the Ralph Lauren shop and wondered how long it would be before she got to do some London shopping.

They walked on the left-hand side of the road, and as they approached the junction with Ixworth Place. Toby told them, "Okay. At one o'clock across the road, that's the My Hotel, that's where they're both staying. They paused very briefly at the junction, enough time for Omar to note the entrance and a few people sitting outside enjoying their breakfast. His view of them, however, was partially obscured by the flower boxes mounted on the hotel's fence.

"Do you know what room they are in?" asked Omar as they continued along the road.

"Not yet, but I think I can find out," Toby replied.

As they walked away from the hotel, Omar surreptitiously checked the GPS tracker app on his phone. It seemed Oleana had brought her Chanel bag with her, and he had a fix.

CHAPTER TWENTY-TWO
Poison Ivy

Beki Harris arrived back at her home on Saint Mary's Road a little after 6 pm. There were three letters on the mat inside the front door. One was handwritten, but it wasn't obvious who it was from. The envelope had a local postmark, so she opened it and took out a small letter.

It read: *'dear rebecca, I have gone away for a few dayS and will be bAck in A weeK or so. don't worry. love mac.'*

She closed the door slowly and called out, "Hardy? Hardy?" The house was silent. She then walked down into the basement and saw Mac's computers sitting dormant. Nothing looked disturbed or out of place.

Under normal circumstances Beki might have just accepted that her husband had been called away on a consultancy job, well aware that client confidentiality was something Mac adhered to rigidly. However, this time she went to her handbag, took out her phone and called the police.

"I think my husband may have gone missing," she explained to the woman on the response line.

"How long has he been missing?" the woman asked, having input Beki's particulars.

"Well, only today," Beki responded, "but he's sent me a letter, and there are two things wrong with it." He calls me Rebecca in the letter, which no one calls me, in fact he always calls me Beck;

and he signs off 'Love', when normally he would always signed off '*LnS*'".

"LnS?" asked the woman.

"It stands for 'love 'n' stuff'," said Beki, a little embarrassed. "It was just our thing. And our dog is missing," she blurted, almost having forgotten this crucial detail.

"Okay, Mrs Harris, I don't think you have anything to worry about," said the lady. "Your husband's left a note and given himself a week's respite. It's in his handwriting, right?" Beki confirmed it was. "In that case he may have decided to take a break with the dog or something. If there are no extenuating circumstances, like medical problems, we would normally give this kind of incident four days before thinking he might be missing. He'll probably call you soon, my love," she added reassuringly.

"He used to work on sensitive government stuff," Beki explained. "The name and the sign off, I know he's trying to tell me something."

"Look, my love, I've made a record of it. If you don't hear anything by this time tomorrow, call us again, and I'll try to put an extenuating circumstance against it."

The call ended. Beki sat down at the kitchen table and unbuttoned her nurse's dress. She looked at the note; the capital letters spelt out 'ISAAK'. "What have you gone and done, you silly bastard?" she muttered. "What are you trying to tell me?"

She went down to the cellar to rummage through his notes.

The quaint village of Wisley was on the whole a peaceful place, except for the constant humming noise of the M25's traffic. It was also a stone's throw from Heathrow Airport, and therefore, despite the acoustic drawbacks of its location, it had become a favourite locale for senior aircrew belonging to British Airways who'd grown sick and tired of a long commute.

John Favour was a well-established member of this 'Wisley Flying Club', as the BA fraternity was known locally. He was no longer the lithe stud he'd been of yesteryear as a Royal Navy Commando pilot; almost twenty years with BA, combined with his frequenting of the local 'clubhouse' – the Anchor pub – had ensured a girth and jowls that made him look far older than forty-nine.

John was not aware of the old adage 'fat owner, fat dog', so he saw nothing wrong with the fact his black Labrador Gibson shared a BMI factor similar to his own. Their walks on Wisley Common represented the full extent of both the man and his hound's exercise regime; when John was working he would sit for hours in a Boeing 747 ingesting at least two meals a flight while his dog would simply sleep, eat and shit, awaiting his master's return.

As Gibson trotted off along one of the common's pathways, John was thinking about his impending trip to Bangkok and the joys that awaited him there during his crew rest. His thoughts of a slim Thai woman jumping all over his Viagra-enhanced penis were abruptly broken, however, as he saw Gibson sprinting towards him with a springer spaniel cheerfully in tow trying to chew at the fat Labrador's ear, the latter fleeing back to the safety of his master.

An exhausted Gibson leaned against John's legs, while his owner stroked the enthusiastic spaniel. "Well, well, where have you come from?" he asked, clearly not expecting any answer. "I bet someone's missing you." He noted there was no collar or ear tattoo to identify the dog.

Together the three covered the remaining route of the common, and, not seeing any sign of a potential owner for the spaniel, John watched with some satisfaction as this new dog leaped into the back of his Land Rover Discovery and sat there panting with Gibson.

Back home John's wife made a big fuss of the new arrival; it seemed perfectly obvious to her this dog must be loved.

"I bet someone's worrying themselves sick about him," John told her as he looked at his watch. "But the vet's closed by now. He must be chipped, so how about you take him there tomorrow and see if we can't reunite him."

"I wouldn't mind keeping this one," his wife replied as she looked at Hardy. "But I suppose we'll have to return you." She went to the fridge and got some cheese; both dogs scurried behind her. As she gave the spaniel some cheese Gibson growled. He didn't like his 'mum' making a fuss of this young pup, and in dog terms he just wished this floppy-eared little upstart would just piss off.

* * *

At the Ivy Ivanna and Maria told the good-looking waiter they wanted to sit at the bar, which was music to the over-booked table manager's ears. Ivanna sat herself one barstool away from the attractive Azerbaijani in the blue jumpsuit and discreetly eyed her up. So this was the woman who had legitimate claim to her lover.

The bartender asked the two Russian ladies what they wanted to drink; Ivanna pointed to Nazrin's martini. "I think we'll have one of those."

Nazrin turned her head to face Ivanna and smiled. "Good decision," she said. "They do seem to make everything better."

"We can drink to that," Ivanna smiled back. "But I love your outfit," she added. "Looking like you do, I can't imagine the world can be that bad."

"Why, thank you." Nazrin enjoyed the compliment. "It's Bebe. I love their stuff, perfect for *girls* our age."

The bartender finished shaking Ivanna and Maria's martinis and proceeded to the theatrics of pouring them.

"*Na zdorovye*; to our health." Ivanna raised her glass and her new friends did the same.

The women then introduced themselves and compared their reasons for being in London. Ivanna explained how she was estranged from her husband, which made Nazrin laugh. "I sometimes wish I was estranged from mine."

"Really?" Ivanna probed.

"You know men," Nazrin went on without hesitation. "They only want one thing from every woman, and it seems my husband is no exception. It looks like he has a lover from your neck of the woods," she added with a sigh.

Ivanna's internal alarm bells were sounding. "From Russia?"

"Tarana here tells me he was with her at a hotel last night. No doubt that means this morning too. Of course, he's denying everything."

Ivanna was now intrigued beyond simply getting to know her love-rival. "Really?" She looked over at Tarana. "You saw her husband in a hotel with another woman? Didn't he see you?"

"He doesn't know me," Tarana told her.

The conversation was interrupted by Maria's phone ringing. She stepped away from the party and outside onto the Kings Road to get away from the ambient noise of the bar. It was Oleana.

"You'll need to sort Shaheen out tomorrow evening," Oleana told her. "He's having dinner with Harry from about 8 pm so he'll be away from his room. I'll tell Harry to get him drunk so he can extract any information we need. Then, once it's done, he won't be able to put two and two together."

"Okay, get me a key to your room, but keep me posted if anything changes." Maria hung up and walked back into the Ivy about five seconds too late to have witnessed Ivanna hand Tarana's phone back to her.

Ivanna had just been shown the pictures of Nazrin's husband with a blonde Russian woman in the Donovan Bar of Brown's Hotel. Of course she recognised both people in the photo. One was her lover, and the other was her former fixer – she knew she should never have trusted that bitch.

"Everything okay?" she asked as Maria rejoined them.

"Yes, just some admin to sort out, and Isaak's in tomorrow," Maria said, reminding Ivanna of something she already knew.

Ivanna finished her drink and reached into her Kelly handbag to hand Nazrin a card with just her name and number on it. "That's my personal card. If you're ever in Chelsea, give me a call. I've enjoyed our chat; we should get to know each other better."

Nazrin grinned at her. This woman had all the trappings of extreme wealth; a friendship with her could be very beneficial. "I'd really like that, thank you." She reached over and picked up one of the bar napkins, and scribbled her number down on it. "And here's my number if ever you need a friend." She held out her hand to shake Ivanna's hand.

As Ivanna stood up she said, "Don't be too hard on your husband. If he is having a fling with that woman, I have a feeling it'll be quite short-lived."

"How do you know?" Nazrin asked.

"Let's just say I have a sense for these things. You take care of him and the rest will take care of itself."

Nazrin watched as the epitome of Russian elegance in the form of these women walked towards the door and left. She turned to Tarana. "Is it any wonder Russian women are so irresistible to men?"

Whatever Tarana's reply was, Nazrin didn't hear it; she was too busy wondering if Ivanna had somehow perceived her intent to kill Oleana.

At about the same time Ivanna was leaving the Ivy, the Italian waiter who worked most evenings in the San Gennaro restaurant wandered into the bar of the Botanist on Sloane Square. He looked around for a familiar face, but saw no one, so he walked up to the bar and ordered himself a bottle of Peroni. As the barman placed it in front of him, he leaned forward and asked, "Is Giovanni in tonight?"

The barman indicated towards the restaurant. "He's over there."

The waiter walked over to the restaurant entrance and saw the man he was looking for in deep conversation with a customer, so he stood to one side of the entrance and loitered. After a few moments, he succeeded in catching Giovanni's eye, who came over to the bar, where the two men greeted each other with a hug and a handshake.

After a few niceties the waiter explained Mr G had sent him, and they were trying to locate a woman called Ivanna who frequented the Botanist with a man called Willie.

"I know Willie," Giovanni explained. "I didn't know the woman was called Ivanna though. They always pay in cash. She's a MILF, I tell you, and a rich one at that – I wouldn't mind getting to know her!"

"You'd get to know anything as long as it didn't have a dick," the waiter teased. "Can you give me a call next time they're in?"

"I can do that, *amico*. When they do come, it's for breakfast and never before ten." He glanced down. "You want another Peroni – on the house?"

The waiter smiled. "*Grazie, ma no*. I need to go." He swigged down the one beer he'd allowed himself. "Don't forget to call." He put the empty bottle down on the bar, smiled, and left.

Giovanni knew better than to forget to call in on a request from Mr G.

*   *   *

By lunchtime the following day Isaak found himself relieved to be saying thank you and goodbye to the Aeroflot flight attendant and making his way through British border controls without incident. He'd only been in the car on the way to his hotel ten minutes when his phone rang. He didn't recognise the Saint Petersburg number but when he answered the call he sure as hell recognised the voice on the other end.

"So you think you can fuck with us?" the Cellist spoke with undiluted malice.

"I'm sorry?" Isaak asked, genuinely surprised by the sentence and its deliverer.

"So you think you can pay us, then suck the money back out to your own accounts and get away with it? Is that it?"

"I'm sorry," Isaak apologised again. "I don't know what you mean."

"Okay, let me spell it out for you." There was a furious tremor in the Cellist's voice. "We had a deal. You paid, we released your boss, we kept our word. But you, you fucking Jewish son-of-a-bitch, have recalled the money back to your account?"

"That didn't happen!" Isaak protested in alarm. "We haven't recalled anything. It must be a banking error."

"I checked with the bank and they say the transfer back was approved from our end. It wasn't. So I'm on to your tricks and here's the deal – either you transfer the money back within forty-eight hours; or your boss goes back to jail for double the time, and this time with you alongside him, *ponyatno?*"

"I understand completely." Isaak could not have been more conciliatory. The call ended abruptly with Isaak in total shock asking himself, "What the fuck's gone wrong?"

He urged the driver to get him to his hotel quickly and rudely rushed the receptionist through the check-in procedure. He didn't bother to tip the bell-boy who helped him with his bags, but instead jumped online as quickly as the hotel's system would allow him.

He stared at the bank accounts. The $20 million had left in two tranches and gone to the Cyprus accounts designated by the Cellist. The transaction had cleared. However, he then saw how just three days later the amounts had come back into the account, only to dwindle the very same day through multiple transfers to banks in Sri Lanka and Panama.

Isaak called the bank manager and screamed down the phone at him. "What the fuck is going on, did you recall the funds? Who authorised these credit and debit transactions?"

The flustered bank manager tried to explain that the bank couldn't recall the funds even if they wanted to, and that all the debits had gone through using... There was a long pause. "It was your coded keypad, Mr Rabinovich."

"It wasn't me, you stupid bastard!" the screaming continued. "Find my fucking money or I swear to God you and your family are history. Do you have any idea who you're fucking with?"

The bank manager knew exactly who he was dealing with, and now clearly he had a big problem. "Sir, please, let's just stay calm, I'm sure we can sort this out."

"Twenty-four hours!" Isaak yelled into the receiver. "That all you have."

He hung up and immediately dialled Mac's phone – it was turned off. "What the fuck?" he exclaimed. He pulled an address book from his briefcase and leafed through it, keyed in a new number and heard Mac's voice on the greeting. After the tone he said, "Mac, your mobile's turned off. It's Isaak. I need to speak to you, it's urgent. I'm in London at the Millennium Hotel in Knightsbridge. Call me as soon as you get this."

He then made another call. "Alexei, we've got a big problem. There's been some sort of fuck-up with our transfers to the Cellist and his boss. They're going nuts. Where are you?"

"Umm, Saint Petersburg, but I'm not alone, if you know what I mean." At his end Alexei looked over at his beautiful Kazakh hooker lying on the bed across the room from him; he smiled and gave her a wave.

"Did you get your visas sorted?" Isaak asked.

"All done."

The words were music to Isaak's ears. "Alexei, get in a fucking car now and get over the Narva border and into Estonia; if they block your passport we're screwed and they'll send you back to jail." The panic in Isaak's voice was palpable.

"What have you done, Isaak?" The tone rising in anger.

"I've done everything I was asked, but someone's fucking with us. You need to get out now. Please, let's post-mortem this when you arrive here in London. Get to Estonia, we'll sort everything from there."

Alexei knew he couldn't take a chance on this one. It was about 140 kilometres to Narva. He paid the Kazakh escort prematurely, regretting not having got his money's worth, leapt into his Mercedes and made a break for the border.

Oleana walked into the My Hotel and proceeded to ooze charm at the trendy, albeit somewhat plump and sparsely bearded receptionist. "I think I've left my key in my room," she pleaded. "Could I have another one, please?"

The receptionist checked her passport and promptly programmed another key. Twenty minutes later she was in the Hour Glass pub just a short walk up the Brompton Road, where she handed it over to Maria.

"Harry's dinner's at 8 pm in Gaucho. I can't see them finishing before 10.30. What's your plan?" she asked.

"Don't you worry about that," Maria told her. "Just remember, Shaheen will take us down if we don't get rid of him." She sipped a sparkling water. "I'll come meet you at 8.30 and we'll take it from there."

"Has Isaak arrived yet?" Oleana asked.

"Yes, he's in the Millennium Hotel. I did call him but he's pissed off about something and said he didn't have time to talk. Are you taking care of that side of things?"

"I am," Oleana replied. "I'm meeting Harry after this."

"Make it soon," Maria told her insistently.

There was a resolute tone to Oleana's reply. "You sort Shaheen – leave Isaak to me."

Harry had had a shit day. He hated it when Nazrin was upset with him, and he was doubly pissed off that Ivanna hadn't even texted him after he'd called her at the Ivy. He wanted to phone up both women, but at the same time he didn't want to seem guilty to one or desperate to the other. So instead he wallowed in his own form of self-pity.

He was almost relieved when Oleana called him and asked him to meet her for coffee in Carluccio's in South Kensington.

"The accountant's in town now," she told him. "I don't think he's spoken to his boss yet, but it's only a matter of time. Do you have anything in mind?" she asked.

"I do, actually," said Harry. "But I need to know whether he knows my face. If he doesn't, it'll be a lot easier?"

"I can try to find out."

"Good," he said. "Suggest taking him up to St James's for breakfast, there are some great places there. Take him by tube from Knightsbridge to Piccadilly, then walk back along Piccadilly itself. I'll plan to follow you into the tube, to see how observant he is. If I lose you at any point, just text me the name of the restaurant and I'll go there."

"My guess is he's not very alert; even though he has your name, I don't think he has a face" Oleana knew Harry was right to do his homework, but didn't want to waste too much time – she just wanted this guy gone.

"Time spent in reconnaissance is seldom wasted," Harry quoted.

As they left Carluccio's she stopped and turned to him. "I'm sorry you had to be involved in this, Harry. You know I still care, right?"

Harry laughed. "Jesus Christ!" he told her. "You lot are like London buses."

"How's that?" she asked with a confused frown.

"Never mind," he said, shaking his head. "Leave the hotel around 9 am sharp, I'll loiter by the underground. If you don't see me, again, just text me the name of the restaurant."

"Oh, one more thing, Harry," she said. "When you've finished with Shaheen tonight, could you text me? I want to be in the bar when he gets back to the hotel."

"Okay," Harry said, shrugging his shoulders. She kissed him on both cheeks and he walked off towards South Kensington station to catch the tube home.

Oleana made her way slowly back towards the hotel, where she called Isaak.

"What?" he picked up impatiently.

"Isaak," she said. "I know you know about the money that went into my account; I want to meet you so we can come to some sort of arrangement. Can we do that tomorrow over breakfast in Piccadilly because I have a mid-morning meeting in that area afterwards?"

Isaak's tone became suddenly more accommodating. "I'm glad you called me, Oleana, but I'm a bit distracted right now." He paused, wondering whether he'd also be able to bed this beauty; perhaps he could even persuade her and Maria into a threesome. "Okay, tomorrow, but we have just this one meeting to sort this arrangement out, and that's it."

"I can pass by your hotel at 9 am," she said. "We can go together and chat about it on the tube. No eavesdroppers there."

Oleana hung up and wondered if she should have told Harry about the Dubai police being in town. She'd decided not to originally, because asking a man to help murder another was quite enough without his having to worry about the likes of Omar Shamoon on his trail.

CHAPTER TWENTY-THREE
Double Jeopardy

Beki Harris sat and stared at Mac's notebook and the number by the name. She was reluctant to call it for whatever it could reveal about her secretive husband. He had, however, clearly tried to give her a message in the out-of-character, poorly written letter he'd sent her, and now there was a name in his notebook that matched – and it had a Russian telephone number.

Beki looked at the clock and googled the fact that Moscow was two hours ahead of British Summer Time. She dialled the number. And heard a man's voice.

"Is that Isaak?" she asked.

The voice simply asked who was calling.

"You don't know me," she told him, "but I'm Mac Harris' wife."

"How did you get this number?"

"Something strange has happened and I don't know what it is."

Isaak could hear the distress in her voice and he listened intently while she recounted the note, the fact that Mac was missing, and how he'd cryptically highlighted Isaak's name in the note.

"Have you called the police?" he asked, hoping she hadn't, but she confirmed that she had. She also explained that they weren't yet prepared to consider Mac missing.

"Are his computers intact?" he pressed, and she assured him they were, and currently on standby; she didn't have the passwords.

"Would he have left the passwords anywhere?"

"I'm not sure," Beki told him, before asking desperately, "How do you know Mac? Why would he highlight your name?"

Isaak went for a broad-brush bluff. "He's one of our consultants, he does IT stuff for us." He paused and thought for a moment. "Leave this with me, we have people that can probably find him. I expect he's fine and just taking a break from stress or something. Give me a couple of days."

He noted down her telephone numbers and was about to hang-up when Beki blurted out, "And the dog is missing – so it must be with him." He once again promised to call her back and ended the call.

"You little bastard," Isaak said out loud to himself. "You fucker!" He immediately called Ivanna.

"Are you sitting down?" he asked her. "Because it seems our friend Mac has stolen $20 million from our accounts and fucking well disappeared."

"What?" she replied in what amounted to a mild scream. "How the fuck?"

"I'd asked him to check out a couple of accounts we needed to make payments to. The payments went ahead but then got sucked back into our account and then dispersed out. It was a classic Mac move, and I'm assuming he thought the other account holders wouldn't be in any position to complain quickly. They were though, and now his wife's just called me to say he's disappeared – he's even taken his precious dog!"

"The British and their stupid dogs, it's so fucked up," Ivanna muttered. "Where would he go? We have to find him. I have a contract with a security company, I'll ask them to get on it."

Minutes later she was on the phone to Harry explaining how Mac had stolen money from them and "done a bunk".

"Jesus Christ," Harry said after this call had ended, which served to get Sid's attention. "Seems your mate Mac just stole $20 million from our Russian client and did a runner."

"No way," Sid spoke firmly. "Mac might be a lot of things, but greedy and stupid is not one of them. He knows better than to fuck with those kinds of sums. Why do they think it was him?"

"Apparently he had access to their accounts, no other suspect mentioned, and they just want us to find him. "I'm heading off to meet the client at a restaurant in Sloane Square. I'll know more in a few hours."

"I do know where Mac lives," Sid told Harry. "I've even been in his house. I could pop down there tomorrow and talk to his wife."

"Good idea," Harry replied.

Sid looked at his watch. "I'll try and call her, and if she's open to it or I can't find the number, I'll definitely go down there. I suppose his phone number will be ex-directory." He bent over his desk and attempted to find Mac's home number on his laptop; there was no trace.

The buxom young vet in Cobham Veterinary Centre was making a big fuss of the springer spaniel who'd just now for the first time in its life sported a conventional collar and dog-lead, instead of a shooting leash. It wagged its tail furiously as she scanned the back of his neck for his chip, and picked up the identification number.

John Favour's wife took his lead while the vet fed the details into the national database and printed off the results.

"He's about thirty miles from home, it seems," she said with an impressed smiled. "I bet he was let off the lead for a walk on the common and ran after a rabbit or something; but he's been not reported missing, which is strange."

She dialled the number on the identification report as the pilot's wife looked on. The vet mouthed "Voicemail" quietly, then spoke after hearing the tone. "This is Maggie Franklin from Cobham Veterinary Centre. We have a healthy and happy spaniel here, and the identification chip provides this as a contact number for his owner. Please could you give me a call whenever you get this message, so that we can get your dog back to you." She recited the clinic's number on to the recording.

She hung up and told the pilot's wife she would contact her whenever the owners called in.

Ivanna was early to the Botanist restaurant on Sloane Square, an unusual sign in itself. As she sat sipping her green tea, questioning whether anyone really enjoyed this shit, she failed to notice the Italian waiter make a call from the maître d's desk.

Harry appeared about ten minutes later; although, out of principle, he wasn't happy to have his back to the door, he sat down opposite Ivanna, who for her part was dying to ask him about his night in a hotel with Oleana. But for now she held back.

"You didn't want to meet at the house?" he asked.

"No, Harry, this is business." Her tone was firm. "You know very well what would happen if you came to the house, and anyway, my accountant's in town at the moment, so he might disturb us." It was half a lie but it would do for now.

"So you think you're safe from him here?" Harry grinned and glanced down at his crotch.

"Well, let's put it this way," she answered, meeting his smile and eye. "If I'm not, then I guess we'll never be allowed back here again."

"Good point." Harry really liked her sense of humour, and he took a moment to imagine them making-out right there and then, before reverting back to reality an instant later. He ordered some Assam tea, and once the waiter was out of earshot, he asked, "So when was the last time anyone saw Mac?"

Ivanna explained everything Isaak had told her; their best guess was a couple of days ago. "You see, Harry, there's a lot you don't know about me. I run a very complex business, and as part of that we have to transfer large amounts of money for shipping and purchase of imports. Mac had access to our accounts because he could ensure we were hedged against the forex risk." She was lying, forgetting the man before her had just spent several years in the financial industry.

"Forex risk?" Harry looked confused. "Why would you ever use Mac to hedge your forex risk? I know guys in the city who've done it for years; Mac's an IT guy for Christ's sake. Did he sell himself as a forex expert?"

Harry searched Ivanna's face for any sign of an expression as she replied. He was steadfast in his belief that, if someone did something illogical, it was for their own gain – and what Ivanna had just told him was totally illogical.

"Mac came to me on my accountant's recommendation," she told Harry, which gave him no reason to think she was lying. "He's worked for us for a few years and done a great job; he's always managed to protect us against loss, and in fact," she added, "he's also made us some good money. I was very happy with him." She sipped her tasteless green tea. "But he was coming very close to retirement, maybe a month or two away, so his disappearing along with $20 million is a bit coincidental to say the least."

"No one who knows Mac has him down as any kind of thief, and certainly not one who would do this sort of job." It was Harry's turn to sip his tea. "How much do you trust your accountant?"

"How much can you trust anyone, Harry?" Ivanna pictured in her mind the photograph Nazrin had showed her of him with Oleana in Brown's.

"Good point," Harry nodded. "I have a good friend from the special forces who insists the only person you can trust is your mother, and even she'll let you down every now and again. But I will tell you one thing, Ivanna." Harry was deadly serious now. "The world is full of high net-worth individuals who've either knowingly or unknowingly been ripped off by their accountants – and that's a fact."

He had stirred thoughts of doubt in Ivanna's mind. She was starting to recount how Isaak had first introduced her to Mac, and the fact that her accountant had perhaps got somewhat ahead of himself in her husband's absence. She now wondered how best she should contain him.

On the far side of the restaurant, a diminutive, tanned man in his late fifties seated himself and ordered a glass of Rioja and some bread with olive oil and balsamic vinegar. He opened a copy of *Global Citizen* and perused the articles and adverts. The Italian waiter brought over his wine and bread, and as he served him, spoke quietly, "That's signora Ivanna, Mr G. The lady with the auburn hair."

"You did well to call me, Giovanni. Your tip will reflect it. Who's the guy with her?" he muttered without looking at the couple.

"I don't know, he's English, I've not seen her with him before. He stops talking whenever I go close to the table, so he's definitely 'waiter-aware', shall we say."

"So he's a criminal or a law enforcer. If he pays by card, you know what to do. So bring me my bill now so that I can leave when she does." He glanced across the room again. The two were locked in serious conversation; she was a beautifully elegant woman, so clearly Russian – and wealthy. He sipped his wine and reflected on how there were only two advantages to becoming an older man: that he became increasingly invisible with age, and at the same time the age bracket in which he found women attractive was ever increasing.

The waiter returned. "This one's on me, Mr G. It's very good to have you in here."

"*Grazie*, Giovanni; and this is for your troubles." He shook hands with the waiter and two £20 notes were slipped to him without anyone noticing.

"My colleague is going to Mac's house tomorrow," Harry was telling Ivanna meanwhile. "He knows Mac better than me. But my advice is watch your accountant like a hawk. This guy knows everything about your business, so if he turns, you have a huge problem. You'll need to act normally, but you also need to make sure he can be marginalised with minimum fuss. Do you think you can do that?"

Ivanna tried not to smile. "I think I can," she told him, and then changed the subject. "Your wife is very beautiful, Harry. She looked lovely in the Ivy last night. I must admit, I'm jealous."

"Have you looked in the mirror, Ivanna? You're a totally beautiful woman." He watched her blush and soften. "When I'm with you, I'm relaxed," he reassured her. "And sadly, all the beauty in the world's no good if the only words a man hears are full of venom."

"So why does she think you're having an affair?" It was a hypothetical question.

"She always does," he answered. "Ever since I've known her. I'm always in the shit, it's only the depth that varies." He paused in reflection. "I suppose there's nothing worse than being accused of doing something when in fact you haven't." Harry's fault was his pathological ability to deny his unfaithfulness to women. "I think it's a man's logic that, if he's constantly accused of cheating when he's not, then he'll take the view he's got nothing to lose if he goes ahead and lives out the accusation."

"It's getting complicated, Harry." Ivanna tone was full of resignation. "In Russia we say that, if a man marries his mistress, then he leaves a void that will be filled. You're that man, Harry. You have a weakness for women, and sadly some women have a weakness for you." She looked around the restaurant, then back. "I want you for myself, Harry, but something tells me that's just impossible – for you or any woman in your life."

Harry remained silent; to speak would have been to condemn himself.

"She thinks you're having an affair with a woman because you met her in a hotel. Her friend was there watching you. Are you fucking her, Harry?"

"Jesus Christ!" The frustration was clear in Harry's voice. "I only met her because she wanted to discuss potential business. She only stayed an hour."

Ivanna stood up to leave. "Well, it was an hour too long – but somehow I believe you. Your wife, however, never will. Make sure you give me whatever you hear on Mac." She retrieved her Prada bag and made her way towards the door leading out onto Sloane Square. Harry turned to watch her go; she was a wonderfully shaped woman who looked fantastic in her Gina shoes and brown leather jeans. At the same time, he tried to attract the attention of the waiter, only to notice the small silver-haired man on the street eyeing Ivanna as she walked past the window of the restaurant towards Belgravia. Harry watched the man's gaze follow her down the street, before he headed in the same direction after her.

Harry got up abruptly and walked across to the waiter. "Could I have the bill, please? I need to leave now."

"We're a bit short, sir, do you mind paying by card. That would be quickest, otherwise I need to go and find some change."

"Fine," Harry said, clearly irritated. He was relieved, however, to see the waiter process the card payment efficiently. He hurried out onto Sloane Square, not too late to see Ivanna in the distance with the silver-haired guy some forty metres behind her, walking at a similar pace so as not to close the distance between them.

"It could be nothing, it could be something," Harry told himself as he trailed them both, little realising the waiter in the Botanist had just written down the name '*Harry N Linley*'.

Ivanna turned onto Eaton Terrace and crossed the road diagonally to enter Eaton Terrace Mews. Harry saw the man quicken his pace as she turned the corner, so he too quickened his.

Mr G turned into the Terrace expecting to see his prey some thirty metres down the road, but she had vanished. He saw the Antelope pub and figured this was the only place she could be. He walked into the pub, looked around, and emerged disappointed. He stared down the mews opposite, but the alley was empty too; there was no sign of her. His thoughts were suddenly broken by a male voice.

"You look lost, my friend." It was the man who'd been with the woman in the Botanist.

Mr G accentuated his Italian accent. "*Grazie, amico mio,* I am a bit. Is this the Kings Road?"

"No, mate," Harry told him. "You're about 180 degrees out. You should have turned right out of the restaurant not left."

"Restaurant?" Mr G asked.

"Yes, we were both in the same restaurant just now, and both happened to walk in this direction." Harry's tone could not have been more friendly.

"*Si,*" said Mr G. "I suppose I must have assumed the beautiful lady was headed to the Kings Road, they tell me they all go there."

Harry smiled. "Well they do; but not that one."

"Your wife? If so, I am sorry." Mr G was now playing with Harry's masculine instincts.

"Not my wife, so no problem." Harry replied.

"So you're going to the pub?" Mr G asked, trying to keep the conversation alive.

"Not today, my friend," Harry told him. "You have a great day." And he continued to walk up Eaton Terrace.

Mr G knew his attempt to see where the woman lived was over. She either lived in one of the houses next door to the Antelope or down this mews. However, he'd been compromised, for now, by whoever this guy was, and to follow him further would blow his own alibi. He walked back towards the restaurant, making sure he wasn't being followed, before retrieving Harry's name from the waiter. After several minutes he walked out of the Botanist and turned right to cross Sloane Street. He immediately made a call and told the person on the other end, "Get me the names of everyone who lives in Eaton Terrace Mews; and go hit the house in Liss – I need the computers."

He was so intent on his call he didn't notice Harry Linley sitting by the Venus fountain in Sloane Square, using his Samsung phone in camera mode.

Isaak didn't recognise the +372 number, so was mildly surprised to hear Alexei's voice.

"I'm in Tallinn, what the fuck is going on?"

"There's been a monumental fuck-up. Mac Harris is missing and so is €20 million," Isaak explained.

"Jesus Christ! So what are you doing about it?" Alexei screamed down the phone.

"We've got a private company trying to find Mac. The UK isn't a big place, we'll find him, Alexei, but it gets worse. The €20 million was sucked back from the payoff for your release, that's why you needed to get out of Russia."

"Jesus Christ!" Alexei blasphemed again. "Have you made good on the amount?"

"Not yet," Isaak told him. "I've asked the bank to sort it out."

"Fuck that, you idiot. Do you know who we're fucking with here? You know how far our president and his fucking Cellist's reach is. Estonia isn't far enough. Pay it again!" Alexei was frantic. "They'll put me back in prison and throw the fucking key away. Pay it again now!"

Isaak didn't feel the need tell Alexei he was echoing the Cellist's intentions for them both. "Okay, I'll do it right now Alexei. I didn't want to send more money without your say-so."

"Pay it," Alexei ordered, "then we can sort out the bank, or Mac, or whoever fucked with us. And do it now, then let the Cellist know right away, then WhatsApp me when it's done." Seeming calmed by this resolution, he changed course. "I'll be in London tomorrow – does Ivanna know anything about this?"

"She knows about the theft but not the details, and certainly not that you're out." Isaak hoped this was the right thing to say.

"Good, let's keep it that way. Hopefully she'll be pleased to see me, so I can sort out this shit for her." He ended the call without another word.

Isaak immediately called the bank and ordered the manager to repeat the transactions to the Cyprus accounts, making sure to remain on the line while the transfers were processed.

"It's done," the bank manager told him.

Isaak went on line and saw the amounts had indeed left the account. He placed a call to the Cellist and politely told him, "It's all back on line, sir, the monies have been transferred; it was a bank cock-up."

"It better fucking well have been," the Cellist menaced.

In Los Mochis the D-Wave quantum computer flashed up a movement from the monitored accounts. Sheetal put down his Red Bull and tapped in the banking coordinates. He called Jorge on his exclusive phone for further instructions. He was told to wait before hitting the accounts again. Sheetal wondered if he could use some sort of blockchain adaptation he'd been working on to effect the transaction – he thought he might just try it out.

Omar Shamoon and Maryam Seyadin sat in Gran Caffé on Basil Street, fitting in perfectly with the preponderance of Qataris who frequented the place, just to be convenient to Harrods.

"We have to scare Oleana again," he told his sergeant. "Otherwise we're going to run out of time. We have two choices – to call her or go to her hotel."

"Or both," Maryam suggested. "Shall I see if her UAE mobile is working?" Omar nodded and she made the call.

At her end, Oleana looked down and recognised the number calling her. "Fuck," she said to herself simply, and put her phone on silent.

CHAPTER TWENTY-FOUR
Dim Mak Attack

S hortly before leaving their home in Richmond to go into town, Nazrin put little Charlie to bed, just as Harry was opening the door to Constance, the teenage babysitter.

Harry told her to help herself to anything in the kitchen, before popping upstairs to check on Nazrin. He walked into their bedroom and noticed a business card on her ladies' desk. It read '*Ivanna Delimkova*' with a telephone number, which of course he recognised. He was still having a flush of anxiety when Nazrin walked into the bedroom. "Whose card is this, baby?" he asked.

"Oh, I don't know," Nazrin said. "Just some rich Russian woman I bumped into at the bar in the Ivy last night. She lives around there so offered to meet up if I was in the area. She seemed very nice."

"I wouldn't bother," Harry told her. "The Russians are legendary for making invitations they don't mean."

"They are? I'd never heard that," Nazrin replied with a shrug.

"If you ever bother calling, I bet you get the cold shoulder," he said, continuing his discouragement, then glanced down at his phone. "Our Addison Lee is here. Let's go eat some steak."

They left the house and got in the car. "Gaucho, Sloane Avenue, sir?" the driver confirmed.

Harry checked his watch – it was 7.30 pm. He knew they'd be on time for the 8 pm reservation, even if the Iranian wasn't.

★   ★   ★

It was about 8.30 when Oleana entered the My Hotel in the company of another blonde woman. She made sure to give her plump male receptionist a passing smile as they entered the lift to the third floor. They both went into Oleana's room, where the second blonde woman pulled her gym kit from a small bag, followed by a plastic container of sleeping tablets in a zip-lock bag, which she tucked into the back of her latex workout pants.

"How are you going to do it?" Oleana asked.

"I'll try to asphyxiate him to the point of unconsciousness," Maria said, removing her wig and tying her hair up into a tight bun. "Then I'll put sleeping tablets under his tongue; that should finish him off; and then I'll put him to bed. It'll look normal." She put on a long sleeved T-shirt and a pair of slip-on beach shoes. "Now go see if the key trick will work."

Oleana went back downstairs to the lobby and smiled broadly once more at the hooked young man behind reception. She saw how he blushed at her very appearance. "Hello again," she greeted him. "Like a fool I put my key in my pocket with my phone, and I think it wiped the programme, please could you reprogram it for me?" She handed him the second key from the room.

"Which room number?" he asked.

"302."

"And your name, ma'am?"

"Oh my God, Matt!" she exclaimed teasingly. "I remember your name and you don't remember mine – I even showed you my passport earlier today! It must be that damn picture; clearly I'm never going to get a date with you!"

"Of course I remember your name!" he lied as every capillary in his face filled with blood. "302 it is." He handed her the reprogrammed key. "And you could get definitely get a date with me," he blustered with total embarrassment.

"Thank you, Matt. You figure out where you want to take me, and if I'm still here on your next night off, let me know. I need to see more of London, and with a real Englishman too."

She spun round and walked back to the lift. He watched her arse move as she went, and it was fantastic. Once she was gone, he tapped '302' into his computer. "Bollocks," he said to himself – she was with a guy. The Chinese-sounding name on the booking puzzled him, however, and he concluded she must somehow be from the eastern part of Russia. His shift ended at 10 pm; he would spend the rest of it fantasising about his first squeeze of that tight arse. Sunday was his next night off.

It was approximately 10.30 pm when the same blonde Oleana had come into the hotel with earlier walked back past the night receptionist. She walked the distance to the Sloane Square Hotel not far away, and just before going in, swapped out her blonde wig for a black one and donned a baseball cap and glasses. The receptionist glanced up and took a mental note that Miss Sedova was back in the hotel.

Harry's reunion with Shaheen in the bar of Gaucho was enough to kill any of his marital tension with Nazrin. Both men were clearly pleased to see each other. Harry had never forgotten that Shaheen had given him his biggest financial break in life, something that had been a game-changer for him. Shaheen on the other hand was just pleased that Harry represented a world away from his in every way. Here was a guy whom he'd trusted multiple times, and who, so far as he knew, had never let him down. He would probably have been less impressed to find out Harry still had Bunny, Shaheen's most beloved Persian cat who he thought had been cruelly skinned and murdered in Dubai. But in his ignorance he was grateful to Harry for presenting him, on the last occasion they had seen each other, with a substitute, Soraya. Little did he realise that this was actually his Bunny's very own kitten.

Nazrin and Lai Xian hit it off almost immediately; both were supremely elegant and confident, and seeing their men so genuinely pleased to see each other caused both ladies to feel totally at ease. Within minutes of being seated all four were thoroughly enjoying the cuisine, atmosphere and each other's company in Gaucho. Lai Xian thought it was the best steak she'd ever eaten and was particularly enjoying hearing all about London from Nazrin.

Shaheen meanwhile, was explaining to Harry how Oleana and Maria had stolen some $30 million from him. When Harry asked how this could possibly have happened, he couldn't explain, but said he had proof they'd been in his apartment while he'd been away, and that was when the money had gone missing. "Can you help me, Harry?" he asked.

"I can try, Shaheen," Harry offered. "Let me have a think about how to tackle this, I'll talk to my partner."

The two couples left the restaurant together, and Nazrin and Harry headed off back to Richmond in a taxi, both knowing there was still enough tension between them to prevent any thought of sex that night. Shaheen and Lai Xian, in contrast, strolled arm-in-arm, and clearly in love, the short distance to their hotel, where they bade the night receptionist good night.

As they entered the room, Shaheen smiled to see the bed had had a 'turn-down service', complemented by a chocolate on each pillow. He watched as Lai Xian slipped silently out of her dress to reveal her thong underneath and that beautiful full-back oriental tattoo; he hoped she was about to get into bed, where he'd be exploring her all over in just a few minutes. To that end, it was time to relieve the pressure on his seminal gland and empty his bladder in preparation. He made his way to the bathroom, already hard, closed the door behind him, and lifted the toilet seat.

He failed to notice the bath towel and robe draped over the shower screen, and was already in full flow when something appeared to move behind him; but it was too late. Maria had come from behind the screen in a flash, and locked her knee up into the small of his back, the straight of her left forearm across his windpipe, her right hand controlling his head and blocking his mouth. She pulled him backwards so he was half-squatted on the floor, totally in control of her victim, and knowing this would be over in less than a minute.

Shaheen tried to call for help but couldn't summon any noise in his throat, nor did he have the air flow to generate it. He kicked out against the toilet but could already feel the life draining from him. He'd no idea a woman could be so strong, or a lock could be held so tightly.

Maria could also feel the life leaving Shaheen's body, acutely aware of how important it was, for the convincing appearance of suicide or accidental overdose, that she should only strangle him into unconsciousness; she could then force the tablets under his tongue and let the chemicals do the rest.

Shaheen's body went limp, but she kept the lock on him for another fifteen seconds, and then released. Hearing the air go back into his starved lungs, she figured she had about three minutes before he would naturally regain consciousness. She eased herself out from underneath him, knowing she'd have to manhandle him out of the bathroom and onto the bed; she opened the bathroom door and immediately felt a crushing blow to her chest, causing her to stagger backwards and fall over the unconscious Shaheen. She stared up in disbelief at the tiny Chinese woman in sexy, black underwear standing above her. Her three concurrent thoughts were: where the fuck had this woman come from; who the fuck was she; and had she actually just delivered a *dim mak* blow?

Maria had been briefed on the *dim mak* during her days in the GRU Spetsnaz, it was a killer blow that would throw the heart out of rhythm. Death could then occur within minutes, or even weeks, according to the chosen technique of the practitioner.

Maria could already tell this Chinese woman's intended time-frame; it felt like someone had just parked a truck on her chest; the pressure on her heart was unbearable. She struggled in vain to get up, but her legs simply wouldn't work. Her attacker didn't strike again; she knew that to do so could disrupt the *dim mak*'s effect. Instead, she simply stepped into the bathroom to watch the effect of the lateral blow of her fist to Maria's chest. It had directly imposed vibrating pressure to Maria's pressure points, throwing her heart into fibrillation and cardiac arrest. Unless another blow could shock the heart back into its natural rhythm the victim would in all likelihood expire.

Satisfied her victim was incapacitated, Lai Xian bent down calmly to feel Shaheen's pulse – he was alive.

"Who are you?" she demanded, looking down at the gasping woman on the floor. "Why do you want to hurt my man? If you don't talk now, you'll die of a heart attack."

Maria met the Chinese woman's eyes. "He was going to kill us, he's killed Russians before, it was either him or me."

Lai Xian had been thinking about giving the woman the blow to the chest that could save her, but the 'him or me' statement had sealed her fate; that kind of shit never went away. She pulled Sha-heen out of the bathroom away from his attempted assassin and lay him in the prone position.

She went back into the bathroom and sat down on the floor alongside her victim, manoeuvring her head so that it was cradled in her lap. Lai Xian gently held her steady and stroked her hair as she started to convulse; she watched the pain wrack the Russian's face as her heart finally gave up trying to oppose the natural elec-tronic signals that had been completely disrupted.

Maria looked up at the woman comforting her as she lay con-fused in her agony; helpless in her last breaths, her final, involun-tary thought was of Isaak and the realisation that the bastard was going to outlive her.

Harry was feeling a bit shabby from a Malbec morning-after, and he was already on his way to rendezvous with Oleana when Sid called him to say he'd spoken with Mac's wife; he was convinced the problem might be greater than just theft.

"His dog was found on Wisley Common," he explained. "That's like one of the last places you can walk a dog in a rural setting before you hit the M25 and head for Heathrow or London – maybe our guy really could have done a bunk."

"Yeah, but why wouldn't he just leave his dog at home? What's the point of taking him thirty-odd miles and then dropping him off? It makes no sense."

"He left a note, mate," Sid went on. "It has a name spelled out in capital letters scattered in the text – clearly written under duress. It spells 'ISAAK'; do you know anyone of that name?"

"Oh Jesus," Harry sighed. "That's the name of some account-ant who just arrived in London, and he's already causing more than a few problems. I think he's up to his neck in it, and may even be the thief; it's nearly always the accountant in this type of scenario. There's some other shit too," Harry added. "Shaheen claims he's had $30 million stolen from his apartment in Singa-pore. He's blaming the women that work for Ivanna. Surely this can't be a coincidence."

Sid said nothing, as he called to mind the asset recovery he and his former SRR colleague had conducted in Singapore at the behest of Mac. He also recalled meeting a Russian accountant and handing the assets over to him in Kazakhstan. "I think Mac could be in on it," he told Harry. "But, you're right, for sure it has to be the accountant too."

Harry checked his watch; he was running behind and was about five minutes late. He loitered outside Harvey Nichols at the top of Sloane Street looking for Oleana and the accountant to appear, figuring he would give it another five minutes before calling her.

Suddenly he noticed people pouring out of Knightsbridge underground station; some looked visibly upset. He jumped down the closet entrance stairs by Harvey Nicks and tried to work his way against the exiting crowd. The underground staff were blocking the entry barriers.

"What's happening?" he asked the stern-looking black woman manning the barrier.

"We just had a jumper, my dear," she told him. Harry stared at her blankly. "A suicide, my love. Someone just jumped under a train. The station is closed."

"Jesus Christ!" he exclaimed. The tube worker assumed he was referring to the thought of the suicide; in actual fact Harry was wondering what else could possibly go wrong.

He exited the station and called Oleana; there was no answer. He walked to the Millennium Hotel and looked around the lobby, but no sign of her. He had a feeling of impending doom and wished he'd asked the gender of the jumper.

Pausing outside the hotel, Harry pondered his next move. Where was Oleana; where was the accountant; and where was Mac? He recalled his mother always telling him how things always happened in threes. His phone rang.

It was Ivanna. "Harry, something's wrong," she told him. "I can't get hold of any of my immediate team, none of them are answering, and I'm still $20 million out of pocket. Come to the house."

Harry dashed across Sloane Street and jumped on the number 22 bus, little realising how much his mother had underestimated her theory.

Alexei had boarded the first available flight out of Tallinn and felt an air of gratitude towards his lawyer, who'd successfully fast-tracked his Schengen and UK visas before they could know there was going to be a problem.

It was 9.35 am when he stepped off the SAS flight at Heathrow, having transited through Stockholm. The border control officer eyed Alexei and glanced at his screen, which indicated the individual was a 'politically exposed person' as a member of the Russian Duma. The officer told him he was going to have to retain his passport a few minutes, and Alexi was asked to take a seat in a small pen positioned between the queueing masses trying to enter the UK.

"Is there a problem?" he asked.

"No problem, sir, but one of our officers just needs a bit of information about your visit." The officer watched Alexei take a seat in the pen alongside a large African woman, before taking his passport back to the control room at the rear of the check area, which overlooked all entry points via two-way mirrors and facial recognition cameras.

Within three minutes two men wearing off-the-peg suits had appeared from the control room. They loitered for a while and studied Alexei's body language; he seemed relaxed and at ease.

Alexei had clocked them as soon as they'd emerged; he knew full well they were the officials who were about to question him.

About an hour and a half later, an MI6 analyst entered Toby's office. He glanced up and was delighted to see it was Tarisai, his absolute favourite female colleague in terms of intelligence and style. She was holding a file in her hands. Originally from Zimbabwe, she spoke immaculate English with a slight African accent, and Toby enjoyed both her voice and her elegant aesthetics.

"A name's come up from one of your old operations," she told him. "Someone on the watch-list has just entered the country."

"Go on," Toby urged.

"It's Alexei Delimkov – the Russian locked up by the president after you blew open the Russian-Iranian uranium enrichment plot he and Shaheen Soroush had hatched in Dubai."

Toby nearly spat out his coffee. "You're joking!" He extended his hand to take the report from her. "Show me. I thought he'd been sentenced to ten years."

"Perhaps he got out on good behaviour?" Tarisai said with a wry smile.

"Yes and perhaps I'm going to be the next pope," Toby retorted sarcastically as he read the notes. "The boys at the airport did a good job. Jailed for three years; just released; politically exposed; reuniting with his wife in their house in Belgravia. He has a year's visit visa, no doubt bought and paid for in Moscow." He looked up at Tarisai. "This could be serious. The Iranian he was in cahoots with is in town right now too, along with a woman who the Emiratis are all over." He looked at the report again; he knew he'd no longer be able to keep a lid on this.

"Well it seems something's going down," Tarisai advised. "You might like to speak to our liaison officers in Thames House and with Special Branch, also our deputy in Moscow; we're probably going to have to ask for surveillance on these clowns, so we'll need as much background as we can get on Delimkov."

"Good idea,." Toby was so glad she thought of this stuff. "Can you sort it?"

Tarisai smiled and nodded. "I'm on it. Are you good for a conference call with them in twenty minutes if they can do it?"

"Definitely." He couldn't help but admire her spectacular figure from behind as she exited his office. Once she was gone, he looked out over the Thames and made a call. "Omar, we've got movement, my friend. The Russian billionaire locked up for dealing with Soroush – he's just entered the UK. Something must be about to happen."

"Interesting," Omar replied. "I just went to Oleana's hotel to confront her, but when they tried to call her room there was no reply. They said she might still be sleeping so I should try again later."

Toby heard movement behind him and he turned to see a smiling Tarisai. "I have both LOs on the line," she told him.

"Got to go, Omar," Toby spoke into the phone. "We're cranking this one up. I'll keep you posted."

The policeman and policewoman from Hampshire Constabulary had taken the short drive from Alton and were now sipping tea at Beki Harris' kitchen table. The policewoman was gentle in her tone as she informed Beki there was no record of Mac having left the country, nor had he used any credit or debit card known to his name. They had also called all the known addresses and associates Beki had provided them with over the phone.

The male officer handled the note using surgical gloves, gently placing it into a zip-lock evidence bag. "Has anyone else handled this letter?" he asked.

"Yes," Beki said mournfully. "One of his friends from his military days who'd heard Mac was missing turned up the day before yesterday to offer to help. He read the note, took a photograph of it, and he also looked over Mac's computers and notes downstairs."

"What was his name?" asked the policeman.

"It's Sid Easton, here, I have his card."

The policeman raised his eyebrows. "Sid Easton DSC," he read out loud. "This guy's seen some action in his time. Did you call him to tell him about your concerns?"

"No," Beki replied. "He just turned up."

"So how did he know Mac was missing?" The policeman pursued his line of inquiry.

"I don't really know," the wife answered, realising she hadn't even thought about this. "I suppose through the military grapevine or something."

The policeman took a photograph of Sid's business card, then asked, "And the dog?" He looked over at the spaniel resting in his purpose-built bed in the corner of the kitchen. "He was found in Wisley, do you know anyone there?"

"Not really, but I did grow up in Ripley," Beki offered.

"Not really or no?" the policeman pushed.

"No," she confirmed. "We don't have any friends or connections there anymore."

"Can we take a look at the computers and notes?" he asked. Beki led them to the cellar door, which she unlocked, turned on the lights and brought them downstairs.

As she turned to point out Mac's supercomputers she froze. "Oh my God!" she exclaimed, putting her hands to her face. "Oh my God, they've all gone!"

The two police officers looked at each other without a word as Beki turned towards them desperately.

"All his equipment's gone. Someone's stolen it!" Beki was in tears now. "And all his notes!"

The policewoman tried to keep her own composure. "When was the last time you were down here, Mrs Harris?" she asked.

"I don't know." Beki was flustered. "Two days ago with Sid Easton. Someone's been in my house and stolen Mac's stuff."

The policewoman walked Beki upstairs back to the kitchen and around the house to see if anything else was missing, including valuables; nothing was. The policeman had already googled Sid Easton's name and pulled up his LinkedIn profile.

He walked outside and called the CID. "Mate," he told the detective on the other end of the call. "We've got a big problem in Liss. A missing guy, five days now; his dog turned up in Wisley unaccompanied; some bloke with a Distinguished Service Cross has been here who knew all about it before we did; and there's been a professional break-in since that specifically targeted the missing bloke's computers and notes. We need to get a SOCO down here and spool up the Met on the military guy, looks like he may have been casing the joint."

Having spent the night using Maria's room in the Sloane Square Hotel, Oleana regretted mistiming her walk and showing up ten minutes early at Isaak's hotel; she regretted even more the fact he was waiting in the lobby, eager to go to breakfast and discuss the money Oleana had put in her accounts. She looked at her watch. Where the fuck was Harry? she thought to herself as she scanned Sloane Street looking for him. She decided she would rendezvous in the restaurant.

They entered Knightsbridge underground via Sloane Street, and once on the platform Oleana had an epiphany. As the train entered the station it would be going at maximum before braking to a halt; she walked with Isaak as far along the platform as possible, taking care to stop directly underneath two surveillance cameras, out of their field of view. She quickly ascertained the camera at the end of the platform had a clear view, but it would be masked by the other passengers.

The platform was moderately crowded, so Oleana stood close to Isaak, who didn't notice her leg extend in front of his as they stood on the yellow line at the platform edge. The sound of an approaching train grew louder, and as it came into view, she looked towards it and muttered, "I like the lights of the train."

Isaak turned his head the same way as hers to comprehend her description, when he suddenly felt her hand in the small of his back. Did Maria's friend actually fancy him too? This could be fun. She was even leaning in now to whisper in his ear.

"This is what rapists get."

As he processed her words, the train emerged out of the tunnel and he felt pressure on his back. He tried to take a step forward to get his balance, but Oleana's leg was in the way. Panicked, he toppled forward as Oleana stepped back.

Isaak's body was left severed in two and smeared along a twenty-metre section of the track, his entrails wrapped around the trains front bogie. The crowd screamed and panic ensued, with the station staff declaring a "Code 2 in progress" and doing everything to calm the distraught onlookers and carry out their well-rehearsed evacuation procedures.

The 'body' would take two hours to clean up, and Oleana hoped to hell the rush hour crush meant no one had noticed the firm but momentary push. Although she'd cleaned up bodies in the past, this was her first kill; she cursed to think Harry should have taken this off her hands; however, since Shaheen had cleared Harry's involvement in her imprisonment, she concluded it was actually only fair she'd been forced to do it herself.

She walked down to the My Hotel where the morning receptionist assumed she'd been out for an early morning walk.

On entering her dark room it was immediately apparent the bed hadn't been slept in. She concluded all had gone well and that Maria had left without bothering to sleep in the room, but wondered why she hadn't returned to the Sloane Square Hotel before Oleana had left to meet Isaak.

She walked into the bathroom and stared at the baseball cap and blonde wig. Why had Maria not worn the wig and hat to leave the hotel as normal? That was strange.

She tried to call her but there was no reply. She wanted to go to Shaheen's room but knew she couldn't. Oleana needed comfort over Isaak's murder, but she now felt isolated. She tried Maria's number again, but to no avail. "Answer the phone, you bitch!" she muttered as it rang.

Oleana tried to gather her thoughts. Where was Maria? Had she even gone to Shaheen's room, or had something gone wrong and she'd had to leave? Was Shaheen even dead? She reasoned that Maria was young, fit and lethal, so it had to be the case – surely?

She decided to go downstairs, make a show of eating a late breakfast, so she would be noticed, and afterwards she'd try calling Maria again.

As she sipped her tea the polite waitress came into the breakfast room and handed her a note. "There was a gentleman asking for you earlier, ma'am, but there was no reply from your room."

Oleana took the note and the waitress left her alone. She unfolded the note. "Shit!" she said under her breath; it was from Omar Shamoon and simply read, '*I'm in town, let's catch up.*'

She sighed; she had no desire to see or talk to this man, but she also knew he was in London, and he knew where she was, and that was no coincidence.

Suddenly she heard a familiar voice pierce her thoughts, asking the waitress for more coffee. She glanced round discreetly at one of the tables behind her to see a demure Chinese woman facing her and smiling towards the man she was having breakfast with. The man turned towards the waitress to thank her.

Oleana felt a rush of panic shoot through her entire body. It was at this point she realised that, whatever the reason Maria wasn't answering her phone, it wasn't good. There was no mistake – the man at the table was Shaheen Soroush.

CHAPTER TWENTY-FIVE
Three Times A Lady

Harry took pleasure in being back in Ivanna's mews house, but he could tell as soon as she opened the door that sex was not on the menu.

Ivanna was as tense as he'd seen her in over a year. Harry showed her the photo Sid had taken of Mac's note and pointed out the hidden message.

"All lower case except for the word 'ISAAK'." He looked at her quizzically.

Ivanna stared at the photo, now in a complete dilemma. Harry had no idea who she really was; if she gave an inch here, did he know enough to join the dots? She couldn't risk it. "Why would he write that?"

"I'm not sure, Ivanna, but I think it's safe to assume this Isaak is directly involved in Mac's disappearance." Harry had just inadvertently thrown her accountant under the bus, little suspecting the man had already succumbed to an alternative mode of transport.

She could hold off no longer. "This is going to seem like such a small world, Harry, but I also have an accountant called Isaak." She tried to dilute the facts as much as she could. "I need to get to the bottom of this." She could see Harry was about to interject so she quickly cut him off and in the firmest of tones said, "Let's get him around here." She picked up her phone and held up her hand as an invitation for Harry to stay quiet.

Harry watched as someone answered the phone. It was clearly not who Ivanna had been expecting in view of the expression she was pulling. "Isaak Rabinovich? Yes, I'm his boss," she said before listening. "No, I don't know his next of kin, maybe they're in Russia, or perhaps Israel. Is he hurt?"

Harry watched her go pale, without knowing she had just heard the words 'accident' and 'non-survivable injuries'.

"He's dead?" she asked in disbelief. "Oh my God." Another pause. "Depressed? Not so far as I know." She listened again. "I'm at 9 Eaton Mews Terrace. Yes, I'll be here all morning." The call ended.

Harry waited for her to explain, but even he was surprised at what she had to tell him. "We have a problem, Harry. Isaak fell under a tube train this morning. That man on the phone was a British Transport Police officer; he told me it looks like suicide. They want to come round here to talk to me and for photo identification."

"Jesus Christ." Harry was trying to compute the events of the morning. "Do you think he knew he'd be the prime suspect in Mac's disappearance and for stealing the money, so he took the easy way out?"

"Who knows?" she said. "But now the police know about our active existence here, and that's not good at all. I'll call my executive assistant again." She tried, but there was still no answer.

"I have a friend who might know this Isaak," Harry offered.

Ivanna was just about to ask "How?" when the doorbell rang.

"That'll either be the police or Maria," Ivanna said, handing Harry a mug of tea.

She opened the door, but it took her another two seconds to recognise the pale, bearded man in front of her, who simply said, "I lost my key."

"Alexei!" she squealed, launching herself at him. "Thank God! What are you doing here? How?"

"Aren't you going to ask me into my own house?" He was relieved she was pleased to see him, little knowing it was for all the wrong reasons.

"Come in, come in," she urged. "Is that your only bag?"

"I left in a hurry," he said as he closed the front door. "We paid off the bosses for my release, and then some bastard stole the money."

"€20 million?" she asked.

"How did you know that?" Alexei's tone was one of surprise.

"Isaak told me that amount had been stolen. Did he know you were coming?" Alexei nodded. "Alexei, my darling," she added softly. "He just jumped under a train and killed himself today. I just found out a couple of minutes ago before you arrived."

"What!" Alexei looked confused. "He warned me to get out of Russia – why would he do that?"

"We don't know yet, Alexei, but that's not all; Mac the IT man is missing too."

Alexei took a deep breath and made his way towards the kitchen, with Ivanna following after him nervously. Alexei stopped in his tracks when he saw Harry, who'd heard the entire conversation regarding the €20 million and stood up as Alexei entered the kitchen.

"Who the fuck are you?" the Russian asked the Englishman.

Harry extended his hand and thought on his feet. "Harry Linley, I'm Ivanna's security advisor," he explained. "And you are?"

"Alexei Delimkov – Ivanna's husband." Alexei also put out his hand, trying at the same time to remember why this man's name seemed so familiar to him. He turned to Ivanna. "So we have a British security advisor, a dead accountant and a missing IT guy? What the fuck is going on?"

Suddenly Harry joined the dots where Alexei couldn't! This guy was the head of the Delimkov cartel and Ivanna was his wife! So this was the source of her income and why her husband had been banged up. Harry had never realised Russian women carried an 'a' at the end of their married names so had never even thought to link hers to the cartel. He had a huge urge to demand "What the fuck?" of Ivanna but knew this was far from the time. At the same time he was instantly mindful of Oleana's warning that the accountant had come to town to confront him over the money he'd earned from Shaheen. Did Alexei know his name; and surely Ivanna didn't know – or did she?

Before Ivanna had a chance to answer her husband or Harry had a chance to blurt anything out, her phone rang. She looked at the caller ID, then back at Harry, then at Alexei. Clearly there was no going back now. "It's his girlfriend," she said, with a curt nod in Harry's direction. She watched him frown with confusion as she answered the call. "Oleana? … No I haven't seen her, have you tried the hotel? … Okay, don't worry, she's probably working out or something. Oleana, something is going on, we don't know what. Make sure you're contactable and I'll brief you later. The call ended and Ivanna told the men, "She can't find Maria."

This was the final nail. Harry was nearly dizzy from the epiphany that was hitting him. Oleana calling Ivanna, who was literally married to the mob, and all linked to Maria, whom he'd previously met in Dubai but he had no idea was in London. Once again all his brain could muster was an urge to blurt, "What the fuck is going on?"

However, this time it was Harry's phone that rang; and again it was Oleana. She had no idea he was with Ivanna, and he had no plans to announce to the room who was calling.

"What's happened?" he asked.

"We have a problem, Harry," she told him. He listened intently as she described Isaak jumping under the train, before moving on to the fact Maria was meant to meet Shaheen after his dinner with Harry, but now she was missing. Harry wanted to curse, but he knew he needed to be discreet in front of his audience. "Where are you now?" he asked.

"Sitting in Aubaine on Brompton Road."

He told her to stay there; he would meet her there in 45 minutes, but as soon as he had ended the call, his phone immediately rang again. He looked at Ivanna and Alexei, mouthing, "Excuse me." It was Sid.

"We have a problem, Harry," Sid opened.

"Several, mate," Harry replied.

"The Met have just been round asking how I knew about Mac going missing. They want to formally interview me. They also asked whether I knew Mac's computer gear had been lifted."

"What? When?" Harry asked.

"Well, they wanted my alibi for the past forty-eight hours, which I have, so I'm assuming it must have happened in that window." Sid sounded calm.

"Look, Sid," Harry said. "The accountant's dead, killed himself this morning under a tube train. Mac's missing, now his computers have gone, and there's another woman connected to them who isn't answering her phone. I think it's safe to say our client is under attack." He had Alexei and Ivanna's full attention. "You've got the Met police on your case," he continued, "and Ivanna's about to be interviewed by the British Transport Police. The whole thing stinks of conspiracy." Harry truly believed what he was telling Sid, but was also very happy to have Alexei think he was truly a security professional and nothing else.

With all calls ended, Alexei took control. "Sit down, both of you." He gestured to the kitchen table. "I don't know what the fuck's going on, but I can hazard a guess and it's important you know." He looked at Harry. "Of course, if any of what I'm about to say leaks out, then I'll know exactly where it came from, and I don't think I need to explain to you the meaning of 'Moscow Payback'." He waited for Harry to nod. He proceeded to explain to them both the fact of his early release, the payoff to the president and the Cellist, the reversal of the funds, and his order to Isaak to repay the money as well as find out where the hell it had gone. "From where I'm sitting now…" – he sipped the coffee Ivanna had put in front of him – "…Isaak's probably dead because he knew he couldn't outrun our president or his lynch-man the Cellist. Do we definitely know he jumped?"

"We have no idea yet," Ivanna told him, "but the police should be here soon. I have to identify him."

Alexei continued. "My guess is it's the IT guy who did all this. We find him, we find the money." He looked at Harry. "If you recover my money I'll pay you thirty percent of whatever you bring back to me. Can you do that, Mr Linley?" There was a suspiciously sarcastic tone to his voice.

"I think I can," Harry said with confidence.

"Good, then get out there and get it done." He put his arm around Ivanna's shoulder. "My wife and I have some serious catching up to do."

Alexei was the only one not to feel the discomfort in the room.

Harry picked up his phone and headed for the door, knowing that, whatever he had ever had with Ivanna had now just ended for good; he wondered just how deep he was buried in this shit.

★   ★   ★

It was unusual for Mr G to eat his lunch at table one in San Gennaro, not least because the restaurant had had to open especially for him, but both he and they had made an exception on this day. Sat opposite him was a woman so voluptuous she could have stepped out of a 1950s movie. He had no idea where she could have procured such a bra, but all he could compare it to was a dead heat in a zeppelin race; and the ample size of the breasts this bra contained was only further accentuated by the thinness of her waist. Her silk neck-scarf was tied like a choker around what was an unblemished and elegant neck, and her thick shoulder-length hair was jet black. She wore bright scarlet lipstick, and if she had dressed to be desired, then it was working well on the Italian in front of her.

"Alejandra." Mr G had wanted to continue a charm offensive, but needed to get down to business. "Have you spoken to your boss Mr Jorge?"

She told him Jorge wasn't her boss, but in any case, no, she hadn't spoken to him.

"There is a payment due in New Jersey," Mr G continued. "It hasn't arrived and I'm concerned."

"If Jorge says you'll be paid then you will be paid, Mr G," Alejandra assured.

"I have no doubt," the Italian answered, "but it seems there were things Jorge didn't tell us, or perhaps know, and my deal was to share any information I acquired from our tasking with him. However, I can't do this until I've been paid in full." He took a sip of his Barolo red wine.

"What kind of information?" the Mexican asked.

"The person we had to take care of for your organisation had two supercomputers, and now we have them. We also have a Greek guy, who's an asshole, but he's our asshole, and one who knows how to…interrogate such computers. He's working on the ones we acquired, and I'm confident we've already identified significant bank records and emails between the controlling accountant and the guy who was operating the computers. So much, in fact, that I think there may have to be an adjustment of price in New Jersey. What do you think?"

"I think my boss might be Mexican, but he doesn't like Mexican-style deals," she told him. "I think you should stick to the deal you had, regardless of what you now know. But!" she emphasised. "If you really want me to take the message back to him, I will, but I warn you, it's ill-advised – my boss is not the gentleman Jorge happens to be. Now can we enjoy our lunch and wine?"

Two hours, three bottles of Barolo and one Viagra later, Mr G lay in the sumptuous surroundings of his Battersea apartment's bedroom watching the Mexican beauty swallow his entire penis into the back of her throat. He reached to unclip her bra and watched in ecstasy as her bought and paid-for breasts maintained their shape as they came uncovered, before she went back to work on him.

Alejandra knew of one bullet-proof way to get a man infatuated with her to the point where he could think of nothing else. It was simple, and she was a third of the way to achieving it with Mr G. She had learned in her early twenties as a flight attendant with Aeromexico that to swallow a man's sperm on three separate occasions was to own him; there were simply no exceptions to this rule she had ever come across – or with.

By the end of this first day, she had already drunk Mr G twice, and the following morning, when they woke at 7.30, she completed the trio. She knew he would think of her all day long and call her over and over again to win a repeat performance.

By the time she'd left his apartment, asking him to call her, she'd also found out the Greek IT guy was called Panos, and he worked in a place called the Ace-1Tech Shop in Chessington. She'd further established that Panos had been ordered by Mr G to obtain all the data contained in the computers, clean them of all evidence, and then dispose of them. This of course would not be good enough for Jorge, who'd want the unwiped physical computers themselves, by any means, to ensure nothing had been hidden from him by the Italians.

It was some four hours later, having ascertained all this with Jorge directly, cleaned herself up, and changed into one of the tightest outfits she possessed, that Alejandra breezed into Ace-1. She perused the shelves and the nametags of the staff.

The tall, unshaven, scruffy man wearing his own tag at an uncaring angle could not take his eyes off this Mediterranean goddess. She was probably the most beautiful women he'd ever laid eyes on. To his surprise, she smiled at him and he smiled back, revealing his nicotine-stained, yellow teeth.

Alejandra hid her disgust and asked, "Could you help me please?" She could see his work colleagues curse the fact she'd picked him.

When he spoke to her his smell matched his teeth; she guessed this thirty-something guy had to smoke sixty a day and washed only once a week, whether or not he thought he needed to.

However, his lack of hygiene did not come with a proportionate lack of self-confidence she'd been expecting, and he clearly thought he had a chance with this beauty.

She asked him where he was from, telling him she'd always wanted to visit Athens, before adding, "Perhaps you'll be there when I finally go?" Groundwork laid, she turned to business. "I have a need for two supercomputers, but I can't afford new ones; do you have any used ones you could sell me."

He told her the shop didn't have any but that he freelanced, and he knew where two could be found, since he happened to have been working on them for the last couple of days. He went on to explain that, once they'd been cleaned up, he expected to be able to sell them.

She asked if they were close-by, and he told her they were. She then suggested they have lunch and perhaps he could show them to her.

The Greek thought for a moment and quickly concluded that no one would find out, and what harm could it do in any case? "Lunch first?" he asked boldly.

She told him she'd rather look at the computers, and then have lunch.

Panos couldn't believe his luck when she walked him out to the Bentley Continental GT Speed Convertible parked outside and told him to get in. He guided her to Davis Road Industrial Park and unlocked one of the units there. Inside was a van, tool racks, some freezers, and a bank of computer screens, with the two supercomputers visible under the desk that supported the screens.

"These are perfect," she told him. "However, please don't wipe anything. I'm told by my people it can mess things up, so we'd like to do that ourselves and we'll pay you well." She winked.

"Could you leave them as they are? Then perhaps I could ask you to configure them for me at my house – if, of course, I were to buy them from you?"

He could already imagine himself on top of her in her own house after having impressed the hell out of her with his IT prowess. "I'll give you the best as-is deal ever," he said in his jarring Greek accent. He was also pleased he wouldn't have to go through the rigmarole of cleaning the damned things, yet still be able to double-dip on a payoff from Mr G and this beauty.

"When?" she pressed.

"I need two more days cleaning them up for my client, then I can come round, and maybe we do dinner also?" He gave her another repulsive smile.

"That sounds wonderful," she said. "Here's my number; perhaps we should have that dinner once your current client is happy, then I can discuss the way I want them configured." They exchanged business cards.

She looked down at his poorly designed card and gave a smile. "'Software Architect'? You should have told me – that's so much more sexy than just being an IT guy."

"I know, right?" he said, not sensing her sarcasm in the least. "It impresses most people. Shall we go for that lunch now?"

"How about we wait for that special dinner?" Alejandra said, reaching up to stroke his unshaven cheek. "That'll be much more fun."

The Greek geek almost ejaculated right on the spot, but his ecstasy was short-lived as she said, "I'd better dash now, can you walk back to your shop?"

Before he could protest she was out the door of the unit and into her Bentley. He cursed under his breath, but reassured himself he would be inside her within a night or two. After all, she wanted those computers.

The Greek was wrong on both counts.

CHAPTER TWENTY-SIX
Duplicitous Slut

A nervous-looking Shaheen got out of a London taxi adjacent to Victoria Bus Station and entered the Hertz rental car shop. He explained that his wife had called to book an Audi A4 Avant for two days, and the pleasant Polish desk attendant asked him for his credit card and driving licence.

A few minutes later he was trying to navigate his car towards Lower Sloane Street on his way back to South Kensington. He was relieved he had learned to master a right-hand-drive car in Singapore already, otherwise he'd have been an accident waiting to happen, and now was definitely not a good time for that.

Lai Xian, meanwhile, had made her way to the Kipling bag shop, convenient to Harrods and bought, with cash, two identical 91-litre black Teagan L bags. She had the shop attendant place one within the other before heading out onto the street and hailing a cab.

When she reached Elystan Street she instructed the taxi driver to drop her off; she could see Shaheen standing by a red estate car. As she approached him smiling, she asked him to open the rear door, and proceeded to leave one of the bags in the car.

Once back in their room, Lai Xian thanked fate the cleaners had obeyed the 'Do Not Disturb' notice, and that Maria was a small woman. She was also very glad that, following Maria's death, she'd managed to keep Shaheen calm and hatch a plan to alleviate them of the body and the crime.

She rightly assumed that whoever knew Maria had come to kill Shaheen wouldn't be willing to go to the police to report her missing. She'd also correctly predicted the onset of rigor mortis, and therefore used four pairs of her pantyhose and stockings to tie the body into the foetal position, and turned the AC to its lowest setting in the bathroom, where they'd left Maria's body in the bath overnight.

Still in shock, Shaheen helped Lai Xian lift Maria's body into the Teagan bag, and together they manipulated the body in such a way as to be able to close it.

While Lai Xian cleaned the bathroom, Shaheen called reception to tell them they'd decided to take a drive in the country and would therefore be checking out.

Although the bag containing Maria now weighed in excess of fifty kilos, Shaheen did his best not to show off its weight as he handled it through reception and to the car.

Within thirty minutes, both he and Lai Xian were on the M4 heading west, having stopped at a home store to buy three pillows, a box-cutter knife, and a large socket toolset.

Oleana felt uncomfortable on several fronts as she sat down outside the Jumeirah Lowndes Hotel, having been beckoned there earlier by an insistent Omar Shamoon. She didn't like the idea of meeting him under any circumstances, but knew that not to would merely encourage his pursuit and his ceaseless inquiries into her activities. The fact she'd committed murder that very morning added to her discomfort; her desperate desire to find out what had happened to Maria was driving her to distraction; and when she saw Sergeant Maryam Seyadin with Omar, Oleana nearly wet her pants.

Had she known that sitting right behind her was an MI6 officer in the form of Toby Sotheby, she would no doubt have decided a postponement of the meeting would be wise.

After initial greetings, they ordered coffee, and Oleana tried hard to avoid eye contact with the female police officer, whom she'd last spoken to in the intimacy of a hotel room in Dubai.

"Why are you here?" Shamoon commenced a direct line of questioning.

"I could ask the same thing," she replied.

"Maybe so," he said, "but I asked first."

"You can't put me in prison here, Officer Shamoon. Don't you think that's good enough a reason for me to be here?" She was indignant.

"Perhaps I can't," the policeman agreed, "but we can make things very awkward for you, and please never forget you may well have to transit through the Middle East again, so if we want you, we can surely get you." He paused to let this sink in. "You're in London; Shaheen Soroush is in London. You're even in the same hotel; we need to know why."

Sergeant Seyadin interjected here. "You left Dubai so suddenly, and we believe the timing of your rendezvous with Soroush was forced by his arrival here. We believe we can show that you're here to perpetrate a crime with him. Perhaps you've already committed it?"

Oleana sensed in Maryam's tone that her priorities were different to her superior officer's, but she knew she had to throw them off any scent of her involvement with Isaak's death. "I never came here to rendezvous with Soroush," she told them emphatically. "In fact, he followed me here to extort some money he'd lost out of me."

"How much?" Omar asked.

"He says $30 million, but he could be blagging, and if not, I honestly don't know who took it from him. What I do know is that he was meant to see my friend last night, who he also suspects, and now she's missing, and not answering her phone."

"Where did he meet her?"

"In his hotel room. He was at breakfast with a Chinese woman this morning, but there's no sign of my friend."

"Could you not ask him?" inquired Maryam.

"He doesn't know I know he was meeting her," Oleana concocted.

Omar received a text message. It was from Toby, who was overhearing the entire conversation from his nearby vantage-point.

"What's your connection to the Delimkovs?" Omar asked, having read the text.

"Delimkovs?" Oleana was buying time.

"Yes, Shaheen's had dealings with them, and it seems they're now enemies, so if, as you say, he's also your enemy, and given the fact you're also Russian, what is your connection?" Omar pushed Toby's request.

"I know Ivanna Delimkova, but not well," Oleana mitigated. "She lives in London."

A man suddenly stood up behind her and sat down uninvited in the seat next to hers. She looked at him with a shocked expression.

"I'm Toby Sotheby, I work for Her Majesty's Government, Miss Katayeva. We're working with our Emirati friends here to ensure our joint national security, to which we suspect you might be a threat." He bluffed. "We know you were in Dubai and linked to Soroush, who was involved with Alexei Delimkov. We also know you were in Dubai with Soroush as major incidents were taking place last year." He reached back to his original table and retrieved his coffee. "So, Miss Katayeva, right now your life comes down to two choices – either you help us regarding the Delimkovs and perhaps we can offer you immunity on crimes you've been linked to..." He purposely paused. "Or we can investigate you for aiding and abetting any crime perpetrated by either the Delimkovs or Soroush. Oh, and by the way, while we're trying to figure all that out, we'll hold you under the Prevention of Terrorism Act." He sipped his coffee to allow her a moment to digest her situation, before proceeding. "So, why is Alexei Delimkov in London?"

"Alexei's in London?" she asked, and all could see she was genuinely surprised.

"He arrived this morning. From Estonia," Sotheby told her. "He told our agents at the airport he'd been released from prison but had run here because he's concerned his president will lock him up again."

"Where is he now?" she asked, now seriously worried about the fact that just a few hours ago she'd pushed Alexei's loyal accountant under a fucking train.

"We believe at his home in Belgravia."

"He's lying about the circumstances," she blurted, almost unable to get her stroke of genius out soon enough. "I think he got out of jail to come and question his accountant, because he believes the man defrauded him out of money while he was in jail. His accountant came here last week, presumably to run away when he heard Alexei was out. That must be the real reason he's here." She'd made the whole thing up on the spot, but this would explain Isaak's suicide quite neatly; she inwardly gloated at the brilliance of her instantaneous diversion.

"Where is his accountant now?" Sotheby asked.

"I don't know," she lied. "But I wouldn't want to be in his shoes." Which was the truth.

"Are you on speaking terms with Mrs Delimkova?" Sotheby asked.

Oleana told him that she was.

"Good, then I need you to go round to her house and find out what's happening. This is my telephone number. You need to call me as soon as you know anything. It's the only way I can help you, Miss Katayeva. Otherwise, my dear, I think your situation will be worse than dire."

"Oleana," Omar interjected. "You have to clean yourself of all of this, and what Mr Sotheby is offering is your only way, do you understand that?"

She did, in more ways than any of them would ever know.

It was very discomfiting for Alexei to find that he'd only been in London a few hours and now the police were already in his house. He was, however, less irritated than he might have been, since Harry had excused himself and left just minutes before the police arrived.

The two uniformed British Transport Police officers were polite, and clearly trying to be sensitive about the fact this couple's employee had just thrown himself under a train.

"These are his belongings." One of the policemen pro-duced Isaak's blood-spattered wallet and passport. "Is this your employee?" he asked.

Ivanna nodded and Alexei said, "That's our accountant. He worked for us for over ten years. A very loyal man."

"Is there any reason you know why he would commit suicide?" The policeman again used the gentlest tone he had.

"I can't think of anything offhand, apart from the fact he was a loner, and a lonely man," Alexei told the policeman, not willing to share any specific detail of anything with the law.

"Okay," the policeman said, making a note of it. "We have extensive video footage from within the station, so we'll be analysing that just to make sure this truly was a self-imposed death. I have to say these things are very rarely anything else."

The policeman handed Alexei his card and asked the Russians to call him if they needed any other information.

As the police car pulled out of the mews, Oleana walked in and rang the bell of Number 9.

Ivanna answered the door; she was none too pleased to see Oleana, who she deemed had probably just been screwing her Harry. "Oleana, what are you doing here? You know I don't meet employees at home."

"Maria's still missing. I don't know what to do." There was a vulnerability in Oleana's voice.

"Come in," Ivanna said gently, and indicated for her to go to the kitchen.

Oleana walked in and immediately recognised Alexei, although she'd never met him.

"Alexei, this is Oleana," Ivanna told her husband. "She was the fixer in Dubai when all the problems started."

Alexei stood to shake her hand. "As I recall," he said smilingly, "you did a good job where all others failed me."

"I tried my best," she told him, "but things got pretty fucked up."

"Tell me about it," he told her. "I've just spent the last three years in jail."

"I did six months myself," she replied. "In Dubai's women's jail. It was shit."

"So what's up?" Ivanna interjected, as she watched this slut now creating common ground between herself and another one of her men.

"We have a big problem," Oleana told them as they sat around the kitchen table, realising she had stumbled on a unique opportunity. "The man you went to jail because of – Shaheen Soroush – he's in London." She could see Alexei's attention pique. "Last night Maria went to meet him to avenge you, but today she's missing, and I've seen Soroush alive and well; I think he may have done something to her."

"Maria knew my plans for Soroush if we ever caught up with him," Ivanna disclosed, looking at Alexei. "Like she says, this is the man behind all our problems, including your time in jail. However, I didn't think she would move so quickly."

"She had to, no one knew how long he would stay; she took it all very personally when she knew he was here and with what he'd done previously to Alexei." Oleana was playing the crowd and actually enjoying it.

"That is so Maria," Ivanna sighed. "Blindly devoted."

"Well I'm afraid that devotion may have cost her dearly." Oleana was genuinely concerned. "She went to his room but now she's missing. What do we do?"

"We need to finish this bastard!" Alexei was clearly angry. "He took three years of my life – we need to take him now, while he's here."

"This is not Moscow, Alexei." Ivanna tried to calm him. "We can't buy the police or the government here."

"That's only because we haven't tried." Alexei sounded bitter. "Let's see what your security guy can sort out. I want to see whether he's any good."

"Harry doesn't kill people, Alexei, it's not that kind of security," Ivanna protested, and watched Oleana's expression change at the mention of Harry's name.

"I wasn't aware there was any other kind," Alexei persisted. "Let's get the guy on him so we can at least know the score on this Soroush. I want him dead, and we'll find someone else if *your* Harry can't do it."

Ivanna ignored the innuendo. "There's more bad news, Oleana. We just learned Isaak killed himself this morning. Jumped under a train."

Oleana looked down at the table and then back up to Ivanna. "I know," she said soberly. "I was with him."

"What? How?" Alexei interjected.

"I think Isaak stole some money, I don't know who from. He asked if I had any money to give him. We were going for breakfast in Piccadilly to have a discreet discussion. I was standing next to him and he just jumped. It was awful, I just ran away. I didn't know what else to do."

"Where did you meet him?" Ivanna asked.

"At his hotel." Despite her calculations, Oleana didn't know where this line of question was going.

"They'll have you on film, Oleana. The transport police were just here, they said they were going to analyse the camera footage. They'll know you were with him."

Oleana tried to keep her cool. She just hoped to God no one saw the gentle shove or trip. "I think I should leave the country. Except..." She trailed off.

Alexei was impatient. "Except what?"

"Before I came here, I had to meet with a detective from the Emirates; he's been tracking both me and Soroush. There was an officer from the British government with him. They want to know all about you, Alexei, otherwise they say they'll make things very bad for me. What should I do?"

Alexei smiled, recalling how efficient Oleana had been as one of their fixers. She'd once again proved her loyalty to him. "You've done the right thing in telling us," he reassured her. "Tell them Isaak was working for Soroush and double-dipping. Tell them I flew in to try to protect Isaak, but clearly he was too scared of what Soroush was going to do to him. That'll keep them busy for a few days. Did you get the name of the British guy?"

"Toby Sotheby. I have his number here." She offered Alexei the business card.

"Good girl," Alexei told her. "Now go and call him. Then go to wherever Maria was staying and check her room." He looked at Ivanna. "You call Harry and get him onto Soroush."

Once Oleana had let herself out, Alexei turned to his wife. "She's a good girl, isn't she? I like her."

"She's a duplicitous slut," Ivanna replied coldly.

Alexei smiled; he'd only been home three hours and already his wife was jealous.

Harry was deep in discussion with Sid when Ivanna called to tell him there was still no sign of Maria and that they needed to get to grips with Shaheen. Harry knew only too well that, if you hung around long enough with Shaheen, then life could get interesting, and not necessarily in a good way.

Within thirty minutes Sid and Harry were in the lobby of the My Hotel, where they called Ivanna back to tell her Shaheen had checked out. There was no sign of Maria and no one answering her description had been seen entering or leaving the hotel.

"My guess is, if something's gone pear-shaped, he'll be making a break for the border. That's his style, to flee. He's with a Singapore national, a woman called Lee Lai Xian. She was in the hotel room with him. Do you want me to call in some favours to see if I can get him stopped or searched at the airport?"

"No, leave it, Harry, I don't want you wrapped up in this. Alexei's clearly jealous of you, so he probably wouldn't mind if you got into trouble trying to help us."

Harry felt a flash of anger at how she appeared to be glossing over the elephant in the room.

"You know what?" he responded without waiting for an answer. "You could have told me you were up to your ears in the Delimkov cartel."

Ivanna knew he was right but they didn't have time for this. "Harry, I thought you knew," she lied. "I honestly did. But I have to go."

The call ended without her saying goodbye.

At the same time, Toby was back in his office in Vauxhall with the lovely Tarisai sitting alongside him as they scrolled the database for anything recent on Shaheen Soroush. There was nothing of note beyond what appeared to be regular travel movements.

His phone rang and he looked down at the phone. "It's our new Russian recruit," he told Tarisai before accepting the call. "Oleana?"

"Alexei is at 9 Eaton Terrace Mews," she told him, "with his wife. When I arrived the transport police had just left. Alexei's accountant committed suicide in the tube this morning. His wife's executive assistant is missing after meeting with Shaheen Soroush. His IT expert is missing and Soroush has checked out of his hotel; we think he's heading for Heathrow." She paused. "The Russian president's still very pissed off with Alexei; I think he may be starting a turf war in London."

"Jesus Christ," Toby said to Tarisai, wondering if he'd got in over his head again, as he relayed to her the conversation he'd just had.

"You need to get someone senior from the Russian desk in here," she told him. "Also pass Soroush's details to border control at Heathrow, let's get a stop, search and hold on him."

"Exactly what I was thinking, Tarisai," he bluffed and told the analyst to execute her own instructions.

While Tarisai was busy gently guiding Toby, Oleana was already calling Ivanna. "Tell Alexei the message has been passed on exactly as he instructed."

Ivanna walked into the bathroom where Alexei had just enjoyed a hot shower; only now could she see how much weight he'd lost in prison. "Oleana's passed it on. Now let me take you to lunch around the corner. We need to feed you."

Mr G sat on the metal chairs on the pavement outside the Butcher & Grill in Battersea, enjoying his mug of tea and a bacon roll. It was a late breakfast, but it was one of those beautiful London mornings under a blue sky peppered with small cumulus clouds. A London cab pulled up in front of him and he saw his Mexican beauty in the back about to pay the driver. He leapt up and told the driver, "I've got this", and passed him a ten-pound note.

Alejandra was, as ever, dressed to kill. She wore a short blue dress with pink polka dots, the upper half of which was see-through, so that her blue bra was clearly visible to all. Her Lanvin high heels accentuated her calf muscles, and her well lotioned legs shone as the sunlight caught them.

She kissed her lover and thanked him for paying for the taxi, then ordered a double espresso. As he watched her sip it, Mr G could think of only one thing he desperately wanted her to drink instead. Her spell had worked, and, unfortunately for Mr G, only she knew her reasons behind it.

"I've spoken to Jorge," she told him. "He assures me the delivery you asked for in New Jersey is now in the States and will be delivered in a matter of days. However," she added, "he wants the computers that belonged to the IT guy before they get wiped. He says the deal was you share information, and that's what must happen."

Mr G looked at her, knowing he couldn't refuse her. He picked up his phone and dialled a number. "Panos, do not wipe those computers. Copy everything, but do not wipe them, you understand?"

"But Mr G," Panos protested. "It's too late, they're already cleaned. I've got all the data downloaded so we can transfer it over to new computers." The Greek knew he had to sell the computers as-is to have a chance of climbing all over the Mexican beauty. She had things Mr G could never offer him.

"Shit, Panos, I didn't need you to be that efficient. Bring the kit containing the data to the restaurant this evening; I also need another copy for us so you can analyse the data later." Mr G's tone was authoritative and not to be fucked with. The Greek would have to be crazy to lie – or at least crazy about a woman.

Panos, as it turned out, had already planned to buy some others as soon as the Mexican woman paid him. These would be clean computers that Mr G would think were the originals.

The call ended and Mr G grinned at his Alejandra. "Although your wish is my command, my dear, we can't do the computers themselves, only the saved data; he's already cleaned the others for security."

Her disappointment was visible, and he thought this was because of the computers; in fact, she'd discovered that she didn't own him completely just yet.

His phone suddenly rang, and a moment later hers did as well. Mr G got up from his chair to take his call and walked a couple of metres down the road.

Alejandra, meanwhile, took hers; it was the Greek again. "Alejandra, I have your computers; if you give me your address, I can bring them today and give you a special price, but I need cash on delivery."

"I'm with someone right now," she told him. "Let me call you back, my dear."

Mr G returned to the table. "Have you had lunch?" he asked.

"You're looking at it." She indicated towards the empty espresso cup.

"Good," he said. "I have to be in a restaurant in Sloane Square. Join me." She smiled, and Mr G used the Hailo app to call a cab; within three minutes they were on their way into Chelsea.

"G?" She put her hand on his knee in the back seat. "Who knows about us?"

The Italian looked at her. "When you say 'us' do you mean 'this'?" he said adoringly, taking her hand in his.

"No, I mean that we're meeting and talking." She turned slightly towards him.

"Your boss, but he'll think it's all business," he told her. "And I guess the guys in the San Gennaro. Why?"

"Because I think your phone is hacked. A Greek guy called Panos just called me and tried to sell me those fucking computers. He knew I was interested in two supercomputers and the information on them. If he's good enough to dig the data off those hard drives, he's sure as hell competent enough to hack into your phone if you ever left it in reach of him for more than a few minutes." She watched the expression on Mr G's face turn very serious; it was intimidating.

"The obnoxious fuck!" he said. "The twat is a software architect, which means he writes code, which means he's hacked this?" He held up his phone. "And no doubt that too," he added, pointing to her phone. "Otherwise how else did he get your number? No wonder the shit wanted to transfer the data and wipe them, he even told me he had a buyer, but of course I didn't realise I was his fucking advertising agency." He paused. "So what else does he know?"

"Is it going to be a problem?" she asked.

"Not for long," he said as the cab pulled up outside the Botanist on Sloane Square.

Giovanni, the waiter, greeted Mr G and smiled broadly at the beautiful woman he'd brought with him. As they entered the restaurant Mr G immediately recognised Ivanna who had her back to the entrance. Sitting opposite her was a slightly dishevelled, tough-looking man in his forties who could hardly be anything else but Russian.

Mr G sat with his back to the Russian couple, which gave Alejandra a very clear view of them. As Giovanni laid the napkins on Alejandra's lap and then Mr G's, he spoke quietly. "She calls the gentleman Alexei; he has a very thick Russian accent. My guess is it's the husband."

"How do you know?" Mr G asked.

"I'm a waiter," replied Giovanni knowingly. "Married couples speak less and never try to impress each other. Trust me, these guys are married." He handed them the menus and described the day's specials.

As soon as Giovanni had gone to fetch the sparkling water, Mr G spoke to Alejandra. "The couple over my shoulder?"

"You mean with the tough-looking guy who can't take his eyes off me?"

"If he's sitting with an auburn lady, then yes. These are the people the guy who stole your money worked for. It's their information that will be on the computers." Mr G paused as Giovanni returned and poured the San Pellegrino.

"So who are they?" she asked.

"Her name is Ivanna, now we know his is Alexei, but your thief's direct boss is a guy called Isaak Rabinovich; our sources tell us he's the accountant for the Delimkov cartel. So you, my dear, are looking at two of the best international smugglers and money-launderers in the world."

A pause again while Alejandra ordered her leek and Emmental tortellini and Mr G ordered the crab linguine.

"Why would they steal from us then?" she asked.

"I have no idea," he said. "Perhaps the computers will tell you that."

"Let me take a photo of you," she told him.

He smiled, knowing he would be crammed well over to the left-hand side of the photograph while the camera's focus would be on Alexei.

"I need to speak to Jorge," Alejandra said after the picture had been saved. She left the restaurant for a few minutes, made her call, and returned to the table where their food had just been served. She took a small notepad from her Tod's handbag and wrote a message using her Montblanc pen, which she then folded up and placed by her bread plate. She watched and waited.

CHAPTER TWENTY-SEVEN
Runs And Hides

It was around 7 pm when Toby received a call and verbal report from border control's duty supervisor at Heathrow. "We have a Mr Shaheen Soroush and a Ms Lee Lai Xian," he explained. "Their tickets to Singapore with a 24-hour stopover in Abu Dhabi are all in order. They're booked business class with Etihad; the only unusual factor is that they were walk-ups for the purchase."

Both men knew this was the most expensive way to buy a plane ticket and was therefore only employed by someone who hadn't expected to travel.

"What about baggage?" Toby asked.

"They've got normal holiday stuff except for one large bag over ninety litres in capacity; with three pillows and their toilet bags. I asked them why they had them, and they tell me that kind of bag or quality of pillow is hard to get in Singapore. What do you want me to do?"

Toby knew he had no grounds to hold Shaheen, and – shit – he only had Oleana's word her friend was missing. He looked at Tari-sai who was listening to the speakerphone. She whispered, "Let them go and then call the Emiratis."

Nothing had been reported officially. "Let them go," he told the supervisor, his voice a tune of disappointment.

He quickly called Omar. "We did the stop on Soroush," he told the Emirati. "They're transiting through Abu Dhabi with

Etihad and taking a stopover. Is there any way you can keep tabs on them and maybe delay them a while if need be?"

"Consider it done," Omar said. "This guy has to screw up sooner or later."

"It seems the Russians are probably having some sort of turf war here; the cartel leader's in town and it seems all his key staff are disappearing or dying. We're not sure why yet but your Oleana is right in the middle of it all, so we should get more – thank you for that asset!" He paused. "It might be better if you head back to the UAE pronto to keep an eye on Soroush. If anything pops here, you know it's going to have some sort of knock-on effect with him."

"We're on our way," Omar said, and the call ended. "Pack up your designer clothes," he said smiling and looking over at Sergeant Seyadin. "We're heading home." He would never know the real reason for her expression of disappointment.

Around the same time as Toby and Omar were speaking, Panos the Greek carried a small backpack into San Gennaro. "I'm for table one," he informed the waiter.

The waiter helped with one of the cases and showed him to the table at the back of the restaurant, where Mr G was already sitting.

"Sit down, my friend." Mr G was welcoming. "Have some red wine."

And before the Greek could refuse, the glass was filled. "Is all the kit in the bags? All files copied onto a hard disk?"

"Yes, sir," Panos said.

"And where are the wiped computers?" asked the boss.

"All still in the Chessington unit, Mr G. All the data is wiped and transferred, but it'll just take a couple of days to ensure they're completely clean with new passwords. By the way," the Greek said, trying to change the subject, "the information you gave was correct on the keyboard pattern passwords."

Mr G didn't really know what he meant by this but smiled appreciatively. "That's great, good job. I wish you hadn't been quite so efficient but I'll have the money to you by this time next week. One of our guys will bring you the cash. Now eat with me."

"Well, I have to meet someone." Panos stuttered as he spoke.

"My friend," Mr G beamed. "I'm Italian, you are Greek. We're neighbours with traditions. You know you can't come into my favourite restaurant and not eat with me."

The Greek knew he was right; the call to Alejandra would just have to wait.

"Have you tried the fungi pizza here?" the Italian asked. "It's the best in London by far."

When Panos said he hadn't, Mr G made a big fuss and told the waiter he wanted the best fungi pizza for his friend, while he would have his usual.

The two men proceeded to share two bottles of red wine while Panos savoured what was probably the best individual pizza he'd ever tasted. By the time he'd finished, he had to refuse Mr G's offer of an ice cream dessert.

The two men shook hands and Mr G thanked Panos for his good work. "We like having you on the payroll, my friend. We'll bring you another job very soon."

Panos left the restaurant and the chef appeared. "Everything okay, boss?" he asked.

"Perfect," Mr G told him. "That Greek's just about to learn you never fuck with anyone whose name ends in a vowel."

Alejandra received two calls that evening. One from Mr G saying the data was ready for collection, and a second from Panos saying he would meet her in an hour to hand over the computers, and that she should bring the cash.

Ivanna knew Alexei would want sex that evening, so she slipped into a Victoria's Secret nightie that would do the trick, and went to retrieve her Chanel perfume from her Prada handbag.

As she took the bottle from the bag she noticed a small, neatly folded note. She didn't recognise it or recall having put it there, so she unfolded it quickly and curiously.

"Oh Jesus," she said as she read it. "Alexei, Alexei!"

He came into the room, and was about to comment on the nightie, when he saw the expression on Ivanna's face. Her arm was outstretched, offering him a piece of paper. He took it from her and read it aloud.

Delimkovs,

You think you can steal from us and we do nothing? Your IT man, your thief, is dead, but before he died he told us everything. You owe us money and now bad things will happen until we are repaid with interest.

Sinaloa.

"Sinaloa?" Ivanna asked.

"It's the fucking Mexicans," Alexei sighed. "Did you steal from the fucking Mexicans, baby?"

"Not that I know of!" she told him earnestly. "But maybe Mac and Isaak did, and somehow they found out. We knew his system would eventually be compromised, but he had built-in measures to detect detection. It was our plan to shut it down in two months just to avoid this kind of thing."

"Two months too late for Mac, it seems. The Mexicans don't fuck about. Where did the note come from?"

Ivanna thought for a moment, trying to retrace her steps that day; she'd only been out of the house once. "When we were in the Botanist today for lunch, I went to the toilet…" She paused in thought again. "While I was in there, a glamourous woman came in; when I said hello, she said '*Hola*'. I thought she was Spanish or Italian, but she could easily have been Mexican. She'd have had time to slip the note into my bag when I wasn't looking. Did you notice her in the restaurant?"

"Not really," he lied. "Was she with a grey-haired, heavily tanned guy? But he wasn't Mexican, was he?"

"Well, now I think *she* was." Ivanna hadn't noticed Mr G to a point of recalling what he looked like.

"Perhaps Isaak dead and Maria missing is part of their revenge too," Alexei said gravely, looking at the note again. "It says bad things will happen until we repay them. So they're sending a characteristic message but they'll have to make contact again to get their money." He thought for a moment. "Call Oleana."

Shaheen and Lai Xian were sitting in business class aboard Etihad, each sipping a glass of Jacquart Brut Mosaïque champagne they figured they'd more than earned. It had been a hell of a twenty-four hours.

Lai Xian had to explain to Shaheen how, far from practising yoga and Pilates at the gym, she actually held a sixth-degree black belt in mixed martial arts, something that had come in very useful with over-zealous clients during her days as an escort. Consequently, she knew how the body's chemistry changed during and after death; it was all part of her training in understanding an enemy's weaknesses.

The disposal of the body, however, was solely down to her genius, and her realisation that the key to a successful crime was more dependent on the escape route than the crime itself.

She had bought two identical bags but only one was ever seen in public or by any surveillance camera. The rental car was the mode of transport to move the body, the 90-litre bag its concealment. The box-cutter knife was to ensure the bag didn't retain air and float, and the socket toolset was extra weighting to buy time. The three pillows were used to fill out the second of the two bags so that, if surveilled leaving the hotel with the large bag, they would arrive and depart the airport with seemingly the same bag.

They had found nothing of consequence in Maria's pockets except for a hotel key, which Shaheen assumed belonged to Oleana. They'd thought about putting Maria's body back in Oleana's room but decided this could end up losing them control of the situation before they left the country.

Following their purchase in cash from the home store, they'd driven along the M4, past Heathrow, and ended up taking Junction 11. Here they double-backed and routed along the A327, only to discover the bridge over the River Loddon. They parked the car just by the bridge, and to any onlooker it would have appeared that this couple were simply admiring the beauty of the river.

Shaheen re-positioned the car heading north between a small red-brick wall forming the end stop of the bridge's railings and some sort of electrical service box. When the road was clear they hauled the 'body bag' out of the car, and in less than two seconds it was out of sight to any passing vehicle. Shaheen then pushed the bag down the steep bank, watching as it slid into the water, which was just deep enough to submerge it, the sedate river current just strong enough to help it come to rest on the riverbed directly underneath the bridge. With luck, it would be days or weeks before the body was discovered.

Satisfied that Maria's body had been successfully disposed of, Shaheen and Lai Xian had then headed for Heathrow and bought a layover ticket to Abu Dhabi and onward to Singapore.

On the down-side, Shaheen hadn't recovered his money, but on the up-side, he was alive, and the love of his life wasn't facing a murder charge or trying to claim self-defence in a foreign land. He'd also learned he now had what was probably the best bodyguard he could ever hope for – and one he got to penetrate on a pretty regular basis.

In the safety of the plane cabin, Lai Xian expressed the concerns she had as they'd been pulled out by the officers in the airport. Shaheen chuckled and looked at her sweetly. "Do you know the worst thing about British law, baby?" he asked, holding her hand reassuringly.

She shook her head.

"It's just. They have this thing called *habeas corpus*. They can't lock you up or detain you without just cause." He sipped his champagne and smiled. "And trafficking three pillows is not just cause."

"I'll drink to that," she told him.

They both laughed, and Shaheen knew Lai Xian was now something way beyond a mere lover; she was a soulmate – and an accomplice.

The Etihad Airbus 380 levelled off at its cruising altitude. Both of them were looking forward to their stay in the Rosewood Hotel in Abu Dhabi, content in the knowledge they had got away to survive another day, together.

Toby's wife sighed as her husband's phone went off. She'd long learned from experience that, if a call came after 10 pm or before 8 am, it seldom represented good news. She watched Toby's expression change as he answered it; it was a woman's voice.

The call lasted about three minutes, concluding with his saying, "Good job, Oleana. Call me if you have anything else." Toby looked at her as he put the phone down. "Sorry, Carla. I have to go into the office." He then called Tarisai to give her some instructions and told her to meet him in Vauxhall in an hour.

It was closer to ninety minutes later when Toby, the Russian and Central America desk officers, and Tarisai were all seated in his office around his small meeting table. The head of stations for MI6 in Abu Dhabi and Moscow were patched in over a secure video link.

"We have a situation unfolding rapidly in London, and I have a reliable source feeding me information as it happens," he reported. "It seems so far that we have Alexei Delimkov arriving in London, and already three of his key people are missing or dead. The Iranian, Soroush, whose file's in front of you, met with one of Delimkov's staff before she went missing. No one knows where she is. Soroush is now inbound to Abu Dhabi as we speak and the Emiratis have been alerted by me. We have one of Dubai's finest detectives in pursuit. Today, while dining in a restaurant, the Delimkovs were surreptitiously delivered a note, apparently from the Sinaloa cartel demanding money and claiming to have killed the Delimkov's chief information officer. Meanwhile Moscow station reports that Delimkov paid off the Russian leadership for his own release, but promptly stole the money back and fled to the UK." He paused, ignoring the note Tarisai had written for him stating it was too early for conclusions. "My conclusion is that the Russian leadership are proceeding with a takedown of the Delimkov cartel, and they've very probably teamed up with the Sinaloa cartel, who are doubtless being paid to do their dirty work in London and elsewhere."

"Have the police been informed?" The question came from the Central American desk officer.

"Not yet," Toby told him. "This stuff is hot off the press and the source is exclusive to us. If we pass on the information, we'll have to blow the source, and it's way too early for us to do that."

The men and women around the table nodded. It made sense.

"Team." Toby took control of the conference-call again, this time reading the bullet points on Tarisai's notepad by his right arm. "I need Moscow to pull in all sources linked to Delimkov and find out the Russian government's intent. Also, can we cut a deal with them to send Alexei and his missus back to them? Let's spool up the head of station in Mexico and get him to inform the DEA that the Russian government has just joined forces with the Sinaloa cartel. Abu Dhabi?" He paused, waiting for an acknowledgment. "Notify the CID that Soroush is coming into town, and that Warrant Officer Omar Shamoon, who knows the case, is inbound from London. Let's see if we can get Soroush to extend his stay without letting him suspect we're onto him. The UAE case officer should try to take control until Shamoon's in place; in the meantime get a team checked into the Rosewood Hotel and let's keep tabs on anyone Soroush meets." The call ended and Tarisai turned off the recorder. Toby leaned back in his chair and said out loud, "Russia linking to Mexico, the clever bastards. Move in next door while a new president's getting his or her bearings, then collaborate, castrate, populate, infiltrate and obliterate."

Tarisai looked at him and quietly muttered, "It is inconclusive, sir, there could be several other scenarios."

"It's obvious," Toby told her. "Russia's fighting a proxy war with the US. It's sourced that they're hacking just about every US system that matters in order to get the American president they prefer. What better way to take it to the next level than to use the criminal element of their next-door neighbour to wreak havoc? I'm guessing the Russians are testing the Mexicans in London, because, if they can do their dirty work here, they can sure as hell do it in the US, where there are fucking thousands of their cousins on the Sinaloa payroll."

Tarisai wanted to shake some sense into him, but she could see the officers around the table were impressed. She couldn't help but wonder how his rise had been so meteoric?

As the officers exited Toby's office, the Central American desk officer walked alongside his Russia desk equivalent. "Is he fucking serious – Russia climbing into bed with the Sinaloa cartel?" he asked.

They stopped at the lift and Russia checked around to make sure no one was in earshot. "They've stalled Ukraine's entry into the EU, they've taken Crimea, they've ensured their bases and access in Syria. The only potential loss they have in terms of territorial influence is Cuba, and if they get a very different US president into power and woo him, then that won't matter. I wouldn't put it past them to use the cartels in Mexico to exert huge diversionary pressure on a new US administration. Sotheby's been right about bizarre shit like this before."

"I suppose your right," answered Central America. "He does seem to have a nose for these things."

The following morning a dark blue Maserati Quattroporte pulled up outside 8 Westbourne Gardens in Bayswater. Mr G got out of his car and dialled the number of the woman he was in lust with. "I'm outside," he told her. "Did he sell you the kit?"

"He did, I'll be right down," the woman replied in her sensual Mexican accent.

Within a few minutes, Mr G and Alejandra were in her second-floor apartment viewing the computers.

"The duplicitous bastard," Mr G said as he stared at the equipment.

"I was under orders to get the actual computers, G; as soon as I realised what was going on with your Greek, I had to take control." She pulled his chin towards hers and kissed him. "I hope you understand."

He shrugged his shoulders. "Hey, you did what you needed to do, so it is what it is. I'd have done the same thing." He smile and placed his hands on her waist.

She kissed him again and offered him coffee and chilaquiles with scrambled eggs; he couldn't refuse.

They sat at her living-room table and enjoyed the simmering salsa and tortilla pieces together. Him because he loved a woman who loved to feed men; her because the rich flavours would mask what she was about to drink.

"What are you going to do with these?" he asked, indicating towards the suitcases.

"They are connecting me to a man," she told him. "Another IT geek, I suppose."

"Did the Greek give you any other information?" he asked.

"No," she told him. "He wanted to come around here and configure them last night but I told him I was having my period, so he'd have to wait a few days."

"He'll never come round here." Mr G spoke with his mouth full.

"I know he won't, but why do *you* say that?"

Mr G looked at his watch. "Because by now he's probably doubled up from vomiting and diarrhoea."

"How come?" she asked with a raised eyebrow.

"Oh, I don't know." Mr G was expressionless. "I heard he was ill."

"Good," she said. "The guy's a Judas. I'm just glad the money I gave him was counterfeit."

"Well, he's got something else in common with that disciple." He took another bite. "He was also at the last supper."

Alejandra said nothing; she'd learned long ago when to stop talking.

"This breakfast is good," Mr G told her. "I'd like to do this a lot more often."

She smiled and brought a fork laden with eggs up to her succulent lips. "This – or something else?" And she popped the eggs into her mouth playfully.

He laughed with delight. "I'll give you a fifty-fifty bet!"

She placed her knife and fork down alongside each other on her plate. "Good," she said. "I love morning sex."

She did not have to repeat herself, and by the time the Maserati's twin-turbo V8 had sprung back into action, Alejandra had become four times a lady.

Eighteen miles away in Chessington, Panos the Greek had called in sick to the Ace-1 computer shop while sitting on his toilet that by now was splattered in fluid excrement and dried vomit. He honestly didn't know anymore whether to sit on the toilet or kneel alongside it, because every time his stomach heaved to empty up contents that were no longer there, he followed through and shat fluid into his boxer shorts and down his legs.

What he didn't know yet was that, within twenty-four hours, he'd begin what would appear to be a recovery period, and the current symptoms would ease to the point where he would again think about procuring the substitute computers with which he could fool Mr G. By then he'd have also been paid by the Italian and be able to take the Mexican beauty on the hottest of dates. This delusion at least compensated for some of his discomfort.

What Panos didn't know was that the apparent recovery was a false horizon precisely delivered by what was about to kill him. In just forty-eight hours, he would enter his terminal phase and be taken into hospital to die four days later of severe liver and kidney failure. The NIIS hospital would put the cause of death down to his lifestyle of overindulgence in drink, cigarettes, and in particular the ample traces of legal highs in his bloodstream. A subsequent search of his apartment would discover nearly £20,000 in counterfeit notes, and he would be judged in death as just another drug dealer who'd overcooked his own habit.

In reality, the *Amanita phalloides* – or Death Cap as it was more commonly known – had been the main fungal ingredients of his pizza with Mr G. From the moment he'd taken a bite, he was a dead man walking; had he spent just a little more time outdoors instead of inside writing software codes, gaming and watching porn, he might have recognised the 'mushrooms' on his pizza had white gills instead of brown.

Here was just another man to die over a lack of interest in the world around him, combined with an insatiable desire for a pussy all too willing to sacrifice him for just about anything else.

CHAPTER TWENTY-EIGHT
Botanist Bunching

Harry turned to Sid. "He's fucking dead, mate."

"Who?" asked Sid.

"Mac! Apparently killed by the Mexicans; some chick covertly left a note in Ivanna's handbag while she was having lunch with her husband in the Botanist in Sloane Square. That was Oleana on the phone. She says we have to find the Mexican."

Sid looked up from his beer. "Are we still on our daily retainer?"

"We are," Harry replied. "And I'm supposing the Botanist is our only start point."

Sid looked at his watch. "It's not closing time for another couple of hours, let's go." Both men swigged their beers empty and walked out of the Sydney Arms, where Sid had been reviewing his racing bets. They would be at the Botanist within ten minutes, putting their plan into play.

Once in the restaurant's bar, Sid quickly scoped out the clientele and spotted what looked like a local leaning against the bar. Harry attracted the barman's attention to order a couple of Peronis.

"I love Chelsea," Sid said, striking up a conversation with the local. "Just wish I could afford to live here."

The local smiled at him sympathetically. "It does suck if you can't."

Sid explained how he'd been in the bar the other night, when he'd got talking to a gorgeous Mexican woman; unfortunately, she'd been with another man that evening, but she'd said that they weren't an item, and that she came to the Botanist a lot; she'd love to bump into him again. "And that's why I'm back," concluded Sid. "Have you ever seen that kind of woman in here?" he asked.

"Fucking hundreds," the local replied. "This place is a pussy-magnet." He turned round and called in a loud voice, "Hey, Giovanni!"

The waiter came over and listened politely as the local described the woman and the guy she'd been with. At that moment, Giovanni recognised Harry as the same man who'd paid for Ivanna's lunch. He shook his head and said, "It doesn't ring any bells. We get a lot of people like that in here. Sorry." And he returned to the kitchen, from where he immediately called Mr G and told him there were two guys, one he'd seen previously with the Russian woman in the bar, asking about Mr G's lady-friend.

Meanwhile, back at the bar, Harry called Ivanna. "Come round right now, we're ready for you," he instructed.

Ten minutes later Ivanna and Alexei were at a table in the bar drinking with Harry and Sid. Now they would wait and see if their suspicions about the bar staff were correct. All four ignored Oleana, who'd been briefed to sit at a separate table and watch proceedings as they unfurled. She wished she could hear their conversation, but the ambient noise put it well out of earshot.

It was about forty-five minutes later when Mr G strolled into the bar. Harry recognised him straight away and muttered, "Stand by, stand by, we're on."

Mr G smiled as he walked up to the table. "*Buon giorno,* would you mind if I joined you?"

Sid stood up commandingly. "Well, it would help if we knew who you were." His tone was firm.

"People call me 'G'." The Italian oozed friendliness.

"Okay G," Sid said with a false smile. "I'm S, this is H, and meet I and A." The sarcasm was very deliberate.

"No problem, S," Mr G replied unfazed, "but if you don't mind, I think I'll just call him Harry, this lady Ivanna, and her husband Alexei. Would that be okay?" The sarcasm had just been reciprocated.

"Sit down," Alexei told him, and the Italian obliged by taking the seat Sid had been sitting in. Harry pulled up a stool from the neighbouring table for Sid.

"So you're Sinaloa."

"No, no, no," replied the Italian. "I've never even been there; I'm simply their messenger."

"And the woman?" asked Ivanna.

"She's just my love interest," said Mr G. "A messenger's messenger, let's say."

"Where are my people?" Alexei asked.

"You mean person…" Mr G clarified.

"No, I mean people. You say you killed my IT man, my accountant is dead, and now I have a woman missing." Alexei's blood pressure was clearly rising.

"First of all, I don't kill anyone, Alexei." Mr G was being truthful. "I'm just the messenger here, and I think you're assuming I know more than I do."

"So what do you want?" demanded Alexei, clearly irritated.

Mr G remained calm. "Sinaloa tells me the price is $25 million with interest."

While they were talking, no one but Harry noticed the elegant young black woman enter the bar. She was beautiful, and he couldn't help but think that behind every such woman there was a husband or boyfriend she must be driving nuts. She walked over to a man standing at the bar, and they kissed on each cheek. Harry knew neither of them, though desperately wished he knew one of them. He awoke from his brief reverie to bring his attention back to the matter at hand.

"How do we pay?" Alexei asked.

"I'll get you the coordinates," Mr G told him. "Who should I use as the contact?"

"Use him." Alexei gestured to Harry.

"Of course, Mr Harry, I should have known." Mr G was making them think he knew far more than he really did. "Your card please?"

"I don't have one," Harry lied. "I can write down my number or give you a dropped call if you prefer."

Mr G reached into his pocket to pull out a Montblanc pen, which he handed to Harry, who scribbled his number down on a napkin.

"All the best things come from a plan on a napkin," Mr G said, folding it and putting it in his pocket. He stood up and politely bid the four of them goodbye.

As he left Oleana got up from her table and exited in tow behind him. Sloane Square was crowded, so Mr G didn't notice her as he walked to the bus stop across the other side of the square. He jumped onto the 452 bus and sat upstairs; Oleana sat downstairs awaiting his descent.

Back at the bar, three parallel conversations were in play. At the Delimkov table they were discussing if Mr G had noticed Oleana walk after him, and whether the guy was for real.

At the bar the black woman was on her phone. "Toby, Tarisai. There was a thin, middle-aged Mediterranean-looking guy with Delimkov and his minders, I've got a photo of him; our girl's walked out after him."

And Giovanni was also taking a call. "They're all still at the table. The only person who followed you was a blonde; she was sitting on her own and paid her bill as soon as she bought her drink. Then she just sat toying with it until you left, when she swigged it down, and left directly after you. She's wearing a brown top, blue jeans, with blonde hair tied back, and carrying what looks like a Chanel bag."

Mr G skipped down the bus stairs, having pressed the bell to alight at Battersea Park station. He spied the blonde in the brown top, but purposely ignored her. He'd made just one phone call from the upper deck of the bus.

He crossed the road to his favourite restaurant, but he didn't go in, nor did he acknowledge the two men standing outside chatting with unlit cigarettes.

As Oleana approached the men, one of them looked at her, as men so often did. "Excuse me," he said. "Do you have a light?"

She was about to say no, when the other suddenly said, "Don't say a fucking word. We know who you're following so we can do this the easy way or the hard way."

Oleana was about to turn and run, but it was over in an instant. A black private-hire minivan had already pulled up alongside her and the slide door opened. She was bundled in and thrown on the floor, the two men leaping in after her; one simply sat on her while the other plasti-cuffed her feet and hands. She tried to scream but the man's huge hand was across her mouth, and she quickly realised any struggle at this point would be futile.

Fifty yards down the road the minivan stopped and Mr G got in.

"So what do we have here?" he asked. "No, don't tell me yet; it would only ruin my fun."

In Los Mochis Sheetal was bored. He hadn't had any instructions from Jorge for several days now, and the IP he'd been tracking in the UK had gone dormant. It appeared the geek in England who'd stolen Mr Jorge's money had shut down his system. Perhaps he'd seen he'd been compromised, or perhaps he'd just taken a few days off.

Sheetal's fingers moved so quickly across his keyboard that they were practically a blur. He'd been distracting himself with the pending US election, unable to believe the likes of Wisconsin, Ohio and Pennsylvania not only used direct recording electronic systems (DREs) for their vote-counting, but also had security that was nowhere near as complex as the banks'; hence the D-Wave had already been able to crack the data locks. Sheetal was, however, fully aware the back door could trace him if he tried to access, remembering from his days at MIT how those who fell afoul of the US government seldom saw the light of day again.

He pondered the Russian accounts and decided to see if he could put in a couple of firewalls and a series of remote IPs in order to make it look like he was somewhere else – in case he screwed it up. He decided the Russian network was favourite, and he went to work.

Within an hour he'd backdoored Ohio's DRE and hacked into the binary counting code. He then figured he could add $1/100^{th}$ of a vote on one side to each ballot without it being noticed, and subtract the same amount from the opposing side. But which side should be which?

He paused before deciding to make a race of it, starting by loading in favour of the underdog. Within six hours he'd managed to backdoor the other two states, for which he varied the plus and minus between $1/100^{th}$ or $1/200^{th}$. The addition and subtraction to each vote would hardly be discernible, and if there was any suspicion later on, he calculated that he was perfectly safe, and that this slight adjustment couldn't possibly make a difference.

He sat back and smiled, satisfied with himself; with this computer he could rule the world.

His little utopia was broken when his phone rang; it was Jorge, asking Sheetal if he could set him up with a data transfer from the UK. Sheetal told him it would be a piece of cake.

The ambiance of the Rosewood Hotel on Al Maryah Island in Abu Dhabi was idyllic by any measure, and Lai Xian in particular was enjoying the full range of designer brands the adjoining Galleria Mall had to offer. The girl's body they'd crammed into a Kipling bag, now rotting in a Berkshire river, seemed a world away – as well it was.

Shaheen was lounging by the pool soaking up the autumn sun, when suddenly he heard a polite Australian accent say his name. He squinted as he looked up to see who was talking to him.

"Mr Soroush, I'm sorry to disturb you; I'm the manager of this hotel, my name is Matthew Wager."

Soroush sat up and said, "Everything is fine, thank you", assuming the manager was simply doing his rounds.

"Well that's fine, sir, but I have some rather good news for you." The manager exuded charm. "You and your wife are the 10,000th guests we've had stay at our hotel, and we'd like offer you a special prize of three complimentary nights in our Royal Suite. Sadly, this is only a here-and-now offer. Would it be possible for you to extend your stay?"

Half an hour later Shaheen and Lai Xian were viewing the hotel's Royal Suite complete with its own dining room, ample lounge, gym, expansive bedrooms, and impressive views of Abu Dhabi Global Market. "Please let's stay," was all Lai Xian had to say to persuade Shaheen to postpone their flight to Singapore by three days.

The manager told the couple he would have all their luggage transferred over. He then went downstairs and spoke to the Emirati who'd given him his instructions. "They're staying, officer," he said. "Three days."

"Good," said Omar Shamoon. "Here's my Amex, charge it to that."

Omar walked to the back of the hotel to view the blue waters, and called London. "Toby, I have them stalled for three days. I'm coordinating with Abu Dhabi Police to have someone on them at all times, so your boys can lift off. Do you think you can get a result at that end in time to find out what he was up to?"

"I'm not sure," Toby told him. "Things are going crazy over here. Your girl Oleana is giving us some good stuff, and it looks like the Mexicans have made contact with the Russians, so some sort of negotiation is in play. Quite where the Iranians fit in isn't clear, but they must be right in the middle somewhere, that's for sure. The fact the Mexicans are involved in London means one thing – drugs. So I'm not sure where they're moving them, but the Russians must be the buyers. Our girl just reported their head-sheds meeting in Chelsea, and two of our people confirmed the meet. Oleana was last seen following one of the Mexican cartel, but now she's not answering her phone, so I'm waiting for her to report back. I've got our Russian desk trying to find out what's going on at that end." He was about to hang up when Omar stopped him, and he immediately grabbed a piece of paper and wrote down a series of letters and numbers. The call ended.

Toby looked at what he'd just written down. "Bingo," he said to himself. He pressed in some numbers on his desk phone. "It's Sotheby; I need a tech guy up here right now!"

It was not widely known that one of the positions in most US embassies was staffed by the Drug Enforcement Agency, and Moscow was no exception. With resources and intelligence on the Mexican cartels way beyond anything the British possessed, the MI6 deputy head of station had met with his American DEA counterpart to explain there was something going down between the Delimkovs and the Sinaloa cartel, and it all seemed to be happening in London.

"Are you fucking serious?" asked the DEA agent. "Sinaloa are in London? Why the fuck would they sell there to a bunch of Russians?"

"We don't know where they're selling, all we know is that the cartel's gone out of its way to meet with the Delimkovs. So we wondered if any of your sources there would know what the hell's going on."

"Leave it with me," replied the DEA agent. "I'll do some digging."

About an hour later the agent was sitting in the Red Café on Sadovaya-Kudrinskaya. His source came in and sat down at his table, and DEA spoke to him in fluent Russian about his family and the weather, before getting down to business. "I hear the Sinaloa cartel are trying to do a deal with the Delimkovs. Do you know anything about that?"

"I don't," the source told him. "The last thing I heard is, having only just paid off the big boss to jump jail, Delimkov's now gone and really pissed him off. Maybe he's planning to flood the streets with Mexican product, but that would be a crazy way to go."

"Can you put the word out on the street to see what you get back?"

"Maybe."

"*Bud'te dobry, schet.*" said the agent, asking for the bill.

When the waitress brought the wallet with the bill in it, the agent placed 7,000 roubles into it and pushed it towards the source. "6,000 for you, 1,000 for the waitress – will that do it?"

"Konechno," replied the source, scooping up all but one of the notes, then getting up to leave without the courtesy of a goodbye.

It was no more than two hours later when a trusted Solntsevskaya Bratva cartel minder walked into his boss's penthouse living room. "Mikhail. We've just received word on the street that the Delimkov cartel's in London, apparently trying to cut a deal with the Sinaloa cartel!"

"The fucking shits!" Mikhail put down his coffee and indicated to his daughter to leave the room. "That bitch came on my boat and guaranteed they would stay out of the drugs game until we met again. Now her old man's bought his way out of prison, and she's obviously feeling emboldened again; they're going to try and ambush the market. They're in London, you say?"

"Yes, boss," the Minder replied.

"Okay," Mikhail sighed. "Let's send them a message. Torpedo the bitch."

CHAPTER TWENTY-NINE
Handy Handbag

The black minivan stopped outside the unit in Davis Road Industrial Park in Chessington. One of the men got out of the vehicle and opened the sliding door for the van to pull up inside.

Oleana was dragged unceremoniously out of the cab; one man held her while the other put a scaffolding pipe between her plasti-cuffed hands. Each then grabbed one end of the pipe and lifted it up onto two stands, forcing Oleana to stand with her arms above her head. She watched on as Mr G rifled through her handbag, from which he pulled her blue passport. She was panicking now, because these guys were making no attempt to hide their faces, which could only mean one conclusion.

"A Saint Kitts and Nevis passport but born in Saint Petersburg, Miss Katayeva. Or is it Mrs Katayeva?" Mr G's sarcastic tone was all too apparent. "Have you ever even been there, or did some sugar-fucking-daddy buy this for you?"

Oleana was trying not to succumb to her emotions, knowing all too well she was in a world of shit. "It's Miss," she told him. "I've never been there, and I don't have a sugar-daddy. What the fuck is all this about? Why have you kidnapped me?"

"Bambina..." Mr G put on his kindest tone. "I was in the Botanist; you were in the Botanist. I got on the bus; you got on the bus. I got off the bus...and I think you know the rest of the story.

Except for maybe one fucking thing." His tone changed completely. "You're a fucking Russian and I was meeting the Russians, so don't fuck with me, I know the Delimkovs were trying to track me back to my home. Do you really think I'm that fucking stupid?"

He walked to the freezer and pulled out a frozen chicken, into which he inserted his fingers, only to pull out what looked like a slither of white meat. "Did you know Mr Hoskins?" he asked.

"Never heard of him." She lied.

"Well, he was also an employee of your organisation, and this…" He held the slither up to her face, pulled down her bottom lip, and brushed it up against her moist inner lip. "This is his ear – and it's all that's left of him. So if you think you're not going to tell me everything, then you might want to think again."

She knew he was right, and was thinking as hard as she could. She had to play for time while she figured out a way to escape. "My hands," she said to him, "I think they've lost circulation. Couldn't you just sit me down and ask questions? I can tell you the shit you need to know without you having to reduce me to a fucking ear."

Mr G looked at the two henchmen and nodded. "Put her on the chair." He looked back to Oleana. "But if you try my patience, then I'm going to leave you with these two for half an hour, and I assure you, lack of circulation to your hands will be the least of your problems."

Her phone rang; Mr G looked at the number. "Who's Toby?"

"He's my boyfriend." Her response was almost instinctive.

"What's your code to this?" He held up her iPhone 7.

"96321."

He tapped in the number and the phone unlocked. "Your boyfriend is keen to speak to you – you have five missed calls." He scrolled through the contacts. "You don't seem to know many people," he said. "But some names in here are familiar to me – and common to the Delimkovs."

"I just got out of jail, that's why I don't have any contacts." Perhaps if the man knew she was a fellow criminal, he'd have second thoughts about harming her. "I'm just a fixer for them, and that's it."

"So what are you fixing in London?" he asked.

"I have no idea because I'm just visiting," she told him. "But you need to know you're messing with the Russians and the Iranians. They've already started killing. So you won't get away with this."

"Miss Katayeva," Mr G explained. "So you're being held against your will – so what? Do you think anyone's going to believe your story when we tell them it was you who murdered Mr Hoskins?" He held up the ear and shook it theatrically.

Oleana's mind was racing; even if they couldn't pin that killing on her, they would surely look into the death of Isaak, with whom she had a known association, and Maria's disappearance too.

"You have no evidence," she told him.

"*Au contraire*." He pulled a chair forward and sat down opposite her. "Your DNA is all over his ear. You brought me here to blackmail us and accuse us of the murder in order to extort money out of us. Your downfall is that I brought my team and we quickly turned the tables." He paused to let this all sink in. "So here's what's going to happen – I'm going to go for a short walk and I may be some time. My friends here are going to persuade you to give us every bit of information on everyone in your contacts list and where they live. When they've finished, they'll call me, and if you're in one piece, then that means you cooperated, and we'll let you go on the basis we can stitch you up at will. If you don't cooperate and it gets messy…well, because we can't exactly have you going to a hospital, can we?" He picked up the chicken and pushed Mac's ear back into the orifice, before getting up and placing it back in the freezer. He looked at one of his thugs. "Call me in an hour, keep her alive."

He walked out of the park and decided to hail an Uber. He was standing some fifty metres from the entrance to the unit when he saw two matt dark grey BMW F800GS motorbikes with riders dressed in matching dark grey jumpsuits leading three plain vans – two white, one blue – into the complex. Each van had two men in the front seats and all were dressed in black. Mr G looked up to the sky and saw a helicopter approaching in the distance. "Holy shit!" he said to himself, and continued to walk away from the complex, praying his Uber would hurry the fuck up.

Oleana had reached 'C' in her contacts list, having given nothing useful to her interrogators, when there was an almighty bang on the small door of the unit. In a moment the room had filled with eight masked and helmeted men with assault weapons pointed, screaming, "Police, get down on the floor! On the floor!"

Neither of the thugs was carrying a gun, so they knew any resistance was futile. Within seconds, they were handcuffed and the police team leader shouted, "Clear!"

One of the female officers cut the plasti-cuffs off Oleana, telling her reassuringly, "You're safe now, we're the Metropolitan Police."

The team paramedic came over and asked if she was hurt; Oleana shook her head. She looked over towards the door as the two thugs were hauled out, and was staggered to see a familiar short man in a tweed jacket and light brown trousers appear in the company of a young black woman, whom Oleana instantly recognised as the woman from the bar in the Botanist.

Toby walked calmly over to the freezer and picked up Oleana's Chanel handbag, before turning towards her with a smile.

"You okay?" he asked.

"You tell me!"

He looked at the paramedic. "Is she okay?"

"Looks like we got here just in time, boss," replied the CTSFO policeman.

"Can you give us a couple of minutes, officers?" As the police team moved away out of earshot, he looked at Oleana and knelt down on one knee in front of her. "You should know, Oleana, that protection of our sources is of paramount importance to us. Although, that said…" He handed her back her bag. "A lady should never go out without her handbag – especially this one."

"Well it is a Chanel." She managed a smile.

"Indeed," he replied. "But this is a very special Chanel thanks to your Emirati friends."

"Say what?" She was genuinely confused.

"Warrant Officer Shamoon and Sergeant Seyadin have in all likelihood just saved your life; before you left prison they put a GPS tracking chip in the lining of your bag. I didn't know this until today, when I called him on another matter and mentioned I was concerned because you'd gone missing after following that Mexican chap; and you can thank that young lady for knowing that." Oleana looked over towards the door to see an elegant African woman smiling at her. Toby continued "And Shamoon very kindly disclosed his little secret to me and…here we are."

"Unbelievable!" Oleana said as she tried to recall every place she'd visited that could have compromised her to the Emirati detectives. Thank God the signal would have been masked in the underground when she'd killed Isaak. She collected herself. "He's a cheeky bastard, that Shamoon, but a clever one too. Is he here?"

"No, Oleana, he's in Abu Dhabi; he had to stay on Soroush." Toby stood up as Tarisai came over.

"So where did the guy you were following actually go?" she asked.

"Well, he went to Battersea," replied Oleana, "but I was rumbled and jumped before I could find out. So I don't know where he was headed; I don't even know if he has anything to do with all this." She was already well aware she couldn't grass him out.

"Boss!" One of the CTSFO sergeants shouted in from the door. "These guys are Italian, not Mexican."

"What the fuck?" Toby looked at Tarisai. "Could this have been a chance abduction?"

"Well, there has been a few incidents in Clapham and Battersea," Tarisai told him.

"You are one lucky girl," Toby told Oleana. "Now let's get you back to wherever you're staying, and all of this can be our little secret."

"Thank you, Toby." She wanted to hug him, but refrained.

"Don't thank me," he replied. "Thank Madame Chanel and the Emiratis."

In the Rosewood Hotel in Abu Dhabi Omar hung up the phone looking pleased. "They got her back," he told Sergeant Seyadin.

"*Hamdulla.*" Maryam was clearly very pleased, but only she knew the real reason.

"But is wasn't the Mexicans," Omar said. "It was the Italians."

"The Italians?" she queried. "How did they get involved?"

"Not sure, but Mr Sotheby thinks it could be just a criminal coincidence."

"And what do you think?" she asked knowingly.

"I think there's no such thing as a criminal coincidence," he replied, half-laughing, but perfectly serious.

The following day Ivanna surprised Alexei when she told him she wanted to go to Harvey Nichols to get a manicure.

"Are you crazy?" he asked. "I don't want you going anywhere until we've got the Mexican thing under control. I'm going to make the calls this morning to let the Mexicans know we're having to contact our banks directly because our accountant is dead. But I need a dollar number from this G guy, and I need to find out what the fuck is going on with the $20 million in Russia."

"Harry can look after me," Ivanna suggested. "My nails are a mess; I *have* to get them done." She looked in the mirror and put her fingers through her hair, adding, "I also need to get my roots done. I'd rather be Mexican than have grey roots and shit nails!"

"No," was Alexei's sharp retort. "I don't want you spending all this time with Harry."

"Why not? He's harmless enough." She paused. "To me anyway."

"I hate how he's got to see more of you in the past three years than I have, I can't help it." Alexei was apologising for his jealousy.

"Darling, everyone has seen more of me than you in the last three years." She walked over, put her arms around him, and kissed him tenderly. "You don't have to worry about the likes of Harry. And let's get real; we haven't refused to pay the Mexicans, so why would they do anything to us just yet? They need us alive to pay them."

Alexei looked towards the window and sighed. "When I found out I was getting out of prison, I was so happy, but ever since I got out, everything's gone wrong. Somebody planned all of this."

Ivanna put her fingers to his chin and gently brought his eyes down to her level. "Everything will be okay, Alexei. We'll pay the Mexicans and anything we owe in Russia. There's a laptop upstairs. Mac gave it to Isaak and called it an 'air-gap' computer. It's never been connected to the internet. Isaak used to update it at least once a month with all the account details and balances. Once we know what we owe, I'll contact the banks and we'll pay out. Baby, we have more money that we can ever use!" She kissed him again. "I'm so pleased to have you back…" She started to grin. "But you'll sure as hell leave me if I don't fix these raggedy nails and old lady roots."

Alexei felt reassured. In fact, for the first time since he'd arrived in London, it felt just like old times with Ivanna.

"Did you hear from Oleana?" she asked.

"Oh yes, I forgot to tell you, she texted me this morning. The guy went to a place called Battersea, but she lost him in a tower complex. She walked back to her hotel, but she's woken up not feeling well – woman stuff and all of that."

"Damn, I was going to ask her to come with me. I wish we knew where the hell Maria was. If only we could call the police." Now it was Ivanna's turn to feel depressed.

"She'll turn up," he reassured her. "If there's one person in the world who can look after herself, its Maria; you know that."

"That's true, but I wish she would hurry up. Either she's gone to sort out her own mission, or something's terribly wrong; I'm worried." She broke away from Alexei and went to rummage through her handbag on the kitchen table.

Alexi poured himself some coffee. "Worrying is like a rocking horse Ivanna; it keeps you occupied but it doesn't get you any- where."

Ivanna knew he was right. "Warrior not worrier, right?" She smiled as she pulled a napkin out of her handbag and reached for her phone and dial a number. "Nazrin, it's Ivanna – we met in the Ivy … I'm thinking about having a bit of a 'me' day today, you know, hair, nails and stuff, and wondered whether you could join me? … Excellent, well that's perfect. You get the little man to his day-care, then call me when you get to Sloane Square."

Alexei sipped his coffee watchfully as she proceeded to make bookings with Nails Inc. in Harvey Nichols and the Skye Norman Hair & Beauty salon.

"Well, I didn't get Harry, but I got the next best thing," she said as she put down the phone.

He gave her an inquisitive look.

"His wife." She was almost boasting, knowing this would actually allay her husband's feelings of jealousy.

"Where's the laptop?" he asked, changing the subject.

"In the bedside stand," she told him. "The password is '*fox-1pheasant*', something to do with Mac's love of hunting."

It was about an hour later, just after Ivanna had left to meet Harry's wife, that Alexei went to explore the laptop in their bedroom. Ivanna had been right; they did have plenty of money spread around in four different countries. She'd made a fortune for him in his absence. He couldn't help but conclude that it must have been the €20 million withdrawn from the Russian account that had caused Isaak to throw himself under the train. Perhaps he'd realised he'd put both the Russian government and the Mexicans onto his boss's trail in one act of stupidity.

As he pulled the drawer open to put the laptop back, the momentum caused whatever was at the back to slide forward and into view. He stared down for a moment dumbfounded, before calmly placing the laptop on the bed. He then picked up one of the flat, square foil packs in front of him, purple in colour with the '*Durex*' logo emblazoned on it. The small print under the logo read: '*1 natural rubber latex condom*', which was then repeated in three languages.

"Bitch!" Alexei said to himself as he reached into his pocket for his phone. He dialled and the call connected. "Harry, it's Alexei. I need a favour. I'm going out on the town tonight and I'll need some condoms. Is there any chance you could buy some and pop them round to the house? … A box of eight or twelve will be fine; please bring them over as soon as you can." The call ended and Alexei replaced the condom with the other three already in the drawer, covering them back up once more with the laptop. He then walked downstairs and poured himself a morning vodka.

CHAPTER THIRTY
Nailing It

Alejandra had been busy in her Bayswater flat. Since receiving her instructions from Jorge and linking up over Skype with Sheetal, she'd learned how to infiltrate Mac's super-computers for him to remotely mine the data each one held.

Sheetal really had enjoyed their conversations and gotten a kick out of Alejandra struggling to keep up with his instructions. Initially she'd used her mobile phone to accomplish the hook-up, and this was when he first got a glimpse of her as she pointed the camera at the connections, before turning it back towards herself. He simply had no idea Mexican women could be so beautiful, as he certainly hadn't seen anything like her since he'd been in Los Mochis.

The only details Jorge had given either of them were that she was in the UK and he was in Mexico. Her task was to do what needed to be done to access the computers; his to extract whatever information was on them.

It was now early afternoon, and the six-hour time difference meant Sheetal had had to bother his minders earlier than usual that day to drive him to the warehouse. They had done so, uncom-plainingly, but in silence.

Within two hours, having previously told Alejandra to buy the fastest internet package available – which happened to be from Virgin Media at 51.4 megabytes per second – and use a cable rather that Wi-Fi, the job was done. Alejandra watched as Sheetal picked up his mobile and called Jorge. When he put the phone down, he said, "Mr Jorge is coming over, he wants to see what we've got. So I'm just separating the obvious files onto my screens."

"Are you enjoying Mexico?" she asked after they'd talked about India briefly. She was asking the question out of genuine politeness, because she could sense from Sheetal's eagerness to talk and his reluctance to end their calls that this guy was lonely.

"Well, I haven't really seen much of it," he told her. "I stay in a villa; it's very nice and two guys drive me here and then they wait outside until I'm done. I suppose there are more exciting places to be than Los Mochis."

"Sheetal!" she interrupted him. "You shouldn't tell me where you are. If anything goes wrong in this business, they always gather up anyone who would have known the information first, then figure out the why and the who by attrition. So you didn't tell me that information and I didn't hear it. ¿Entiendes?"

"I'm sorry," he told her, "it just slipped out." He seemed genuinely contrite. "I'm pretty lonely here and quite bored lately, so you and this transfer are the only distractions keeping me from thinking about home." He was about to continue when he felt the air-pressure change in the warehouse. "Wait a minute, someone's here." He minimised her screen so she was no longer visible, but still on camera, as she watched him take off his headphones, get up and walk out of shot.

He returned a moment later with two men, but she could only see them from hips to chest. She waited to see what would happen but could only hear muffled voices. The men came closer to the camera, but she still couldn't see their faces. One of them leaned forward, presumably to point at one of the screens, and finally she heard the voice say, "And what does this mean?"

She saw the man's round, moustachioed face come into view, and she almost shit herself. Immediately she hit the end-call button.

"Ay Dios!" Archivaldo was in Los Mochis, was he fucking crazy? The stupid arse was going to get himself caught again, and it would be the people of Los Mochis who would pay in blood, first to the government for having harboured him, and then to the cartel for betraying him. Alejandra sat back in her chair and literally prayed he hadn't realised she could see him.

She picked up her phone, stared at it for a few seconds, then called her mother. "*Mamá*," she said. "Everything's okay and I can't talk for long, but you need to leave Los Mochis today, just for two or three weeks." Her mother wanted to know why, and when Alejandra refused to tell her, she in turn refused to leave. "Please *mamá*!" Alejandra begged. "There's a bad man there, the whole world is looking for him, and if they catch him in your town, you know there'll be a bloodbath. Please, go to your sister's."

"Archivaldo is here?" her mother asked, not realising her daughter had deliberately avoided his name. "In Los Mochis? He wouldn't come here; it's too obvious!"

Alejandra knew she needed to finish the call quickly. "*Mamá*, I've seen him there on live video, he's there, I swear; now get out, and call me when you're at your sister's. I have to go. I love you." And she ended the call.

Once more she slouched back in her chair, trying to analyse what had happened in the last few minutes. She wondered if that smart Indian boy had a clue what he was playing with. If he got out of there alive, it would be a miracle. She just thanked God she wasn't in the USA and subject to all the NSA eavesdropping Snowden had exposed to the world.

Sadly for her, she hadn't heard of the Investigatory Powers Act 2016, otherwise known as the 'Snooper's Charter', which gave the UK government *carte blanche* to listen to or collect any communication made within its shores. There had been three collation elements in her call to bring it to the attention of a GCHQ analyst: that it was made to Los Mochis, the home of a notorious international cartel; that 'Los Mochis' was a keyword, which would elevate the call's status above simply passing interest; and that the name 'Archivaldo' had been mentioned.

Within an hour the call data had been pulled and the recording reproduced; within another two hours Toby Sotheby had received the information; and within three hours the information was with the DEA representative in the US Embassy on Grosvenor Square.

*   *   *

Mr G was in an unusual situation; he now had two women on his mind – Alejandra because he was infatuated; and Oleana because of the feedback he received regarding the police questioning of his two men.

He was not surprised to hear that neither of the two had implicated him in the 'unlawful confinement' charges being brought against them. He was, however, pleasantly surprised to learn the Russian woman had told the police that only these two men had been involved in her kidnapping, and no one else. Additionally, she was insisting she did not want to testify in court as a witness, saying she believed it was all a big mistake, she wanted to forget about it, and this sort of shit was run-of-the-mill in Moscow. If she continued along this route, both his men would get off with a 'caution'.

He sat in his luxurious Battersea apartment and stared at Oleana's Saint Kitts and Nevis passport. He'd put it in his back pocket after leaving her behind in the industrial unit, but of course hadn't been able to return it as intended once he'd got the answers he wanted. He looked at her photograph; she was a beautiful woman who'd clearly seen better days. He thought about her responses to his questions, her courage, and her acceptance of what might happen to her. If it had gone the wrong way for her, she could have ended up in the same condition as Mac, and she'd known it; if she cooperated and had chosen to work for them, then she would have gained a reprieve. He couldn't be sure how it would have turned out.

He was asking himself how the police could have known she was there. Was there a snitch, or did they have the unit under surveillance? He reasoned that, if it was the latter, it would all be over for him now. They would have to vacate the place, probably for good. He called his quartermaster and told him to move the cover business to a new location, and to close Chessington down.

But now he found himself wanting to give the woman back her passport; he wanted to find out why she hadn't given him away; and he wanted to thank her. He needed to figure out a way to find her. Little did Mr G realise how little she cared about this passport, however; she still had her Russian equivalent, and she would simply report the other lost.

Omar was exploring new depths of boredom hanging around the Rosewood Hotel. It wasn't that there wasn't plenty to do; it was just that Shaheen and Lai Xian were clearly using the Royal Suite to its full potential, and 'christening' every bed, soft chair and couch in the place. They hadn't surfaced in the public rooms of the hotel until mid-afternoon, after which they spent a couple of hours visiting each of the designer boutiques in the Galleria Mall so conveniently attached to the hotel. Now he and Sergeant Seyadin were seated in Bentley's restaurant, watching Shaheen and Lai Xian giggle like young lovers as they sat at the bar.

Lai Xian sipped her Bombay Sapphire and tonic, which had been specially mixed with a slice of grapefruit and slithers of ginger for her, her low-cut dress once again giving an ample display of her oriental back tattoo. Shaheen was drinking a beer.

"You know the problem with Arab dress?" she asked Shaheen.

"No, what's that, my baby?" He wondered what the hell she was going to say.

Her response was innocent. "It makes them all look the same."

Shaheen nearly spat out his beer and started to laugh.

"What?" she asked defensively. "It does!"

"Maybe so, baby, but the joke amongst stupid and untraveled white people is that all Chinese look the same, so coming from you, that statement is a breath of fresh air!" He had a broad smile on as he reached up and touched her shoulder.

"Well," she said, half-indignantly, "I'm just saying, because there's an Arab couple sitting in the restaurant drinking coffee, and I could swear I've seen them before. Don't look round," she quickly added. "It'll be obvious."

"Where do you think you've seen them?" asked Shaheen.

"Well, I haven't been anywhere in this country except the Taj Hotel in Dubai and here, so I guess it's there." She paused and shrugged. "But maybe they really do just all look the same."

Shaheen asked the barman for directions to the toilet and the young man pointed him to the far end of the restaurant. He stepped off his barstool and turned around, and as he did so, he scanned the restaurant and made towards the toilets. He tried not to take any notice of the local couple but simply take a snapshot in his mind. Lai Xian was right – there could be no doubt. This was the same Arab couple who'd sat across the restaurant from them when he'd met Graham Tree in the Taj Hotel; or at least he thought it was.

Over at the table Sergeant Seyadin said, "He just checked us out."

"I know," Omar told her, "but I didn't want to look. Any recognition?"

"Maybe," she said. "He held his glance just a fraction too long; should we leave?"

"Not yet. Let's brass it out."

His sentence was interrupted by his phone ringing. He inserted his ear-piece and Maryam listened in.

"So tell me, Toby. Does she still have the bag or do you? … The Italians? Where do they fit in? … Surely not?" Then the subject changed. "We're eyes-on now, but in danger of getting burned. I don't think they're up to anything here, so if we're to hold them, I need a reason from your end." They said their good-byes and Omar hung up.

"It was definitely the Italians who lifted her, not the Mexicans," Omar told his sergeant. "They made it look like a mistake, but I bet they've got wind of the drug sale or something, and are trying to get in on the action." He stood up abruptly. "Let's end this cat and mouse."

Omar walked over to the bar where Soroush had just returned. He could see the Chinese woman eyeing him as he approached; she mumbled something to Shaheen.

Omar stood back from the bar but in arms-reach of them. "Mr Soroush, Ms Lee. I'm Warrant Officer Omar Shamoon of the Dubai Police. We've been asked by the British to ensure your safety while you're here. Do you know of any direct threat to you in the UAE?"

"Did they ask you to look after us in the Taj as well?" Shaheen said without answering the question.

"Perhaps." Omar was as cool as ever. "If you saw us, then yes, if not, then no."

"So we'll take that as a yes." Shaheen was feeling belligerent.

Lai Xian stepped in to ensure things didn't get any worse between the two sparring males. "I don't think anyone is threatening us, officer, so how can we help you?"

"My detective sergeant here" – he beckoned to Maryam to join them – "and I have been tasked to ensure your safety during your stay. It would help if you would cooperate with us, rather than us having to chase you around, which makes our job more difficult. If you could let us know of any possible danger to you, or why you were just in London, it would be a big help to me."

"And just why should I help you?" Shaheen was indignant, seemingly over what appeared to be an affront to his privacy, but the real reason was the matter of Maria's murder. Had they found the body; had they put two and two together?

"The reason you should help me, Mr Soroush, is because I don't believe you and Miss Lee here possess a marriage certificate, and, that being the case, it seems you're cohabiting as an unmarried couple in the same room. That is illegal in this country, and punishable by one year in prison – for both of you."

"But they let us check in!" Shaheen protested. "They didn't ask us for a marriage certificate. We even won an upgrade."

"That's probably all true, Mr Soroush, because under the law the hotel is not required to implement a married-only policy; that's the job of law enforcement, which, it won't have escaped your attention, we are. You see, Mr Soroush, Ms Lee, my country has many laws; however, most of them we simply get to choose when to implement. Does that make sense?"

"Well, not really," Soroush muttered defeatedly. "But I guess you have us over the proverbial barrel there, so what do you really want from us?"

"I want your side of the story, Mr Soroush, and I'm even willing to buy you and your wife dinner and wine to hear it. Why don't you come and join us so we can all understand what's happened? You do that, you have my word you'll fly out as planned. If not, then I could make you stay, without the dinner and wine, for considerably longer." He looked around him. "And in a significantly less salubrious environment. Shall I ask for a table for four?"

Shaheen looked at Lai Xian and was about to protest again, when she spoke first. "For fuck's sake, Shaheen, take the fucking dinner option and don't be an idiot!"

When the doorbell rang at 9 Eaton Terrace Mews, Alexei opened the door fully expecting it to be Harry with the condoms; so he was surprised to be faced with Oleana.

"Is Ivanna here?" she asked.

"No, she's gone to get her hair and nails done," he told her.

"Nice, I could do with a bit of that myself!" She let out a glimpse of a laugh.

Alexei asked her in and they sat down at the kitchen table, where he poured her a coffee.

She explained how she'd been lifted by two thugs before getting a chance to track down where the tanned man was going. "Luckily," she lied. "It seems someone saw them push me into a van and called the police; the vehicle was stopped within about ten minutes. It was harrowing, to say the least." She went on to tell Alexei there was no doubt these were the men who'd killed Mac – they'd made it quite clear – and if they were somehow tied in with Soroush as some sort of defensive action against Ivanna and himself, then she wouldn't be surprised if Maria had gone the same way.

Alexei thought she was going to cry when she looked him straight in the eye and proclaimed, "I've had enough, Alexei, I want out! I did everything that was ever asked of me and more to protect the cartel, but it's done nothing to protect me in return. I gave up the man I loved because I had to leave Dubai when you were messed up with Soroush; then my lover was killed in a plane crash; I've been attacked by Iranian agents, thrown in an Arab jail and half-starved; I've lost my best friend, seen a man throw himself under a train, and now I've been kidnapped." She took a sip of her coffee. "And on top of all that, the man I truly love is married to another woman here in London. I'll never win him, so I want to go home to Saint Petersburg and live a normal life." She gave a bittersweet smile. "You know, that same man did once teach me something very important: what matters isn't worrying when to get in, but knowing when to get out. And, Alexei, I should have got out a long time ago."

Alexei reached across and took a gentle hold of her arm. "I'm sorry all this happened to you, Oleana. You were one of our best fixers, ever. I think, if I hadn't been in jail, I could have protected you, but I was, so I couldn't."

"I don't blame you, Alexei. All that's happened is of my own making. I used to be lucky, but somewhere and somehow that luck left me. Now I have to ease back until I can find it again. I hope you and Ivanna will understand." For the first time in a long time Oleana was not acting.

"We all need to do what you're doing, Oleana. It's obvious to me we need to scale back operations and morph ourselves into something else before whatever's happening right now takes us all down. You go back to wherever you like and look for your luck. I have a feeling you'll find it."

They were interrupted by the doorbell ringing. "Oh, that'll be Harry," Alexei said casually as he got up.

Oleana looked shocked. "Harry? Here?"

Alexei was already on his way to answer. "Yes, he's bringing me some stuff."

The very next moment Harry was joining them for coffee at the table. Alexei popped upstairs with the Boots pharmacy bag Harry had brought for him. He took the fresh box of condoms out of the bag; it was purple and read 'Durex Elite' across it – perhaps he'd got it wrong. He tore off the plastic cover and pulled two joined condom packs from the box. He opened the drawer of the bedside stand, reached in to the back to retrieve the others, and held the new and the old packs against each other to compare – they were identical.

Alexei knew that, so far as condoms went, men were habitual and had their favourites. These must be Harry's choice, and it was surely no coincidence his wife's security advisor's brand matched those languishing in her night stand.

He went back downstairs to the kitchen, now figuring out how he could draw out and then punish Harry and Ivanna.

"Oleana was just telling me she's leaving London." Harry was as pleasant as ever, completely unaware he had just spun his own web for Alexei.

"I think we'll all be sad to see her go." Alexei was about to call Harry out when his phone rang. He picked it up and answered in

Russian. Oleana and Harry stopped talking. "Artur Kiselev, how are you? … What? … Who? … When? … Jesus Christ!"

"Something's gone wrong, Harry." Oleana was looking intently at Alexei, trying to get more clues from what she was hearing. Harry was now glued, though he couldn't understand what was being said.

"Thank you, Artur, thank you," Alexei continued in Russian as Oleana translated. "I'll repay you for this." Harry assumed this must be something to do with business. Alexei ended the call and looked at them, all the colour had drained from his face.

"That was an old friend I was in jail with; he's in Moscow now. He's very loyal, it seems – the word on the street is that Mikhail, the boss of the Solntsevskaya Bratva cartel, has put out a contract on Ivanna."

"What?" exclaimed Oleana. "What for?"

"Apparently he believes she's muscled in on one of his operations and double-crossed him."

"Does he have the capability?" Harry asked.

By now, all thought of revenge had been driven from Alexei's mind. "You better believe it, Harry. These guys make all of us look like angels. They're into everything from drugs to people-trafficking, no morals, no boundaries. Ivanna must have pissed them off and now they're going to take her out to send a message to everyone."

He was already dialling her number. "Come on, come on," he urged as it rang and rang, before she finally picked up. "Baby! Where are you?"

"We're in the hair salon, we're just having a nice day, my love." She sounded happy.

"Where is it?" he asked.

"It's called Skye Norman, on Old Church Street, down the bottom of Kings Road. We're planning to go to the pub next door afterwards, do you want to come?"

"Baby, do not under any circumstances leave the salon, just stay where you are! Harry and I am coming to get you." Alexei could not have sounded more serious.

"Oh, Jesus Christ, the Mexicans?" she asked.

"No, baby, worse – Solntsevskaya Bratva; there's a contract out on you because they think you've rained on their parade. It's a mistake, but we just need to get you back here until it's all sorted out. Just stay calm; we're on our way." Satisfied she'd understood the severity of the situation, Alexei hung up and reached for his jacket. "Okay, Harry, let's go!"

Harry stood up and walked over to the Xinzhou kitchen knife set adjacent to the cooker. He picked up the wooden holder and offered it to Alexei.

"Pick your weapon of choice," he insisted.

"You actually want me to take a knife to what's probably going to be a gun fight?" asked Alexei incredulously.

"You know what they say in these parts?" Harry said knowingly. "Guns for show, knives for a pro." Pausing a moment, Alexei then pulled a long, broad, thin blade from the holder.

Oleana stood up and said, "I want two."

"Oh no, you're not coming," Harry told her.

"To hell I'm not! If it really is the Solntsevskaya Bratva, then you're going to need all the knives and all the friends with knives you can get – unless of course you have friends with guns?"

"Give her the knives and hand me that meat cleaver," ordered Alexei. "And Harry, I forgot to mention – your wife is with Ivanna."

"What?" Harry and Oleana spoke in unison.

"I don't know, they're having a girls' day out or something," explained Alexei.

Harry was already on his phone to Sid, who was parked out on Eaton Terrace. "Sid, bring the car around! We've got bad fast ball; Ivanna and Nazrin are in deep shit and we need to extract them. I'll brief you on the way in."

Oleana wanted to call Toby to see if he could help again, but knew Alexei would never approve.

The Solntsevskaya Bratva cell in London was one of the brotherhood's most established anywhere in the world. Most of the team lived and worked in the city under some guise or other, and all kept a low profile. They worked exclusively for the cartel and sorted out any business in London that needed their attention.

The surveillance team was normally used to follow rivals or cartel members visiting the city in order to establish on which side they really were. Consisting of just four men who'd been selected for their inconspicuous looks and style, and then trained by former KGB agents who'd served in London during the cold war, these men were as good as any. When operating they would simply call into a secure local conference call facility through a local number and take advantage of uninterrupted communications for the extent of their serial.

Their task was to simply to watch and report. They would never go overt or bring attention to themselves; to do so would mean the end of their operational effectiveness. They all knew that, if they could 'house' the target person, then there were 'honey-monsters' on hand to do whatever dirty work happened to be on the cartel's menu that day. What they didn't know, they couldn't grass, and that was just fine with all of them.

Earlier in the day, when Ivanna had gone to meet Nazrin, she'd thought nothing of the ordinary London black cab parked up with a driver and passenger in the front.

However, closer examination of the taxi would have led her to notice that the orange light on its roof didn't have '*TAXI*' written on it; and its white taxi license plate had been replaced by one reading '*private vehicle*', with a duplicate registration number of the vehicle itself. Of course, only the most astute onlooker would ever notice this, and local cab drivers were all well aware that savvy celebrities and members of the royal family owned such vehicles in order to travel around the city incognito.

As Ivanna walked past the 'taxi', the 'passenger' alighted – he was the 'Foxtrot' or walking element of the team. Aside from the driver, there were two members, one with a moped, the other with an Oxelo New Town 9 folding kick scooter.

Foxtrot sat on the wall outside of the Royal Court Theatre and watched Ivanna as she loitered outside Sloane Square station. Once they'd established she didn't intend to catch a train, the team went into stake-out formation so that, no matter which way Ivanna went, she would always be walking towards them. Additionally, like any normal human being, they knew she wouldn't be looking for somebody following her ahead of her.

Nazrin appeared from the station and the two women walked across the square to the bus stop on Sloane Street.

Scooter had placed his practical conveyance inside his carry-bag and moved to blend in with the grouping at the bus stop. The women were busy chatting and got onto the number 22 bus. Scooter got on the bus after them and sat on the back seat, mumbling in Russian into the microphone and earpiece rig of his mobile.

Meanwhile, Foxtrot got back into the taxi, which was now positioned behind the bus. Moped rode ahead to make sure he was through a traffic light ahead on the bus's route.

As the bus approached the Knightsbridge bus stop, Scooter could see his marks were about to alight. He called it in, and the taxi pulled up short of the bus stop; Foxtrot got out. Scooter remained on the bus. Moped had pulled into Basil Street in case the women were going to Harrods.

As predicted, the ladies got off the bus and walked up towards Basil Street, but then changed course and crossed Sloane Street.

Foxtrot did not follow them across, but continued walking, watching them as they entered Harvey Nichols, chatting casually all the while. Only then did he cross the road and called in to say he was going 'complete' to see if he could hazard a guess as to how long they were going to be.

Meanwhile, 'Taxi' did a U-turn, and reported he had the Saville Street exit covered. Moped called in the same for the Sloane Street exits, and Scooter announced he was off the bus and rolling his way down Knightsbridge from Hyde Park Corner to cover the Knightsbridge exits. With all of them in position, if the ladies did leave the store, the team would be on them.

About five minutes later Foxtrot called in to say they were having their nails done; he estimated it would be a twenty to forty-minute stop if they had nothing else planned. He left the store and returned to the taxi.

Exactly thirty-five minutes later the women emerged back onto Sloane Street and walked to the bus stop, browsing the shop widows as they did. By the time they'd boarded the number 19 bus, Foxtrot was already at the stop, having been dropped off on Harriet Street, where Taxi remained, engine running.

Moped was back in Basil Street on his ride; Scooter already paralleling Sloane Street using the speed of his scooter to get back down to the square.

The team's surveillance technique was identical to pre-Harvey Nichols, except this time Scooter was front running the bus stop by stop as it entered and then made its way along the Kings Road with the ladies on board.

Foxtrot called in the women alighting at Carlyle Square, and Scooter doubled back, before folding his vehicle and slipping it back into his bag. He changed his hat for a black baseball cap. Moped had now parked up the street before the bus stop and was walking at pace to get within a respectable distance of the women.

As the latter turned into Old Church Street, Moped informed the team he "had" the target under control, and Scooter stopped to look in a shop so as to give him some space.

Shortly after, Moped had called in the women "complete, Skye Norman hair salon on Old Church Street."

Two minutes later, Scooter walked by and could see them each sitting in separate salon chairs being tended to by stylists.

The team decided to rendezvous at the river end of Old Church Street. The debate was whether to call the executive team in. The women were clearly there for the long haul – they guessed at least an hour and a half – the location was discreet, and a one-way street. The only problem from Moped's point of view was the massive mansion behind the wall directly opposite the salon, which was heavily surveilled by cameras on the street; Scooter quickly pointed out, however, that the lens covers were seriously tinted from age, which would obscure clarity.

"Can you reach any with tape?" asked Taxi.

"There's one on each gate, easily reached," Moped told him. They all realised this was as good as it was going to get in London.

Taxi called it in. "Advise motorcycle, expect some camera coverage, but we will mitigate where possible. Recommended escape route – Battersea Bridge, then south."

The Solntsevskaya Bratva Controller took the message and then called Mikhail for confirmation. He got it.

* * *

The Mexican Marines had been on the trail of Archivaldo for six months now. In their and their president's view, the short-arsed drug lord had successfully humiliated the entire system, and so as soon as they received the tip-off from MI6 that their quarry was hidden in plain sight in Los Mochis, they began calling in every source and favour they had to track him down.

GCHQ had also identified a large data transfer between a Bayswater address and Los Mochis the day of the intercept, though it had appeared to run through a Russian firewall, which was probably just masking.

The Marines got hold of every commercial address with access to the fastest internet connections in Los Mochis. They would raid every one. Additionally, since the tip-off, every known connection to Archivaldo had become subject to phone monitoring, and when they established that Jorge González was in Los Mochis and not Costa Rica as suspected, they knew the Brits had probably nailed it.

It took three days to hone in on the right house, and at 4.30 am, seventeen Special Forces Marines swept in to grab their quarry, supported by fifty soldiers. No one was taking any chances.

Archivaldo's minders did their job and immediately engaged the intruders, but they were outgunned and out-skilled. Two of them were dead within seconds; another three would be dead within minutes.

The boss, however, was gone, once again slipping the net via a tunnel that had been built as a contingency for just such an event. Once out of the house and into the pre-positioned Ford Fiesta, he drove out onto Highway 15, which also had the honour of being part of the pre-planned escape route. Archivaldo should have been cut and dry, but just to be sure, he called Jorge to tell him to bring in the quick reaction force, which comprised of forty assassins and thugs. Another mistake, and the call was instantly intercepted.

Jorge activated the force, confident they would cause enough distraction to save his boss. So he moved his thoughts onto Sheetal and called him up – this too was intercepted.

Within minutes Jorge had picked Sheetal up from the villa in his car and they were at the 'office'. "Wipe it," Jorge told him urgently. "Wipe everything, unless you can encrypt it so well that no one can get into it."

Sheetal's fingers blurred across the keyboard, before he finally pressed a button shutting everything down. Jorge could hear the computer coolers winding down. "Done?" he asked.

"Done, except one thing," Sheetal told him. They walked to the computer and Sheetal removed a rack. "Without this the system probably can't be cracked, and without me I'd say it can't be cracked at all."

"Good man, Sheetal!" Jorge told him. "You carry the rack, I'll turn the lights off."

Sheetal turned to head for the door but didn't even make it one step; Jorge had grabbed him by his hair and jerked his head back. Sheetal was so shocked, he didn't even see the pistol sweep round under his chin; by the time the sound had escaped the room, the bullet had already decimated his brain.

Jorge lowered Sheetal's body to the ground and watched the pool of blood grow around his head. He then wiped off the pistol, took Sheetal's right hand and wrapped it around the gun, placing his finger on the trigger. He let the dead man's hand drop naturally so that it would release the grip on the pistol. Finally, he wiped the blood splatter from his own face and picked up the D-Wave rack, turned out the lights and went back outside to his car.

He left the industrial estate and drove north.

Meanwhile, south-bound on Highway 15, a police patrol had received an alert regarding a white Ford Fiesta. They spotted it, they stopped it, and they arrested the most wanted man in all of Mexico. They then waited nervously on the roadside to see who would turn up first to relieve them of their prisoner - the Marines or the cartel.

CHAPTER THIRTY-ONE
Skye Blues

Sid pulled his Porsche Macan Turbo into Eaton Terrace Mews and sounded his horn. He was surprised to see Oleana and Alexei emerge from the mews house with Harry, and even more surprised to see Alexei wielding a meat cleaver.

Alexei and Oleana got in the back seat while Harry took the front. He instructed Sid to take them down Kings Road and then take a left onto Old Church Street, just before the cinema. As they drove, he explained the entire situation to Sid.

In the midst of all the tension, Alexei didn't notice Oleana press the call button on her phone, and, because she'd muted it, no one could hear Toby Sotheby on the other end saying, "Hello? Oleana, are you there?"

Toby looked at Tarisai. "What the fuck is going on?" he asked. She took the phone from him, and it took her less than four seconds to assimilate the fact Toby was meant to be listening and not speaking; she scribbled frantically as she heard Harry talking, before the voices suddenly became muffled; Alexei had looked across at Oleana, so she'd quickly put her phone in her pocket.

"There's a potential hit going down," Tarisai said calmly, "but we don't know where; Oleana's phone is still open, run a trace on it right now, sir."

Toby called in the emergency to the Met Police and placed an immediate live track on the number.

As the Porsche eased its way along the snail-pace traffic on the Kings Road, no one took any notice of the Honda NC750X cutting down the middle of the road with rider and pillion.

The Honda reached the turning into Old Church Street, where both riders hoped the watcher team had done their job by putting masking tape on the camera lenses within reach. They needn't have worried.

The rider pulled up just past the red frontage of the Skye Norman salon, and the pillion got off and walked back the few yards to the door. Their target would get no warning of his arrival.

As he walked through the door dressed in leathers and full face helmet, the effete receptionist said, "Can I help you, sir?"

At the same moment, Ivanna, who was towards the back of the salon, looked around and immediately knew this was her adversary. "Get down!" she screamed at everyone around her. "Get down!" Then she watched, as if in slow motion, as the man pulled a Makarov pistol from inside his leather jacket; this all looked too easy.

Nazrin was seated at a stylist's stand to the gunman's right; she saw the gun in the mirror and instantly remembered what Harry had once told her: "The only part of a gun that can kill you is the little hole at the end. If you can make that hole point somewhere else, then it can't kill you."

In this case the hole was being brought to aim straight at Ivanna.

Nazrin spun in her chair and leapt the five feet to the gunman's side, concentrating solely on the pistol – she had to make it point somewhere else.

The gunman's peripheral vision was limited by his helmet, and as the woman in a black hairdressing robe hit his hand and grabbed the pistol, it discharged, causing all but Nazrin and Ivanna to scream. The man grabbed his assailant's hair with his left hand and tried to pull her off his arm; but she knew, like a cowboy riding a rodeo bull, she had to hang on for dear life – literally.

As he tried to shake her off, he didn't notice Ivanna pick up a pair of scissors, but he did hear a crash outside.

* * *

The Porsche had finally reached Old Church Street, and was slowing to a stop outside the salon; it was then they heard a gunshot.

"We're too late!" Alexei immediately lamented.

As the car drew up, Harry could see the motorcyclist inside the shop struggling with something or someone. He flung his door open, and as he leapt out, he shouted to Sid, "Hit the bike, hit the fucking bike!"

Sid knew exactly what to do; he floored the turbo and the Porsche punched into the bike, which turned and started to topple sideways. Sid kept going, accelerating at full power with the bike and rider unable to free themselves from the momentum. He accurately slammed them into a lamppost on the left-hand side of the street.

"Oleana, don't let him get away, fucking stab him if you have to!" Sid shouted. "Alexei, with me!"

Both men ran back towards Skye Norman as Oleana turned her attention to the wreckage of the bike and its rider.

Inside, Ivanna had already buried a pair of scissors into the assassin's shoulder, and was about to stab him again through his thick leather jacket when she saw Harry burst through the door.

Harry, seeing both his wife and his mistress fighting to bring down their attacker, immediately grabbed the assassin's helmet from behind and took control of his movements by pulling him backwards and twisting. The gunman was now completely off-balance, with the second woman still hanging onto his gun and arm. As he fell backwards, Nazrin fell with him, and the tension coupled with his survival instincts made him squeeze the pistol as hard as he could, pulling the trigger twice, thereby discharging a further two rounds.

Harry felt the shots ring out, followed by a whimper, as he saw Nazrin slump from the gunman's arm. She looked over at her husband, who was on the floor gripping the helmet; he could see the helpless fear and shock in her eyes, but was powerless to help her for the moment. The gunman, right arm now free, started to bring the pistol round to bear onto Harry, who instantly knew his only option now was to change his grip and concentrate on the 'hole'.

He was about to launch himself at the pistol, when one arm followed by another came and grabbed it – it was Sid. The next moment he saw the flash of a broad steel blade come slicing horizontally through the air, and he, Sid and Ivanna all watched as the meat cleaver hit the gunman just under the thumb and took the path of least resistance straight through his hand.

They heard the muffled scream from within the helmet and watched as the pistol and the entire hand attached to it – except the little finger – flew up into the air. Before the man had time to react, Alexei leapt at him and pinned him to the floor. "Move again and I'll chop something else off."

They then heard a crash to their right, and realised the petite male receptionist had tentatively stood up, only to faint back down onto the glass coffee table.

There was a tense silence for a moment as the scene settled, before Sid broke it. "Nice one, Alexei – he's never going to play the piano again."

There was a peal of nervous laughter, before everyone realised Harry had scrambled desperately over to Nazrin and rolled her gently onto her back; she was unconscious with blood dribbling from the corner of her mouth.

"Jesus Christ!" said Sid. "Has she been hit?"

Harry tore off Nazrin's hairdresser's robe and the bloodied blouse beneath it; the two entry wounds were in the centre of her chest and her right breast. There were no exit wounds.

He looked at one of the stylists standing by in shock, and said in a quiet voice, "Call an ambulance."

The salon door blew open to reveal Oleana standing in the doorway with a bloodied blade in hand. "The sirens are coming and I wanted to see what was going on, so I stabbed the fucker in both legs. He's not going anywhere unless he's crawling." She then absorbed the scene of Harry cradling his unconscious wife and talking soothingly into her hair. Oleana knelt down beside them and simply said, "Oh my God."

Time stood still as they heard Harry plead with Nazrin in a desperate, mournful voice. "Please don't leave me, baby, please don't go. I'm sorry for everything, don't leave me like this, not like this. I love you so much." Silent tears were rolling down his cheeks.

Sid stepped in. "Mate, we need to get her onto her right side to control the internal bleeding and plug these holes. She's still breathing and she's still got a pulse, let's keep it that way." Harry loosened his grip on her reluctantly. He was in bits; he was used to violence and blood and guts, but not hers, not this way.

Ivanna looked at Alexei and Oleana wide-eyed. "She saved my life." She burst into tears. "I'm so sorry, Harry, it should have been me."

Oleana moved to comfort her.

The Metropolitan Police had sealed off the road outside, but had to wait for an armed response team in order to approach the crime scene. The salon door was pushed open. "Armed police officers! Lay down your weapons and show us your hands."

"It's okay," shouted the salon owner, having now shakily gotten to her feet. "It's all over, but we have a dying woman, she's been shot. Please get an ambulance quickly."

Two armed policemen with Heckler and Kochs trained into the salon appeared at the door. One looked to his left and said, "Looks contained, get a medic, we have one female casualty, appears VSI, and one male with a hand amputation."

The ambulances were there in minutes and the three casualties almost instantly triaged. Already on a drip and oxygen, Nazrin was blue-lighted to Chelsea and Westminster Hospital, where she was taken straight for emergency surgery. Harry and a policeman accompanied her.

The other ambulance crews were treating the motorcyclists and tending to the shocked salon staff, when Toby Sotheby and Tarisai pulled up in unmarked car with blue lights and sirens. Toby showed his credentials to the policemen, who by now had a triple cordon in place. He walked into the salon and looked at the blood on the floor, and then at Oleana, Ivanna and Alexei. "Any of that blood yours?" he asked.

"No, it's Harry's wife's," Sid said, having just turned from talking to a police officer.

"Shit," Toby said. "Sid? What are you doing here?" Toby knew Sid Easton as a former SRR officer of considerable repute.

"We manage the Delimkovs' security here in London," Sid sighed.

"So I guess you're going to be fired," Toby retorted, to be met with a stony silence. Coughing awkwardly, he asked, "Is Harry's wife going to be okay?"

"I don't know." Sid looked gaunt. "She took two point-blank rounds to the chest from a Makarov. A lot will depend on the type of round he was using. If it was hollow point, it'll have shredded her insides; if it's ball, then maybe not."

"Who did it?" Toby asked.

"I'm sorry, who are you?" Alexei interrupted.

"This is Toby Sotheby," Sid told him. "He's a big kicker in MI6, we used to be in the military together. He's here to help." The last comment was more a prompt for Toby than anything else.

"This is the work of Solntsevskaya Bratva cartel," Alexei said, taking up the reins of the conversation. "And these guys aren't fired. If it weren't for them, my wife would be dead."

"Do we know why?" asked Toby.

Ivanna now joined the conversation, stepping forward. "I guess I must have pissed them off."

Toby looked at Oleana. "And are you okay, young lady?" he asked, pretending not to know her.

"I've had better twenty-four hour periods," Oleana responded, before giving him a brief nod of thanks for his discretion.

A police officer intervened. "Do any of you ladies and gentlemen require medical treatment?" They all shook their heads. "Okay, I'm going to have to ask you all to come to the police station with us to make statements. There's a van outside waiting to take you all." He looked at Sid. "We'll get your car towed, sir."

As the group walked out onto the street, the amount of police and emergency vehicles waiting to meet them was astounding; they were ushered to the van. Toby grabbed the police officer's arm. "Are you leading the investigation, inspector?" he asked, purposely using the officer's rank out of respect.

"At this stage I am," the inspector told him.

"Good, because all these people are MI6 sources, and I need the line of questioning to reflect that. This was all self-defence, and my best guess is that there'll be no charges."

The inspector knew precisely what Toby was saying. "Why don't you come down to the station, sir, I reckon with your help we can get this one cleared up pretty quickly."

CHAPTER THIRTY-TWO
Cé La Vi

The next morning at 4 am, ten officers from the Metropolitan Police drugs squad rang the doorbell of the first-floor flat in 8 Westbourne Gardens in Bayswater, announcing themselves and asking the occupants to please open the door. There was no response, so they forced entry.

They entered the flat screaming "Police!", but very soon stopped – there was nothing and nobody there; the flat was completely empty of any contents. The lead sergeant got onto his radio to confirm the address. "They've gone, boss. Whoever was here must have heard what went down in Mexico and done a bunk."

Further inquiries with the neighbours established there had been a Hispanic-looking lady living there, but nobody knew her name. It seems she'd moved out yesterday. It had already been established the flat was owned by a Cayman Islands company, with a law firm in Panama holding the directorship and shares. There was no known lease on the property.

Across town in Battersea, Mr G lay under his duvet watching the area around his crotch move up and down. He groaned in ecstasy, and there followed a spent silence of about twenty seconds. The movement of the duvet came up towards his head, and Alejandra's thick, black hair emerged, followed by her beautiful face and naughty smile. "So I've had my breakfast, but no coffee?"

"Well, we can't have that now, can we?" he said as he rolled out of bed and grabbed his bathrobe. "I'm glad you've decided to come and live with me, my darling," he told her. They had barely had a moment to speak since she'd arrived on his doorstep the previous night and moved straight to the bedroom. "But why the sudden decision?"

"I finally concluded you and I will be a lot more powerful working together than apart," Alejandra responded, omitting the fact her conclusion had been rather forced.

"And what of your other bosses?" he asked.

"There are big changes in Mexico, and they're in big trouble, so I'm guessing they can't use the information we have on the Russians. We'll need to find a good IT guy and find out everything that's on those computers." She nodded towards the two super-computers in the corner of the bedroom.

"It's a job well done," replied Mr. G. "Between the value of that data, the payoff to my cousins, and outing a two-timing employee, it's been a good few days' work – and everyone who needed to got out clean as a whistle." As he spoke, something on the muted television caught his eye, and he picked up the remote to flick up the volume on Sky News. They both watched aghast as the young male reporter with an Irish name stood on Old Church Street, describing what was rumoured to be a Russian mafia hit. He described the gunfire and an apparent struggle that had left the mother of a small child fighting for her life in hospital, and the resulting amputation of one of the assailant's hands under confused circumstances.

The reporter then walked down the street and interviewed a man who'd been drinking in the Pig's Ear pub. The Chelsea-accented local described how he'd just been having a glass of Prosecco when there was an almighty bang that sounded like a gunshot, followed by a Porsche SUV colliding with a motorcycle and then ramming it into a lamppost; two men had then leapt out and run back up the road, while a woman holding a carving knife had walked calmly over to the sandwiched rider from the car and stabbed him in both legs, before jogging back up the road herself.

The journalist asked him whether he could confirm the rumours that the biker was Russian, to which the enthusiastic interviewee said, "Well, I'm not sure, but he was screaming something like '*suka blyat, suka blyat!*' … Whatever that means," he added with a sheepish grin.

The reporter turned to the camera and told the viewers they expected a statement from the Metropolitan Police later that morning.

Mr G was about to turn around and comment, when the news anchor went straight into international news to a report that the leader of the Sinaloa cartel in Mexico had just been captured in the town of Los Mochis, and that dozens of people had been killed in the arrest and ensuing operations.

As the pictures of Archivaldo flashed across the screen, along with street scenes of bodies and blood, Mr G turned to Alejandra, who was sitting fixated on the television. "Mmm," he said. "I think we'll let sleeping data lie." He walked to the bedroom door. "Do you take milk and sugar, baby?"

Later that morning Toby Sotheby was having a 'Tale of Two Cities', best of time-worst of times kind of morning. Just about every five minutes he was being congratulated for his role in bringing the Mexican-Russian link to the notice of the authorities, which in turn had led to them being on the ball with regard to a crucial intercept out of London that had led to the capture of the Sinaloa leadership and the disintegration of that particular cartel. The discovery of a quantum D-Wave computer in Los Mochis, which was the recipient of the data transfer from the UK, had astounded all US, UK and Mexican intelligence agencies, and the self-inflicted death of a former MIT authority in quantum computing was a clear indication the cartel had successfully become a world leader in cyber-crime, even, it seemed, penetrating the world's banking system. And now the culmination of the cartel war that had resulted in the Old Church Street hit was set to close down one Russian cartel and cleanse the other from the streets; the fact Toby had called it all in as it was actually going down, thereby allowing a rapid police response, had been an apparent stoke of master spy genius.

Once again Toby Sotheby's ostensible skills and guile had put him ahead of the curve, or at least this was what 'C' had told him earlier that day.

Riding high and, for now, forgetting Tarisai's input, Toby had then taken a call from Omar Shamoon in Abu Dhabi, who told him about his dinner with Shaheen Soroush; it seemed they'd all miscalculated Soroush in every possible way.

Omar explained that Shaheen's only debts to the Russians had been from real-estate, and never anything to do with a nuclear deal involving their respective countries. He'd also previously been attacked by two Iranians in Dubai, presumably as a punishment by the regime for his commercial interests in pornography. The man had lost his wife and daughter in the Malaysian Airlines crash over Ukraine; Oleana had been his dead wife's lover; and he believed her and the Russians had stolen many millions of dollars' worth of physical assets from him. And that was what had brought him to London – nothing more, nothing less.

By the end of the call, for the first time in his career, Toby realised he'd only ever survived by luck and not by skill, and if he'd been rewarded appropriately for his ineptitude, he wouldn't even have qualified to man the security barrier at the entrance of his iconic building. Alone with his thoughts, he stared out at the view across the Thames and thanked God even Omar hadn't been able to join all the dots on this one.

He surmised that Shaheen Soroush's urgency to leave the country meant he would never come back to the UK again, but was glad in any case to know from Omar the Iranian was on his way back to Singapore. He just hoped dearly that Omar's account would never fall on the ears of any other member of Her Majesty's Secret Intelligence Service.

His thoughts were interrupted when Tarisai walked in beaming. "What's up?" he asked her.

"I was just chatting to C's executive assistant, and she asked me if I was looking forward to getting her job?" Tarisai explained.

"What! Are they taking you away from me? That's not right." Toby knew she deserved it but was clearly irritated.

"Not at all, I'll still be working for you…"

"I don't know what you are saying." Toby sounded impatient.

Tarisai rolled her eyes and spelled it out for him. "I'm saying, Toby, that C is retiring in three months, and you, *Sir* Toby, are the clear frontrunner to take over from him." She could see he still didn't get it. "Toby, she's telling me you're the only person in the running to take over the top slot. And you better take me with you!"

Toby thought again about his qualification to man the barrier, and quickly concluded that being grossly over-promoted was something he could live with. It seemed that only by fooling myself could he have fooled everyone else. He searched his brain for a dignified response.

"About fucking time! Now my wife might actually be proud of me – especially if she gets a title."

Alexei Delimkov's lawyer called the Cellist to inform him that their banks had transferred a total of €40 million back into the designated Cyprus accounts for the benefit of the Cellist and his 'best friend'. It was twice what they owed them.

The following morning at just past 3 am, the Moscow Police breaching team smashed through the door of Mikhail's penthouse. He and two high-class escorts were hauled from the king-size bed by the black-clad assault team. The hookers screamed and Mikhail protested, telling the officers they'd made a grave mistake that would cost them their lives. They let him have his one phone call before throwing him into the waiting police van, but his call to the Cellist went unanswered.

In the back of the van, handcuffed and livid, he glared at one of the balaclava'd policemen sitting on the bench opposite him. "What is this?" he demanded. "Where are you taking me?"

The anonymous blue eyes looked over at him. "To your new home, Mr Mikhail. You may have heard of it as Krasnoyarsk prison. Your accommodation has been paid for by Alexei Delimkov and approved by your president. The lesson you should take away here is that, if you have a score to settle, then you settle it with the man, not his wife, and you don't embarrass your president with your thugs in a foreign land." He paused, smiling invisibly under his balaclava. "I hope those hookers gave you enough to think about for the next five years, you rotten bastard!"

Shaheen and Lai Xian sat underneath a square parasol in Cé La Vi SkyBar overlooking the cityscape of Singapore. Shaheen's membership in the club-lounge had ensured them a table at this most prestigious of nightspots on the roof of the iconic Marina Bay Sands towers.

They both looked towards the city they loved, taking in the view while holding hands, until their thoughts were disturbed by a duo of beautiful waitresses. They turned to watch one of them lay out the plates of crispy oysters and tempura mushrooms as the other showed Shaheen the bottle of 1988 Salon S champagne and announced its name and vintage.

Shaheen beamed as he tasted it, and they proceeded to fill Lai Xian's flute, while he in turn waited for his own glass to be charged. She raised her glass. "Cheers, my babe."

"Oh, I nearly forgot," he said as he reached into his pocket and slipped halfway off the chair to land with his knee on the floor. "Please will you be my wife?" Between his thumb and forefinger he held a five-carat, square-cut diamond ring. He watched as the tears welled up in her black but so very beautiful eyes. Her bottom lip quivered.

"Of course I will, Shaheen! You have no idea how much I wanted you to ask me this. You're the best and kindest thing that ever happened to me." She paused. "But I have something to tell you."

Shaheen's mind raced. Oh God, what now?

"We might need a bigger apartment," she told him. "I'm six weeks pregnant." And now it was her turn to beam as his eyes filled with tears.

Suddenly he looked at her glass and laughed. "Should you be drinking that then?"

"Not until you've put that thing on my finger," she teased. "And I can go dry from tomorrow." He took her in his arms and they kissed deeply.

Unbeknown to both of them at that moment, Lai Xian would give birth at full term to a little girl, and in doing so would end Shaheen's mourning over the daughter he'd so tragically lost. Her birth would transform him into a man who lost his greed and lived every day to be with his son and new family.

Shaheen Soroush would never again return to Dubai, and so would never know that Omar Shamoon had settled back into his old habits of tracking serious criminals across the UAE, as good at his game as he'd ever been.

Nor would Shaheen ever know of his and Omar's simultaneous decisions to marry their partners, or that both their wives had
been attracted to the same Russian woman – a woman they'd all
chased halfway around the world, but who refused to be caught.

CHAPTER THIRTY-THREE
Greater Love

The Russian Orthodox Church in Chiswick was packed to capacity. The Azerbaijanis – Christian and Muslim – had all turned out in force. The caring residents of Chelsea were taking up standing room only, and hairdressers from all over London had taken a day off to attend the service. The people of Richmond had crowded there, and members of MI6 and the Metropolitan Police patrolled inside and outside the church, while media teams stood providing quiet commentary on the arrivals.

Harry, Graham Tree, Sid Easton, Alexei, and Nazrin's brother and father carried her coffin into the church, led by the Orthodox bishop. Once the coffin had been laid on the stand at the front of the church, Harry gently opened the half-lid of the casket to reveal his beautiful wife lying in peace. She was wearing one of her favourite dresses with a burial shroud folded on top of her. Over her forehead was draped a headband with the words '*Holy God, Holy Mighty, Holy Immortal, Have Mercy On Us*'. And in her hands she held a crucifix.

Harry walked back to his seat by Nazrin's mother, who was holding Charlie in her arms, sobbing as she handed the little boy back to his father. The choir sung Psalm 118, before Nazrin's brother stood to read from the scriptures.

Finally, it was time for Harry's eulogy, and he stood up, handed Charlie back to his grandmother, and stood by the coffin to face the congregation. His voice trembled as he spoke, trying to hold back his tears.

"Greater love has no one than this: to lay down one's life for one's friends." He looked down at her. "And that's what you did, my angel. You went out to get your hair done, but instead you did this." He choked, then tried to hold it back together. "When I first laid eyes on you, you were the one. When I was weak, you were strong; when I was in doubt, you were resolute; when I failed, you made me pick myself up. You gave me our son, you made our house a home. You moved halfway around the globe to be with me. We had our laughs, we had our tears, we had our moments." The tears were rolling down his cheeks now. "But I didn't think you'd ever be the one to go first. You see, Charlie and me, we need you. We need you to somehow reach out to us from beyond death. We want you there in bed in the morning, to snuggle in the evening, we want your smile, we want your love." He took several deep breaths and reached into each of his jacket pockets, pulling out his SAS beret and a small blue teddy bear. "This is my special forces beret, my love. As it turns out, you earned it more than I ever did." He placed it gently in the coffin. "And this is Charlie's first teddy, the one you bought when we found out we were having a little boy." He set it alongside her head as if it were nuzzling into her hair. "So now it's goodbye, baby. You were just the best wife any man could hope for. We love you so much, and I'll try so hard to be the mother you would have been for little Charlie." Harry gave a single, abrupt sob. "I'll tell him all about you." He bent over her and kissed the crucifix and her forehead. And then he lost it. He broke down, dropped to his knees, and wept like a baby.

A few weeks later, back in their Moscow apartment, and still solemn from the effects of Nazrin's funeral, Alexei and Ivanna had decided to wind down their cartel positions. They already had more money than they could spend for the rest of their lives, and given what they'd both seen and experienced in London, they'd decided their life together was truly too short. They both had a lot to forgive and forget with each other, and that was precisely what they planned to do.

Ivanna had set up a trust fund for little Charlie that would ensure he would go to the best British schools and universities money could buy, with another £5 million to be released to him at the age of thirty. She had also found a full-time (but not too good-looking) nanny who spoke Russian, Azerbaijani and English to fulfil Nazrin's wish that her son would grow up fluent in all three languages.

In Saint Petersburg, despite the cold Oleana took long walks every single day. She mourned the disappearance of Maria, and wondered if the girl would ever just turn up one day. There was hardly an hour when she didn't think about Harry or his sorrow; she cried a lot these days. She so wanted to reach out to him, just to hold him, but whenever she called him, which wasn't as often as she wanted, he either didn't answer or sounded like a mere shadow of his former self.

For Harry was a broken man now. One of his favourite sayings had always been 'If you're lucky in life, you can have it all… but you can never have it all at once.' But he'd learned that to be unlucky in life could most certainly happen all at once. He lived with Charlie, Bunny, and a plump, kindly nanny, either working with Sid or tending the two things left in his life that he could love unconditionally. Harry could see no end to the dark tunnel of grief or guilt that lay before him. And until the inevitable healing time would so surely bring for him, this current life of mourning and brave faces for his son and his friends was just how it was going to be.

EPILOGUE

In Limón, Costa Rica, Jorge González was still trying to figure out who the hell had snitched his boss to the authorities. They'd been so careful with his security, and all the killings and interrogations since had come to nothing.

Jorge was watching CNN as the counts came in for the US presidential election, and was amazed that states like Wisconsin, Ohio and Pennsylvania had all swung in the underdog's favour. Neither he nor the rest of the world had any idea that sitting in the garage of that Costa Rican villa was the D-Wave rack holding the key that had entered the three states' electronic counting systems through a Russian VPN in order to skew the votes.

Jorge shrugged his shoulders and spoke with a smirk to his television. "So go ahead, build your expensive wall, gringo." He took a bite of his honey melon. "Don't you know we go under it, not over it!"

Acknowledgements

My profound thanks to:

Mina – for the fruit, the tea, and literally everything else

Bunny – for still being real

Anthony – for meteoric future sales and the trilogy pack

Dominic – for his skilled editing at arm's reach

Bernie D – for all things Mexican

Ms Caliente – for her attention to past-perfect

Anastasia, Kasyap and Rania – for their Russian, Hindi and Arabic

The team at San Gennaro – for an idea and Italian

The Persian Advisors

The Russian Gurus

The Battersea Boys

The Flats, the Walts, Box and the Shakies

The characters – only the cat is real, but you know who I know

The Producer – for signing the film option for Persian Roulette, Moscow Payback and Mexican Standoff

London, Singapore, Abu Dhabi and Dubai – for being such great cities